# THE

AMERICAN ROYALITY

# KENNEDYS'

IN THE GREATEST CITY

# NEW YORK

IN THE WORLD

## TIM ENGLISH

# ALSO BY
# TIM ENGLISH

*Popology:*
*The Music of the Era in the Lives of Four Icons of the 1960s*
*(JFK, RFK, Martin Luther King and Thomas Merton), 2013.*

*Sounds Like Teen Spirit:*
*Stolen Melodies, Ripped-off Riffs, and the Secret History of Rock*
*and Roll, Revised and Expanded 2016 Edition.*

*John Lennon:*
*1980 Playlist, 2020.*

# CONTENTS

# INTRODUCTION

ALTHOUGH IMAGES OF CAPE COD and Palm Beach often come to mind when we think of the Kennedys, *The Kennedy's New York* will prove that New York has at least as much of a claim on the family as those places do. The Kennedys were New Yorkers by choice. Joe Sr. moved his family to the Bronx in 1927. By the mid-1960s, all of the surviving Kennedy children — except for Rosemary, who was institutionalized in Wisconsin, and Eunice and Ted, who lived in the Washington DC area — were Manhattan residents. All of the Kennedys spent their formative years as residents of New York State — first in the Riverdale section of the Bronx and then in Bronxville, in Westchester County.

Rose later explained that the family moved to New York in 1927 because Joe's "business was exclusively in New York at that time," but that was hardly the whole truth. Having grown up amid anti-Irish prejudice in Boston, Joe was never exactly enamored of his hometown. "Boston is a bigoted place," he bluntly wrote to a friend. In explaining why he moved his family to New York; Joe later told a reporter that "Boston was no place to raise Irish Catholic children." Joe found New York's Wall Street to be a welcoming meritocracy where one was rewarded for their smarts and hard work without regard to their background.[1] New York was the family's home from 1927 to 1941.

Former *Washington Post* executive editor Benjamin C. Bradlee once described his friend JFK as "about the most urban — and urbane — man I have ever met." After observing both candidates up close, Senator Jacob Javits later described the election of 1960 as the "First time in history Americans had elected a big city fellow (JFK) over a smalltown boy (Nixon).[2]

From the time his family moved to Riverdale when he was ten in 1927, JFK was never away from Manhattan for very long. As a college student in the 1930s and 1940s, he hit nightspots like the Stork Club. In the 1950s, he went to society dances at the Plaza and the Waldorf and enjoyed the city's finest French restaurants, such as Le Pavillon. JFK spent considerable time in Manhattan as President, using the Carlyle Hotel as a home base.

Jacqueline Bouvier was raised in Manhattan and acquired a sophisticated appreciation for the finer things in life, be it jewelry, clothes, art, or fine food. New York's artistic and cultural organizations had no better friend than Jackie, who lent her time to so many good causes through the years. Uplifting the cultural life of U.S. citizens was a crucial part of what JFK sought to accomplish as President, and Jackie carried on this mission after she left the White House.

Interestingly, Bobby and Jackie moved to New York simultaneously in 1964 when Bobby decided to run for the New York Senate seat held by Kenneth Keating. Jackie made a home at 1040 Fifth Ave.

---

1    David Nasaw, *The Patriarch*, p. 105.

2    Jacob K. Javits, Oral History Interview, JFK 1, April 26, 1966. https://www.jfklibrary.org/asset-viewer/archives/jfkoh-jkj-01

for the rest of her life. Bobby would only serve as a New York senator for three and a half years. Still, during that time, he sought to assist the poorest of his new constituents while also partaking in Manhattan's glamourous nightlife. Accused of being a carpetbagger during his 1964 Senate campaign, Bobby liked to remind critics that he'd lived a third of his life in New York. As a senator, Bobby had an apartment at the fashionable new United Nations Plaza building on the East River while maintaining the family home, Hickory Hill, in McLean, Virginia.

John Jr. spent all of his life in Manhattan save for his first three years in the White House and his time away at prep school in Massachusetts and college in Providence, Rhode Island. Raised a famous child of privilege on the Upper East Side, he managed to maintain his humility and a comedic sense of the absurdity of his situation in life that endeared him to his fellow New Yorkers. They sensed that he was one of their own when they saw him playing frisbee in Central Park or biking around Manhattan in his suit and tie. After graduating from Brown University, John eventually got his own place on the Upper West Side and later settled downtown in 1990 in the then-emerging neighborhood of Tribeca. He never returned to reside on the Upper East Side, although he did spend the final nights of his life sleeping blocks away from his childhood home on Fifth Avenue. John's celebrity ramped up after he was designated *People* magazine's "Sexist Man Alive" in 1988 and went to stratospheric levels when he secretly married Carolyn Bessette in 1996.

A *New York* magazine tribute to him after his death was titled "Prince of the City" because that's how residents treated him, and that's how he carried himself. One of a precious few figures seemingly above politics, John's death came at the start of an era of conflict and mean-spiritedness that has only worsened in the past decades.

In examining the lives of the Kennedys following the cataclysm of JFK's assassination, one is struck by how they tried — each in their own way — to carry out his life's work. Bobby and Ted in Washington, Jackie with her support for the arts and cultural institutions, Caroline's 21st-century role as U.S. ambassador to two of America's most important allies, Japan and Australia, and John Jr.'s efforts to get regular people interested in politics with *George* magazine and his largely unheralded efforts to assist the working poor via the Reaching Up organization that he founded. These efforts continue in our time, which is why you will find website links to the organizations to which they devoted their time and efforts.

*The Kennedy's New York* will demonstrate the myriad ways in which New York impacted the Kennedy family story. Each place has at least one story to tell, many of which are not widely known.

*The Kennedy's New York* is your guided tour to the New York the Kennedys knew: from Joe Sr.'s Broadway office at 46th St. where he ran his Hollywood film studios, to John Jr.'s office four blocks north at Broadway and 51st where he ran *George* magazine more than six decades later, and from the city's most exclusive address at 740 Park Ave. where Jackie once lived, to the seedy Harlem hotel where Bobby's son David scored his drugs. It's a tale of triumph and tragedy, of the glamorous and the mundane. Much of the New York they knew in the 1960s or even the 1990s is gone, but not all of it. *The Kennedy's New York* will guide you to the places they knew and loved.

In thinking about the lives they led, the sacrifices they made, and the example they set for us, perhaps we, too, can be inspired by the line Bobby often quoted by Alfred, Lord Tennyson: "'Tis not too late to seek a newer world."

**NOTE:** Be advised that many of the locations mentioned in this book are private residences that are NOT open to the public. If you attempt to enter such properties without permission, you will be trespassing and subject to arrest and prosecution.

**FORMAT:** Entries are presented in a north-to-south direction within each section.

"IN THE CITY,
THE PAST BECOMES
VISIBLE."

—UNKNOWN

# UPPER EAST SIDE EAST OF FIFTH AVE., AND NORTH OF 59TH ST.

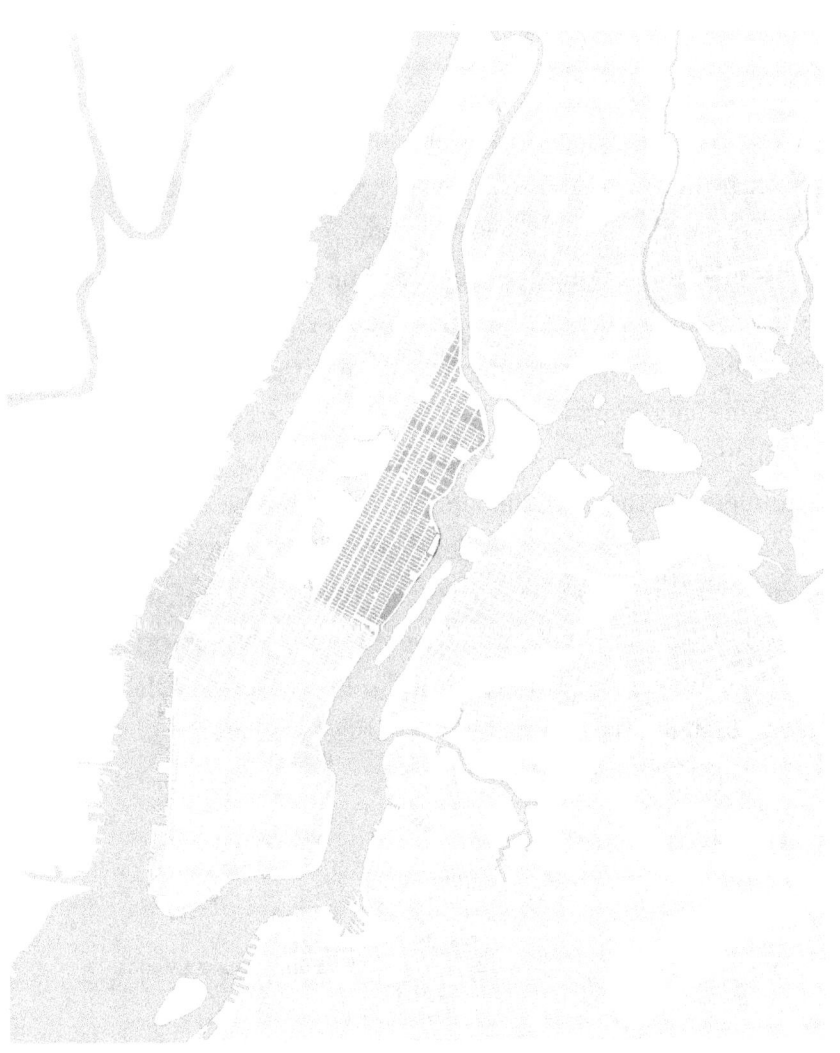

# RAO'S

## 455 E. 114TH ST. @ PLEASANT AVE. EAST HARLEM

THIS IS A TINY OLD-SCHOOL southern Italian restaurant, long a favorite of New York's power elite. Hachette-Filipacchi CEO David Pecker hosted a small dinner here to celebrate the financing of John Jr.'s *George* magazine in February 1995. John was spotted arriving on his bike and leaving late that night the same way. Pecker later told *New York Magazine*, "As he was going down 114th St. in the middle of the night, the photographers were all chasing him."[3]

In initially convincing a skeptical Pecker to back *George*, a magazine focused on the intersection between politics and celebrity, John reminded him that JFK thought he might become a newspaper publisher upon leaving the presidency and that Jackie had spent years in the publishing industry, so it was in his blood. Upon his departure from *George*, John and Carolyn were reportedly at a sort of farewell party for Pecker here in March 1999. Pecker left Hatchette to Run America Media Inc., the publisher of the *National Enquirer*.

---

3    Maer Roshan, "Prince of the City," New York Magazine, August 2, 1999.

# WILLARD D. STRAIGHT HOUSE; FORMERLY THE INTERNATIONAL CENTER OF PHOTOGRAPHY

## 1130 FIFTH AVE @ E. 94TH ST.

IN 1974, PHOTOGRAPHER CORNELL CAPA, the younger brother of famed war photojournalist Robert Capa,[4] founded the ICP. The museum's purpose was to feature "concerned photography," which the ICP defines as "socially and politically minded images that have the potential to educate and change the world." The ICP has carried out this noble mission ever since.

A former professional photographer herself, Jackie penned an anonymous article in the *New Yorker's* "Talk of the Town" section promoting the museum's opening. This was a part of Jackie's sometimes quiet efforts to elevate the cultural life of New York and the United States, work that carried over from her time as First Lady.

Jackie was an ardent supporter of the ICP and a key part of the museum's fundraising efforts for many years. She attended numerous functions here including annual anniversary parties in the fall. Jackie edited Diana Vreeland's book *Allure* for Doubleday, and on October 13, 1980, she celebrated its publication here.

---

4   Robert's photo of a Spanish Loyalist soldier taken at the moment he was shot to death in 1937 is one of the indelible images of the 20th Century. In 2007, the ICP acquired a lost trove of negatives - known as the "Mexican Suitcase" - taken by Capa, Gerda Taro, and Robert Seymour during the Spanish Civil War.

1130 Fifth Ave. is now a private home. The ICP moved to a Midtown location in 2000 and is now located downtown at 70 Essex St.

www.icp.org

# ST. THOMAS MORE ROMAN CATHOLIC CHURCH
## 65 E. 89ᵀᴴ ST. BETWEEN MADISON AND PARK AVES.

A GOTHIC REVIVAL-STYLE BUILDING DATING from 1870, St. Thomas More resembles a church one might find in the English countryside. Along with Jackie, Andy Warhol was also a parishioner. [5]

Pat and Peter Lawford were married here on April 24, 1954. A huge crowd gathered outside the church to catch a glimpse of the couple and all the other Kennedys in attendance. Lawford — a star in his own right — had appeared in Hollywood movies for a decade and was then co-starring in director George Cukor's hit romantic comedy *It Should Happen to You* along with Jack Lemmon and Judy Holliday. Joe was not crazy about his daughter marrying an actor, and a non-Catholic, British one at that! Perhaps his instincts were right because although the union produced four children, the marriage only lasted a decade.

Stephen Smith's funeral was held here on August 21, 1990. He passed away at the age of 62 after battling cancer. Ted praised his late brother-in-law in the eulogy:

---

5   In *The Andy Warhol Diaries*, Warhol records that he attended mass on more than fifty occasions.

*"Without (Steve) there would have been no Camelot.
...Mother and Dad came to love Steve as a son....
When Jack and Bobby left us, it was consoling that
we still had Steve."*

Although this was the church Jackie attended regularly, her memorial service was held at St. Ignatius Loyola because it has a seating capacity of 1,500 as opposed to Thomas More's 350. Jackie often came to mass alone here. Upon her death, the pastor, Rev. George Bardes, said this about her to the *New York Times*:

*"She was a religious person. The circumstances
of her life were so often trying and difficult — the
bitter with the sweet, the pain with the laughter. I
believe she called upon the deep religious resources
inside her very often."*[6]

Bardes also recalled that Jackie took time to exchange pleasantries with the priests following mass here.

In May 1995, John and Carolyn were photographed leaving a memorial mass for Jackie a year after her death.

A private memorial service for John Jr. was held here on July 23, 1999, before 350 invited attendees. Because the remains were not present – their ashes having been buried at sea the day before near the site of the crash - this was technically not a funeral but a memorial service. Then-President Bill Clinton was there along with First Lady Hillary Clinton and their daughter Chelsea. Rev. Charles

---

6    https://www.nytimes.com/1994/05/23/nyregion/fond-adieu-to-jacqueline-onassis-at-her-home.html

O'Byrne, who had presided over John and Carolyn's wedding on Cumberland Island, Georgia, less than three years earlier, gave the homily.

Ted Kennedy's memorable eulogy for his nephew began on a humorous note when he stated:

> *"Once, when they asked John what he would do if he went into politics and was elected President, he said: 'I guess the first thing is to call up Uncle Teddy and gloat.' I loved that. It was so like his father."*

The outpouring of grief in the days following John's death affirmed that something more than three young lives had been lost when his plane went down. The country had lost a man who occupied a unique place in the national psyche. He was admired by people regardless of where they stood politically, one of the few such figures in the increasingly partisan 1990s. He was lost when the country's political divide was becoming ever more bitter, a process that would only accelerate in the coming decades.

Ted concluded with this passage:

> *"We dared to think, in that other Irish phrase, that this John Kennedy would live to comb gray hair, with his beloved Carolyn by his side. But like his father, he had every gift but length of years."*

Wyclef Jean of The Fugees sang the Jimmy Cliff song "Many Rivers to Cross," a favorite of John's. The song is the title track of the 1972 movie starring Cliff that helped popularize reggae in the U.S.

Carolyn's friend Hamilton South eulogized her as follows:

*"Her famous phrase was, 'We need to talk.' That would be the beginning of a two- or three-hour telephone odyssey... that revealed a range of interest that left you spinning — from this new book to that museum, from fashion to Walt Whitman, from what's in the paper to what's uptown. She could be high-brow and low-down. It left you breathless, exhausted, and hungry for more. To spoof herself and to cover up what she was really doing, she'd say of these talks, 'Now let's remember, it's all about me.' But... it was never about her. When you talked to Carolyn, it was all about you, and all about life.'"*

7    https://www.townandcountrymag.com/society/tradition/a28187331
     /john-f-kennedy-jr-carolyn-bessette-last-days-plane-crash-true-story/

# SAINT DAVID'S SCHOOL

### 12 E. 89TH ST. BETWEEN FIFTH AND MADISON AVES.

THIS INDEPENDENT CATHOLIC SCHOOL FOR boys was founded in 1951. John Jr. began classes here in February 1965. He was a student here until the fall of 1968 when he transferred to Collegiate School. His cousin William Kennedy Smith attended here at the same time, marking the beginning of a close lifelong friendship.[8]

The school's mission statement is "...That they be good men," a phrase that seemed to imprint itself on John's consciousness. As an adult, John sometimes told friends that he believed being a "good man" was a more worthwhile goal than becoming a "great man" and wondered if being the latter made it more difficult to be the former.

---

8  Perhaps this explains John's presence during two days of jury selection at Smith's 1991 rape trial in Palm Beach, Florida. Smith was acquitted following a ten-day trial.

## LEMOYNE BILLINGS RESIDENCE
### 5 E. 88ᵀᴴ ST. BETWEEN FIFTH AND MADISON AVES.

OFTEN DESCRIBED AS "JFK'S BEST Friend," Billings lived here — just steps from the Solomon R. Guggenheim Museum and three blocks up from Jackie's home on Fifth Ave. — from the fall of 1969 until his death here on May 28, 1981. "Lem" and JFK met as teenagers when they attended Choate, a prep school for boys in Wallingford, Connecticut, and the pair remained close until JFK died. Lem even had his own room at the White House when JFK was President. Although some speculated about Lem's sexual orientation, he was very discreet about his private life.[9]

JFK was apparently confident that Lem would never bring a scandal upon him. Lem was devoted to JFK — to the point that writer Gore Vidal (who knew both men but wasn't exactly a fan of either) once described him as JFK's "slave" — and helped see his friend through the numerous illnesses JFK experienced as a teenager and beyond.

---

9    Although several biographers have claimed that Billings was gay, Robert F. Kennedy Jr. — who knew him as well as anyone — denied ever seeing any evidence of this in his 2019 book *American Values*.

Lem later said of JFK: "Jack was more fun than anyone I've ever known, and I think most people who knew him felt the same way about him."[10]

Lem was devasted by JFK's death and, by all accounts, was never the same after it. He was also close to Bobby and served as a pall-bearer at his funeral. Brokenhearted, Lem descended into alcohol and drug abuse later in life.

---

10    Michael O'Brien, *John F. Kennedy: A Biography* New York: Thomas Dunne, 2005.

## GRACIE MANSION
### EAST END AVE. @ E. 88<sup>TH</sup> ST.

THIS IS THE OFFICIAL RESIDENCE of New York City mayors since 1942, when urban planner Robert Moses convinced then-mayor Fiorello La Guardia to move in. The grounds offer a sweeping view of the Hell Gate channel in the East River. On May 20, 1962, JFK met here with a group of mayors, rallying them to support his bill to establish a medical care program for senior citizens.

Bobby announced his candidacy for the U.S. Senate here on August 25, 1964. A Senate run was Bobby's best option once the possibility of his being selected to join LBJ's ticket had been taken off the table when LBJ announced he wouldn't choose any member of his cabinet to run with him.

Picketers outside carried signs reading "Go Home Bobby!" and "New York for New Yorkers." Quirks in New York State law enabled Bobby to be elected to the Senate (which required only that he be an "inhabitant" of the state) but prohibited him from voting in the November 3 election because of a six-month residency requirement. So, neither Bobby nor Ethel voted in the 1964 election! Bobby was flanked by Mayor Robert Wagner, who had initially opposed Bobby's candidacy. Brooklyn native Steve Smith strongarmed Democratic Party politicians in New York to clear the field for his

JFK addressing a meeting of U.S. mayors at Gracie Mansion on
May 20, 1962. New York Mayor Robert F. Wagner stands behind him.
Cecil Stoughton. JFK Library, Boston.

brother-in-law. This announcement culminated months of speculation about Bobby's future that included his statement on June 23
— when he was still serving as LBJ's Attorney General and hoping
to pressure the President to select him as his Vice-Presidential running mate — that he would *not* seek the New York Senate seat held by
Republican Kenneth Keating. Now, a visibly nervous Bobby said he
said that he was running because:

> *"All that President Kennedy stood for, and all that*
> *President Johnson is trying to accomplish...is*
> *threatened by a new and dangerous Republican*
> *assault."*

Thus began Bobby's first run for public office and a new phase of his career.

## SCHRAFFT'S RESTAURANT
### 1221 MADISON AVE. @ 88TH ST.; CLOSED

THESE RESTAURANTS, BEST KNOWN FOR their ice cream, were once ubiquitous around New York. They were affiliated with the Boston-based candy company and also had a few locations in Boston and Philadelphia. John Jr. and Caroline loved to eat here when they were kids. A cashier later told of Jackie coming here in a fur coat and ordering $8 worth of donuts and ice cream for her kids. By the 1980s, the restaurants and the candy company were all gone.

# DR. MAX JACOBSON'S OFFICE
## 56 E. 87TH ST. BETWEEN MADISON AND PARK AVES.

THIS PREWAR BEAUX-ARTS BUILDING WAS where the good doctor's patients were said to line up day and night to get their fixes... err, I mean their vitamin shots! Yes, this building housed the office of the notorious Jacobson whose patient list included many prominent celebrities such as Eddie Fisher, Maria Callas, Gov. Nelson Rockefeller, Marilyn Monroe, Leonard Bernstein, and most famously, JFK and Jackie. By some accounts, JFK visited the disheveled Dr. Max at his office here sometime prior to the first 1960 Presidential debate, held in Chicago on September 26. JFK sought relief from his back pain as well as the rigors of the campaign. The problem was that Max's secret concoction contained a high level of amphetamine, and it appeared that many of his patients soon became addicted. Nevertheless, Dr. Max became a frequent visitor to JFK's White House — his name appears in White House logs more than thirty times — and even traveled with JFK and Jackie to Paris and to the high stakes Vienna Summit with Soviet leader Nikita Khrushchev on June 4, 1961, a main topic of which was the stalemate over Berlin.

Dr. Max ministered to JFK before the meeting, and by some accounts, loaded him with too high a dose. JFK told the *New York*

*Times* columnist James Reston that the summit was, "The worst thing in my life. (Khrushchev) savaged me." Many historians now point to Vienna as an important factor in JFK's insistence that the U.S. — in the wake of the Bay of Pigs fiasco and the building of the Berlin Wall that August — needed to make a firm stand *somewhere* against communist aggression, a belief that reinforced his commitment to the government in South Vietnam.

Jackie also became one of Max's patients while battling depression following John Jr.'s birth. Dr. Max saw JFK regularly until Hans Kraus, the President's New York-based orthopedist, threatened to go public with what Dr. Max was doing, telling JFK, "No President with his finger on the button has any business taking stuff like that."[11] Kraus put JFK on an exercise regimen in 1961 and 1962 that proved highly beneficial in healing his back.

Regular patients didn't need to trek to the office; Max gave them syringes and showed them how to shoot themselves up. Following a front-page *New York Times* exposé in 1972 that documented the enormous quantities of amphetamine ordered by Max's office, the good doctor lost his license in 1975 amid charges of fraud. He died in 1979.

11   Peter Keating "The Strange Saga of JFK and the Original 'Dr. Feelgood'" *New York Magazine*, November 22, 2013.

## THE CROYDON; FORMER LOCATION OF
## CROYDON BOOK SHOP
12 E. 86TH ST. BETWEEN FIFTH AND MADISON AVES.

JACKIE REGULARLY SHOPPED AT THE bookshop here during the 1960s, purchasing numerous books for John and Caroline. The store even maintained a list for her lest she buy a duplicate copy. Jackie was once spotted shaking her head disapprovingly as she perused a paperback of the 1964 book *Jacqueline Kennedy: A Biography* by Gordon Hall and Ann Pinchot.

# JACQUELINE KENNEDY ONASSIS RESIDENCE
## 1040 FIFTH AVE. @ E. 85^TH ST.

AFTER PURCHASING IT FOR A reported $250,000, Jackie lived in her fifteenth-floor apartment here from September 1964 until she died here on May 19, 1994.

She resided here longer than anywhere else in her life. (After moving out of the White House with its fortress-like protection, she had to endure curious pedestrians peeking into the windows of her house in Georgetown.) Her apartment had fourteen rooms — including five bedrooms — and took up the entire fifteenth floor. It offered a breathtaking view of the Metropolitan Museum of Art and the Central Park

The entrance of 1040 Fifth Ave. as photographed in 2023.

Reservoir, which now bears her name. The family nanny, Maud Shaw, thought the family felt more comfortable in New York than in Washington: "People seem to accept the presence of the Kennedy children without staring at them or doing anything so ridiculous as asking for their autographs." Secret Service agent Clint Hill observed that native New Yorkers were so focused on their own activities that they were less likely to infringe on the Kennedys' privacy.

Eager to display his closeness with Jackie, LBJ interrupted his campaigning to stop here for a half-hour visit on the evening of October 14, 1964. The unannounced meeting was widely trumpeted in the press the following day,[12] along with a photo of Jackie, LBJ, and Bobby standing together beneath the building's front canopy.

Bobby was a regular presence here. He turned up on the night of November 9, 1965, while New York was in darkness due to the Northeast Blackout. John Jr. and Jackie were photographed waving to Bobby from their apartment window as he kicked off his presidential campaign by marching in the St. Patrick's Day Parade down Fifth Ave. on March 16, 1968. Jackie must have been filled with apprehension that day because we've since learned that she advised Bobby not to run, telling him that "the same thing that happened to Jack" would happen to him.

News photographers often photographed Jackie entering or leaving "1040," as she referred to her home, notably her nemesis Ron Galella, who was, by his admission, "obsessed" with Jackie. Whatever one thinks of his methods, there's no doubt that Galella captured some of our most iconic images of the object of his obsession, nota-

---

12  In a subsequent phone call with LBJ, Jackie expressed her astonishment at how affable LBJ had been during this visit, considering that he'd just found out that his long-time close aide Walter Jenkins had been arrested on a morals charge in a Washington DC public restroom, a potentially devastating scandal given public attitudes toward homosexuality at the time.

bly his famous "Windblown Jackie" photo, taken on Madison Avenue on October 7, 1971.

Standing on the sidewalk outside the building's entrance on May 20, 1994, John Jr. announced to the world that Jackie had died the previous evening:

> *"She was surrounded by her family, her friends,*
> *and her books — the people and things she loved.*
> *She did it in her own way and on her own terms.*
> *We all feel lucky for that."*

Billionaire businessman and political activist David Koch purchased Jackie's apartment for a reported $9.5 million after her death. He rebuilt the interior and listed it for $19.5 million when he moved out in 2006, bound for another of Jackie's old addresses, 740 Park Ave.

# ENCORE CONSIGNMENT

## 1132 MADISON AVE. BETWEEN E. 84TH AND 85TH STS.; CLOSED

THIS UPSCALE SECONDHAND STORE (ISN'T that an oxymoron?) was founded in 1954 by entrepreneur Florence Barry. Jackie was said to have both bought and sold clothes here. When she married Ari, Jackie had carte blanche to spend as much as she wanted on clothes plus a $30,000 monthly "allowance." Jackie often blew through the $30k by the middle of the month and soon had to revert to a clever sort of money-laundering scheme she'd first utilized when married to JFK. Jackie would take expensive garments she'd worn a couple of times (if at all) and have one of her aides sell them to Encore in her own name. After depositing the funds in their account, the aide would write a check to Jackie, who would then pocket the cash. Jackie's White House personal secretary Mary Gallagher, later reported that she performed this duty for Jackie during the early 1960s.

Encore was conveniently located just three blocks from Jackie's Fifth Ave. home. After seeing a bill for $9,000 that Jackie had spent with the designer Valentino, a frustrated Ari barked: "What does she do with all the clothes? I never see her in anything but blue jeans."[13]

---

13    Nicholas Gage, *Greek Fire: The Story of Maria Callas and Aristotle Onassis*, New York: Alfred A. Knopf, 2000, p. 305-6.

Encore moved out of its Madison Avenue home in 2020. An online iteration of the store is still in business.

https://encoreresale.com

## JACQUELINE BOUVIER RESIDENCE

1 GRACIE SQUARE; SOUTHEAST CORNER OF E. 84TH ST.
AND EAST END AVE, YORKVILLE

THIS WAS AS FAR NORTH as Jackie ever lived in Manhattan. After separating from Black Jack Bouvier, Janet moved here in 1939 with Jackie and Lee. The Rosario Candela-designed building was completed in 1929. Located across the street from Carl Schurz Park, today, the building has 22 units on its 15 floors. Jackie and Lee had a short walk to Chapin School, located caddy-corner across East End Ave. Janet and her father plotted PR tactics for her divorce here. Things soon got ugly, with Janet accusing her husband of serial infidelity and Black Jack firing back with allegations (supported by the household staff) that Janet was violent and abusive toward her daughters. For all his faults, it's instructive that the daughters both strongly preferred their father's company to Janet's. Later in 1940, the divorce was finalized in Reno, Nevada.

# THE CHAPIN SCHOOL
## 100 EAST END AVE. @ E. 84TH ST.

THIS IS AN ALL-GIRLS K-12 school whose motto is *Fortiter et Recte* (Bravely and Rightly). Jackie was a student here starting in September 1935, attending from grades one through seven. Jackie and her family lived steps away from Chapin after moving to One Gracie Square in 1939. Here, she met her lifelong friend and later close aide, Nancy Tuckerman. The student body was predominantly Protestant at the time. One of Jackie's teachers described her as being "Very clever, very artistic, and full of the devil." Janet Felton, a classmate of Jackie's here who later worked with her in the White House, said of her:

> "She was naughty as everything, she would disrupt whatever she could, but very talented. ... She'd be sent to the headmistress every week because she was so naughty. ... She had the best sense of humor and of the ridiculous throughout her life."[14]

---

14 Sarah Bradford, *America's Queen: The Life of Jacqueline Kennedy Onassis*, New York: Viking, 2000.

Jackie's parents separated in 1936 and were divorced four years later. Following her mother Janet's marriage to Standard Oil heir Hugh D. Auchincloss in June 1942, Jackie and Lee moved to their stepfather's Merrywood Estate in McLean, Virginia, just outside of Washington DC. Thus, Jackie's years at Chapin were the only time she attended school in New York City proper, although she later attended Vassar College in Poughkeepsie for two years before graduating from George Washington University in Washington DC in 1951 with a Bachelor of Arts degree in French literature.

www.chapin.edu

# CHURCH OF ST. IGNATIUS LOYOLA

980 PARK AVE.; SOUTHWEST CORNER OF PARK AND E. 84TH ST.

THIS ROMAN CATHOLIC CHURCH WAS built from limestone in 1899. Because two planned hundred-foot bell towers were never constructed, the building has a somewhat stunted appearance. Jackie attended mass here as a child and was baptized and confirmed here. JFK and Jackie attended Sunday mass here on February 10, 1963. Due to its larger size, Jackie's funeral took place here instead of at the St. Thomas More Church on East 89th St. where she was a parishioner. At her funeral, John Jr. read from the Book of Isaiah. Caroline read **Edna St. Vincent Millay**'s "Memory of Cape Cod" and Maurice Tempelsman read C.P. Cavafy's "Ithaka," two of Jackie's favorite poems. Opera singer Jessye Norman sang a pair of hymns. Mike Nichols read a Bible passage. Ted eulogized her as follows:

> *"During those four endless days in 1963, she held us together as a family and as a country. ... Robert Kennedy sustained her, and she helped make it possible for Bobby to continue. She kept Jack's memory alive as he carried on Jack's mission."*

Pat Lawford's funeral was held here in 2006.

# METROPOLITAN MUSEUM OF ART

## 1000 FIFTH AVE. @ 82ND ST.

WITH THIRTY-TWO ACRES OF FLOOR space, this is the largest museum in the Western Hemisphere. Conveniently located just across Fifth Ave. from her home, Jackie had a long association with "The Met," long regarded as the most prestigious museum in the United States. Jackie came here often and was friendly with many of the curators.

When John Jr. was a youth, the steps out front of the museum were his favorite place to hang out with friends. "We used to hang out there for hours outside at night," recalled John's pal Jason Beghe. The group would eventually make their way to the park where they engaged in "some good, some naughty" activities, according to Beghe.[15] The characters on the CW television series *Gossip Girl* (2007-2012) often hung out on the steps here, just as John and his pals had done decades earlier.

As First Lady, Jackie was responsible for bringing Leonardo Da Vinci's *Mona Lisa* to the United States. During JFK's state visit to France in the spring of 1961, she used her perfect French and knowl-

15    Maria Hinojosa, "JFK Jr. Remembered as a Regular New Yorker", cnn.com. July 22, 1999. edition.cnn.com/US/9907/22/jfk.growing.up.in.nyc/

edge of the country's history to charm French Minister of Cultural Affairs, novelist André Malraux. She convinced Malraux to ask the Louvre to lend the painting — considered a national treasure in France — to the U.S. They agreed to do so the following year, and the Mona Lisa arrived in the U.S. with much fanfare in December 1962. Taking no chances, JFK ordered the Secret Service to guard the painting 24 hours a day. The *Mona Lisa* created a sensation when it was exhibited; first, at the National Gallery of Art in Washington — where JFK and Jackie viewed it with Malraux on January 9 — and then here. The *Mona Lisa* was displayed at the Met from February 7 to March 4. It was seen by 1,077,521 people, many of whom waited in line for hours. Along with Jackie's televised White House tour, the *Mona Lisa* exhibits were a vital part of her efforts to uplift the nation's cultural life.

Jackie attended countless events here through the years, perhaps the most famous being "The Glory of the Russian Costume" preview benefit that she chaired here on December 6, 1976. She was escorted by museum director Thomas Hoving. The pair had journeyed to Russia the previous summer with the Costume Institute director Diana Vreeland in a successful attempt to get curators at the Hermitage to share their valuable clothes with the Met for Vreeland's exhibits. That summer, Jackie was editing the book *In the Russian Style* that was to be released in conjunction with the exhibit, and, in explaining the necessity of the trip, Vreeland told Hoving that Jackie "demands to see what she's writing about."[16] Hoving later opined that the visit benefitted the show "immeasurably" and helped facilitate future exchanges with the Soviets.

Jackie was a regular at the Fashion Institute's December galas here.

---

16   Ibid.

On December 12, 1977, Jackie was the chairwoman for the opening night party celebrating Vreeland's Costume Institute's "Vanity Fair" exhibit. Bianca Jagger and Ronald and Nancy Reagan were among the attendees at the opening night party whom Jackie greeted while working the receiving line.

Jackie attended the Costume Institute's gala for the opening of the "Fashions of the Hapsburg Era" exhibition on December 3, 1979.

For Vreeland's Costume Institute exhibit "Eighteenth-Century Woman," Jackie commissioned an accompanying book by Olivier Bernier published by Doubleday and the Met in 1981.

As First Lady, Jackie lobbied JFK to urge Congress to approve $10 million for the UNESCO fund for the Temple of Dendur, a Nubian temple in southern Egypt dating from 10 BC that the construction of the Aswan High Dam would have drowned. This would result in Egypt awarding the Temple to the United States as a gift. Therefore, it was ironic that Jackie was said to have complained about the floodlights shining into her bedroom after the exhibit was installed in the new Sackler Wing at the northern end of the Met in September 1978. Or perhaps it wasn't so ironic given that Met director Hoving claimed in his memoirs that in 1965, when he was lobbying LBJ to award the Temple to the Met rather than to the Smithsonian, Jackie was adamant that they go to the Smithsonian in homage to JFK. Hoving claimed Bobby — newly elected to the Senate — offered him little assistance, and Jackie's position was undoubtedly why. LBJ awarded the Temple to the Met in the summer of 1968. Maybe Jackie just got used to them in time, but the spotlights apparently didn't bother her in later years.

In December 2021, the Met announced that the Sackler name would be removed from the wing due to their ties to Purdue Pharma, the maker of oxycontin.

A wildly popular exhibit of the fashions Jackie wore as First Lady named *Jacqueline Kennedy: The White House Years — Selections from the John F. Kennedy Library and Museum* ran here from May 1 to July 29, 2001.

# 995 FIFTH AVENUE;
## FORMERLY THE STANHOPE HOTEL
### 995 FIFTH AVE. @ E. 81ST ST.

FOLLOWING ANOTHER ARGUMENT WITH CAROLYN, John Jr. spent his final nights here in Room 1511. Although moving out of your home to a hotel would seem to indicate that the marriage was in trouble, some who knew the couple described it as a mere cooling-off period before they reunited. This was reportedly not the first time John had spent the night here instead of at home with Carolyn. When asked why he needed a room, John jokingly (?) told a clerk, "My wife kicked me out." John was up to his ears with work — including coming up with a new business

The entrance of 995 Fifth Ave. as photographed in 2023.

plan to satisfy Hachette and getting out a new George issue that was to feature Rob Lowe on the cover — and might have decided it was best to work at the Stanhope to avoid the distractions of home. (Of course, his workload wasn't large enough to prevent him from going to Yankee Stadium to catch a baseball game that Thursday night.) George maintained a corporate account at the Stanhope, and photo shoots and meetings were sometimes held here. John's friend Robert Littell later wrote that he found it poignant that John returned to a place so close to his childhood home at 1040 Fifth Ave. in moments of despair, almost like he was trying to "go home."

In what would prove to be a fateful event, John, Lauren, and Carolyn had lunch at Café M here on July 14. Lauren reportedly initiated this meeting in an attempt to play peacemaker between the arguing couple. She hoped to convince a reluctant Carolyn to accompany John to his cousin Rory's wedding at Hyannis Port that weekend, which John had already committed to attend. Perhaps hoping to serve as a buffer between them, she even offered to go along. Unfortunately for all concerned, Lauren proved persuasive, telling her sister, "Oh, come on now. We'll have fun!" (By at least one account, it appears that the plan was always for Lauren to be dropped off at Martha's Vineyard.) At least part of Carolyn's reluctance to go was because John had recently purchased a new, more elaborate, Piper Saratoga plane. Carolyn had only flown in it once, and on that trip to the Cape a couple of weeks earlier, there was a flight instructor on board.

Several sources report that John had breakfast with ex-paramour Julie Baker at Café M the next morning. However, this claim is contradicted by the *Globe* tabloid that published photos of John purportedly outside his North Moore St. home on that Thursday morning and its claim that he ate breakfast at a restaurant nearby in that Tribeca neighborhood.

Baker was a Wilhelmina model whom John dated for two years. They reportedly had their first date in 1989 when they attended an Andrew Dice Clay comedy show. (How romantic!) They were spotted out in New York again in late 1994. The pair reportedly[17] got together for lunch regularly, even after John was married. Baker later remembered John as "a normal and humble great guy."[18]

John had breakfast by himself at Café M on the morning of July 16. Perhaps John and Carolyn's relationship was best summed up by Carole Radziwill:

> *"He loved her. And she loved him. And they drove each other crazy."*[19]

The Stanhope became a co-op in 2005. It's now known as 995 Fifth Avenue.

17    Beller, *Once Upon a Time.*

18    ABC-TV *The Last Days of John F. Kennedy Jr.* Jan. 3, 2019.

19    https://www.closerweekly.com/posts/john-f-kennedy-jr-s-lovers-recall-memories-after-his-death/

# PETER AND PATRICIA LAWFORD RESIDENCE
## 990 FIFTH AVE. @ 80TH ST.

A JULY 1964 NEW YORK Times story described the couple's purchase of a 14-room co-op here for $140,000. A board had earlier rejected them at another East Side building that was wary of "people in show business and Democrats." One doesn't imagine the couple having had too many happy times at their new abode since they divorced in February 1966.

Knowing of their marital woes, JFK had requested that Pat and Peter not go public with a separation until after the 1964 election. JFK's death was a shattering event for the entire family, but Pat was said to have taken it particularly hard. The assassination and divorce sent Lawford on a downward spiral, both personally and professionally. After years of drug and alcohol abuse, he died at the age of 61 in December 1984.

# MADISON PUB

## 1043 MADISON AVE. @ 79TH ST.; CLOSED

KNOWN FOR HAVING THE BEST jukebox in New York (a lot of Sinatra, Patsy Cline, Jimmy Durante, Louis Prima's "Just a Gigolo" and the like) the Madison was frequented by Jackie, John Jr., and Ari. It was a small dive, the last of its kind on the rapidly changing Madison Avenue of the 1990s. The door to the pub was located in the entryway to the old brownstone still located here. The Madison was renowned among locals for its great burgers and friendly atmosphere. Perhaps not coincidentally, it closed as NYC's smoking ban took effect in 2003.

This was the location where a deceased author of several gossipy Kennedy books claimed to conduct his possibly imaginary meeting with John Jr. a few days before his crash. Subsequent investigation revealed that the staff had no memory of either man having been here in recent years. That didn't prevent some media outlets from running with these tall tales.

This is also the location of another possibly apocryphal story of a couple entering the bar only to observe that the place was nearly empty, with only three patrons at the bar. "Let's go; there's nobody here," said the man as he exited. Jackie, Ari, and Peter Lawford were thus left to themselves.[20]

20  "Madison Pub, Classy Dive, Closes; Now the Avenue Belongs to Armani" by Nick Paumgarten, The New York Observer, November 8, 1999. https://observer. com/1999/11/madison-pub-classy-dive-closes-now-the-avenue-belongs-to-armani/

# LENOX HILL HOSPITAL

## 100 E. 77TH ST. BETWEEN PARK AND LEXINGTON AVES.

JOHN JR. CAME HERE TO have surgery on his broken ankle after he injured it in a rough landing in what Carole Radziwill described as his "flying lawnmower" on Martha's Vineyard over Memorial Day weekend 1999. John had the cast removed here on the morning of July 15. A seemingly mundane occurrence that would prove to be of profound importance in setting off a chain of events that would lead to the deaths of John, Carolyn, and Lauren the following evening. For had the cast come off, say, the following week, John would almost certainly have taken a flight instructor with him on the trip to the Cape via Martha's Vineyard, just as he'd done when he flew to Toronto on July 12. In fact, John took a call early Friday afternoon at his *George* office inquiring if he'd need a flight instructor for that evening's flight, but he declined, telling his instructor that he wanted to "go it alone" that night. John was said to be elated to have his cast off, knowing he could now make the flight by himself. Even with the cast off, John left Lenox Hill on crutches, just as he'd been using for the past six weeks.

# J.J. KLEJMAN GALLERY
## 982 MADISON AVE @ 77ᵀᴴ ST.; CLOSED

JFK OFTEN STOPPED HERE WHILE staying at the Carlyle Hotel just across Madison Ave. The Polish-born John Klejman operated this well-respected, high-end gallery. JFK made a quick stop here during a busy day in New York on May 23, 1963. While at the Carlyle that afternoon, he had slipped out to the gallery "apparently without knowledge of the protecting police," according to an account in the next day's *New York Times*. He reportedly made an undisclosed purchase.

Before delivering an address to the United Nations on the morning of September 20, 1963, JFK stopped here and admired a statue of a life-size bronze of a handsome athlete dating from the 4th century, BC. Klejman had placed the figure on a pedestal and bathed it in floodlights. Greek bronzes from the Hellenistic period are very rare. When Thomas Hoving of the Metropolitan Museum of Art expressed interest in purchasing this "breathtaking" statue, Klejman told him: "It's already placed. The President has fallen in love with it. He plans to raise the money for the National Gallery to acquire it."

According to Hoving,[21] the statue later went missing, although

---

21 Thomas Hoving, "Making the Mummies Dance," New York: Touchstone, 2004.

he figured it would turn up again someday. For Christmas 1963, Klejman sent Jackie a beautiful little bronze horse that JFK had seen in the gallery and planned to get for her for Christmas. Klejman's closed in 1974.

## CORDIER & EKSTROM GALLERY
### 978 MADISON AVE. BETWEEN E. 76TH AND 77TH STS.; CLOSED

THIS GALLERY CHAMPIONED IDIOSYNCRATIC AND innovative artists such as Marcel Duchamp, Man Ray, and Isamu Noguchi.
It was the site of a show by David Webb that Jackie attended in the
autumn of 1966. Her appearance was mentioned prominently in a
*The Saturday Evening Post* article[22] in its March 11, 1967, issue. The
article described how supposedly sophisticated New Yorkers were
starstruck in her presence. The gallery lost its lease and relocated to
417 E. 75th St. in 1979, where it flourished for more than a decade.
Gallery director Arne Ekstrom died in 1996.

22    Alan Levy, "Jackie Kennedy: A View from the Crowd," *The Saturday Evening Post,*
      March 11, 1967.

# THE RAVEN PUB; FORMERLY AMERICAN TRASH
## 1471 FIRST AVE. BETWEEN 76TH AND 77TH STS.; CLOSED

AMERICAN TRASH WAS AN UPPER East Side dive bar, but a charming one. Ted got into a late-night altercation here in January 1989 with a fellow patron — who, like Ted, was probably feeling no pain. While arguing with Ted, the patron accused him of being: "Nothing like your brothers." Unsurprisingly, Ted took exception to this comment and tossed his drink in the man's face. Both men decided to take the dispute outside, but when the man took out his wallet to show his ID as a former cop, Ted knocked it out of his hand. At that point, bouncers intervened, cooler heads prevailed, and both men returned to the bar. Ted was said to have called it a night (or a morning) at 4:30 a.m. This was the period before he "cleaned up his act," met his soon-to-be wife Victoria, and issued a mea culpa for the sometimes-questionable choices he'd made in his personal life in the wake of the William Kennedy Smith Palm Beach rape accusation in March 1991. He also had a seemingly tough re-election fight on the horizon in 1994.[23] American Trash closed in January 2022.

---

23    Ted defeated Republican Mitt Romney that year with 58% of the vote to Romney's 41%. This marked the first time since 1962 that a Republican had held Ted to less than 60% of the vote in Massachusetts.

## JEAN AND STEPHEN SMITH RESIDENCE
### 950 FIFTH AVE. @ 76TH ST.

BECAUSE IT WAS CONVENIENTLY LOCATED just a block away, even as President, JFK would sometimes walk here from his suite at the Carlyle. He did so on Sunday morning, February 10, 1963, to pick up Caroline and his nephew, Stephen Smith Jr., and take them for a brief walk in Central Park. The next day's *New York Times* front page showed JFK standing on Fifth Ave across from the park. This casual sort of scene would soon become a thing of the past with the increased levels of Presidential protection in the wake of the Dallas tragedy. According to George Plimpton's wife, Freddy, JFK was dropped off at the back entrance here by taxi following a visit to the private Raffles Club in the fall of 1963. Bobby had an election night gathering here on the evening of November 3, 1964, that Jackie and other friends and family attended.

# THE CARLYLE HOTEL
## 35 E. 76TH ST. @ MADISON AVE.

THE FAMILY'S DUPLEX APARTMENT HERE served as JFK's home away from home when visiting the city as President. The family's apartments occupied the entire 34th and 35th floors and featured stunning views and two terraces. Secret Service agent Clint Hill later wrote, "The magnitude and majesty of this apartment was almost overwhelming."[24] JFK no doubt appreciated the privacy and discretion the Carlyle — to this day — takes pride in providing its guests. He was well protected when he visited here as President. During his September 1963 visit, for example, fifty NYPD officers were assigned to the hotel. (A group of demonstrators decrying the recent Birmingham, Alabama, church bombing had gathered outside the hotel.)

JFK often conducted official business here while President. He met with Cambodian Prince Norodom Sihanouk on September 25, 1961, and Argentina President Arturo Frondizi on November 2, 1961. On September 26, 1961, JFK signed the Arms Control and Disarmament Act here. It established the U.S. Arms Control and

---

24   Clint Hill and Lisa McCubbin Hill, *My Travels with Mrs. Kennedy*, New York: Gallery Books, 2022.

Disarmament Agency, which existed until 1999, when it was merged with the State Department.

The famed Bemelmans Bar here features the paintings of its namesake, author and artist Ludwig Bemelmans, on the walls and ceiling.

Jackie, Caroline, and John Jr. lived here briefly after moving from Washington DC but before settling in at 1040 Fifth Ave. in September 1964. They lived on the 14th floor because Jackie wanted a different suite from the one she'd stayed in with JFK when was President. Bobby lived here while running for Senate in 1964, living and working out of Room 11E on the 11th floor. He stayed here regularly before moving to his United Nations Plaza apartment in 1966.

Writer Herb Gardner (*A Thousand Clowns, I'm Not Rappaport*) later recalled[25] having dinner with Bobby and Jackie in the Carlyle Lounge during the 1964 campaign. When the pianist took a break and approached Jackie at the table, he asked if she'd mind if he played some music from *Camelot*. Jackie, smiling "her most radiant smile," replied, "Yes, I would." The pianist quickly took his leave. Soon, a man approached the table and shook Bobby's hand. He wished Bobby well in the campaign while apologizing for intruding on their privacy. He then asked Jackie to forgive his intrusion because "I had to tell you of the great affection and sympathy we feel for you."

Jackie and Ari were entertained by the hotel's mainstay singer/pianist Bobby Short here in 1971. In January 1977, Jackie met with reporters in a private dining room here to promote *In the Russian Style,* the book she'd edited for Viking.

In her 2012 book *Once Upon a Secret: My Affair with President John F. Kennedy and its Aftermath,* JFK's college-age paramour

---

25    Gerald C. Gardner, *Robert Kennedy in New York*, New York: Random House, 1965.

Mimi Beardsley (later Alford) claimed she'd met with JFK for the last time here on November 15, 1963, at which time he gave her $300 to go shopping. When JFK said he would call her when he returned from Texas, Mimi reminded him that she was getting married in January. Never one to let marriage vows get in the way of a good time, JFK replied, "I'll call you anyway." Alford wrote that her affair with JFK had begun in the summer of 1962 but — concurrent with the death of his son, Patrick, and her engagement to another man — had become nonsexual by the end of the summer of 1963.

After moving to nearby Fifth Ave. in the fall of 1964, Jackie was said to regularly stop in here for lunch. Her usual order was a gin and tonic and a Cobb salad, with which she'd enjoy a cigarette. John Jr. got his hair cut at the hotel barber shop when he was young.

In later years, John Jr. often roller-skated in for lunch. John met here with Princess Diana (then separated from Prince Charles) when he unsuccessfully tried to convince her to appear on the cover of George. Their meeting occurred in June 1995 as John prepared to launch George. Incredibly, the pair showed up together and walked in Carlyle's front door, correctly anticipating that paparazzi — having sniffed out that something was up — would be gathered at the side entrance on E. 76th St. Diana inquired about Jackie's parenting methods, saying that she was likewise attempting to give her two sons as normal a childhood as their circumstances would allow. Diana later told Vogue editor Anna Wintour that she wished she could have gotten married in the private way that John and Carolyn had but the Royal Family would never have allowed it. For his part, John found Diana to be "Very nice, shy, a little coy," and "taller than I thought." [26]

---

26  https://www.hollywoodreporter.com/movies/movie-features/john-f-kennedy-jr-george-magazine-stars-share-stories-project-1200375/

JFK and Jackie exit the Carlyle Hotel, September 26, 1961. *Robert Knudsen.*
*White House Photographs. John F. Kennedy Presidential Library and Museum,*
*Boston*

Carolyn was understandably shaken up by Diana's death on August 31, 1997, due to a car crash in a Paris tunnel that occurred as paparazzi followed her. Just weeks earlier, on July 22, Carolyn had sat directly behind Diana in the Milan Cathedral for the funeral of fashion designer Gianni Versace,[27] although the two women spoke only briefly. (It surely couldn't have been lost on Carolyn that Versace — who was assassinated outside his Miami mansion by a crazed stalker — was a victim of his own fame.) As a daily target

---

27 Donatella Versace later recalled John and Carolyn's being overnight guests at her brother's home on Lake Como in 1995. In one of his last interviews, Versace named Carolyn – along with Madonna, Courtney Love, and Priceless Diana – as the four women who most inspired him. Noting that each of the four had different needs, he stated, "...You have to produce something chic for Carolyn Bessette."

of paparazzi photographers herself, Carolyn identified with Diana. She anxiously watched hours of cable news coverage about her in the days following Diana's death. "That poor woman," she'd sigh whenever someone mentioned Diana's name. With Diana dead, Carolyn now feared that the media scrutiny of her and John was bound to increase. Speaking of his wife's reaction to Diana's death, John told his friend Billy Noonan: "I'm not sure what I'm going to do about Carolyn.... She's really spooked now."[28] Understandably, Carolyn identified with Diana. Like Diana, she'd married a "prince," — albeit an unofficial one — who'd been famous since the day he was born. Like Diana, she found the almost overnight transition from private citizen to worldwide fame to be daunting.

Diana and John also had a lot in common. Both knew universal fame in a new era in which public figures were granted little privacy by increasingly intrusive paparazzi eager to satisfy an audience with a seemingly insatiable appetite for news of the rich and famous. Both had once enjoyed a cloak of protection by government security agencies. Secret Service agents protected John until he turned sixteen, and Diana declined to utilize her palace security staff except for when she attended public events following her divorce in 1996. Both were thus left to fend for themselves. Finally, both of their deaths were at least indirectly caused by the fact that they were so famous: John was flying his own plane in part to avoid gawkers at airport terminals. Diana's crash would likely not have happened but for the presence of photographers chasing her. Perhaps Carolyn had a premonition of her own fate as she considered what had befallen Diana?

John's *George* colleague Elizabeth "Biz" Mitchell detected John's

28  William Sylvester Noonan, *Forever Young: My Friendship with John F. Kennedy Jr.*, New York: Viking, 2006.

emotional response to Diana's death, later recalling that he'd been "finding it difficult" to deal with her unexpected passing. As Mitchell planned how the magazine should cover the tragedy, John uncharacteristically blew off the meeting where the subject was to be discussed. Then, after days of delay, he finally said, "I don't see why this needs to be a story."[29] In the end, *George* published a photo essay on the people mourning Diana in London.

29  https://www.hollywoodreporter.com/movies/movie-features/john-f-kennedy-jr-george-magazine-stars-share-stories-project-1200375/

## THE SURREY HOTEL
### 20 E. 76TH ST. BETWEEN FIFTH AND MADISON AVES.

USING AN ASSUMED NAME, JOHN Jr. began staying at this luxury hotel in February 1994 to be close to Jackie when she was ill. It's a short walk to his old home at 1040 Fifth. After undergoing an extensive renovation, the Surrey is scheduled to reopen in 2024.

https://www.corinthia.com/en-gb/new-york/

## SPLENDIFEROUS

OPENED IN 1963, THIS WAS "One of the largest, fanciest boutiques in town," per a June 1968 *New York Magazine* article. Terence Ryan and Jerome Goldfarb were the proprietors. A November 1965 *New York Times* article detailed a two-hour shopping trip that Jackie made here. They even included a sketch of the dress she had purchased, a "Shaker knit dress in zing green" designed by Rudi Gernreich. Gernreich was the Austrian-American avant-garde designer whose fashions celebrating sexual freedom included the thong bathing suit and the "Monokini" topless bikini. By early 1967, Goldfarb claimed that Spendiferous had sold more topless bikinis than any other store in the country. In March 1967, *Look* magazine listed the boutique as one of Jackie's favorite places to shop in New York. In February 1967, Spendiferous opened a second, larger location in a five-story townhouse at 16 E. 56th St. Goldfarb and Ryan closed the business in 1973.

# MORTIMER'S
NORTHEAST CORNER OF 75TH ST. @ LEXINGTON AVE. CLOSED

OPENED BY GLENN BERNBAUM IN 1976, this brick-walled bistro quickly became a favorite of rich and famous Upper East Side residents, including Jackie and John Jr., who were regulars here. Bernbaum modeled the place after P.J. Clarke's, so it's not surprising that Jackie enjoyed eating the cheeseburgers here, just as she did at Clarke's.

Admission was dependent on an okay from Bernbaum so Mortimer's became known for its exclusivity, to the point that it was effectively a private club. Bernbaum loved to seat Jackie and other prominent diners like designer Bill Blass at table 1B near the entrance where passersby could see them from the sidewalk.

# THE WHITNEY MUSEUM OF AMERICAN ART

945 MADISON AVE. BETWEEN E. 74TH AND E. 75TH STS. MOVED

THE HUNGARIAN-BORN, BAUHAUS-TRAINED MARCEL BREUER designed this building along with Hamilton Smith. It's listed as among the "must be seen" buildings in New York, according to the American Institute of Architects (AIA). The five-story Brutalist structure makes no effort to integrate itself with surrounding buildings, making it beloved by some locals and hated by others since 1966.

Founded in 1930 by Gertrude Vanderbilt Whitney, the Whitney showcases new American art. The Whitney had previously been located at 22 W. 54th St. near the Museum of Modern Art. It took over the space when the Whitney vacated it.

Jackie was elected a trustee of the Whitney in 1962. In 1965, she was appointed to head the museum's national committee charged with expanding the museum's presence in the artistic community and among art dealers. On October 21, 1965, Jackie visited the newly expanded museum's construction site here to call attention to the need to raise additional funds to complete the construction and acquire additional artworks. She was joined by Breuer and Flora Whitney Miller, the museum's president.

On September 27, 1966, Jackie was among the officials at the ribbon-cutting ceremony on the new building's opening day here. A photo from the event appeared on the front page of the following day's *New York Times*. The new Whitney's first exhibit was called "The Art of the United States: 1670-1966."

Like his mother, John Jr. frequently attended events at the Whitney. John and Carolyn attended the museum's 30th anniversary party held here on November 4, 1996, celebrating the Breuer building. A *New York Times* story on the event focused on the newly married Carolyn and was titled "A Debut of Sorts at the Museum". Evelyn Lauder, whose husband Leonard was the museum president, told Carolyn, "You're not unnerved by all of this. You must be a pro." John made an amusing speech, although he didn't ask Carolyn to dance.

John and Carolyn attended the opening night party for the Andy Warhol exhibition here in November 1997. Of course, Warhol's 1964 "Nine Jackies" painting, consisting of photos taken before and after JFK's assassination, was one reason the pop artist skyrocketed to fame.

John and Carolyn were also at the "Brite Nite Whitney" gala benefit for the museum here on March 9, 1999. The event was designed to attract a younger and more diverse audience to the museum. They mingled with the likes of Martha Stewart, investor Ron Perelman, and designer Carolina Herrera while being entertained by "I Will Survive" singer Gloria Gaynor and teenage rapper Foxy Brown. After dinner, John approached the third-floor stage after Brown had done a song and pronounced himself a big fan of the artist: "I was in Korea two weeks ago and couldn't sleep. I turned on the television and saw Foxy Brown doing 'Hot Spot.'" The song is on Brown's 1999 album *Chyna Doll*, which topped the *Billboard 200* album chart upon its release. This made Brown only the second female rapper to achieve that feat, Lauryn Hill was the first in 1998 with her album *The Miseducation of Lauryn Hill.* Later, when John told Brown he liked her music, she replied: "Shut up! You don't listen to rap." John told her, "No, I don't listen to rap, but I listen to you." As if to prove his point, Brown said John then proceeded to rap a couple of lines of "Hot Spot".[30] (John once surprised one of his *George* co-workers by knowing every word of a Puff Daddy song that was playing.)

The Whitney relocated to its new and much larger quarters downtown on Gansevoort St. in the Meatpacking District in 2015. This building reopened in 2016 as the Met Breuer, displaying modern art from the Metropolitan Museum's collection until the Met closed it in 2020. The building was known as the Frick Madison from 2021 until March of 2024, when it temporarily housed the Frick Collection during renovations to the Frick Museum on E. 70th St.

www.whitney.org

---

30    Michael Musto "Foxy Brown: Hip Hop's Fashion Diva," *Paper* Magazine, September 1999.

## JOHN "BLACK JACK" BOUVIER RESIDENCE
### 125 E. 74TH ST. BETWEEN PARK AND LEXINGTON AVES.

AFTER HIS MARRIAGE TO JANET ended, Jackie's father lived in an apartment in this elegant 10-story building that was built in 1929. There were two daybeds in a guest room for when Jackie and her sister Lee stayed over. As she grew into a teenager, Jackie loved listening to her father speak of his amorous conquests, including an assignation with millionaire heiress Doris Duke on his honeymoon bound for England on the *Aquitania*. She was also said to enjoy quizzing him to learn which of the mothers of her fellow students at Miss Porter's School in Farmington, Connecticut, he had bedded. Thus, two highly impressionable teenage girls would enter adulthood with a somewhat warped idea of what constituted acceptable behavior in a husband.

# JACQUELINE BOUVIER RESIDENCE
## 790 PARK AVE. @ E. 74ᵀᴴ ST.

HAVING MARRIED IN EAST HAMPTON in July 1928, Jackie's parents moved into an apartment here as newlyweds. The marriage got off to a less than auspicious start when Black Jack got into an argument with his new father-in-law, James T. Lee, at the couple's wedding reception. James and other family members were dubious about the union, fearing that Black Jack was only after their money. Then, on their honeymoon cruise, Black Jack — who at 36 was sixteen years older than his new bride — got drunk, gambled, and openly flirted (at a minimum) with heiress Doris Duke, who was then a teenager. While not the most ambitious of men, Black Jack purchased a seat on the New York Stock Exchange and was lifelong friends with songwriter Cole Porter.[31] Jackie was born on July 28, 1929, in Southampton Hospital, and spent her first couple of years here before her family moved down the street to 740 Park.

---

31  Asked to name her favorite songs in 1960, Jackie said Porter's "Down in the Depths (On the 90th Floor)" was among them.

# HENRY FONDA RESIDENCE

## 151 E. 74ᵀᴴ ST. BETWEEN LEXINGTON AND THIRD AVES.

IN A MARCH 17, 1961, article on Fonda and his wife, Afdera, the *New York Daily News*[32] reported that this 6,000-square-foot four-story East Side townhouse was a popular gathering spot for the Fonda's friends. So much so that...

> *"One night, President Kennedy evaded his Secret*
> *Service guard and slipped down the stairs of the*
> *Carlyle Hotel to attend a party given by the couple."*

The Fondas' former home is four blocks away from the Carlyle. The *Daily News* story implied that JFK was on foot that night, but it doesn't specifically say so. JFK's escapade was noted only in passing, an indicator that an incident that today would be regarded as an appalling lapse in Presidential security wasn't such a big deal in 1961. Fonda was starring in *Critic's Choice* on Broadway at the time, and JFK took time to see the show in December 1960. The main focus of the *Daily News* article was Fonda's impending divorce from

---

32  Nancy Randolph, "Split, but Still Fonda Each Other," *The Daily News*, March 17, 1961.

Afdera, his fourth wife. He was 55, and she was 27. The couple married here in 1957.

Fonda's former home went on the market in 2016 with an asking price of $11 million.

# SOUP BURG RESTAURANT

## 922 MADISON AVE. @ E. 73ᴿᴰ ST.; CLOSED

THIS DINER WAS JACKIE'S FAVORITE place to get a cheese-burger, one of her favorite foods. It dates back to 1948, but Greek immigrant Peter Gouvakis purchased Soup Burg in 1964 and ran it during the years that Jackie dined here. This location closed in 2006, and the two other locations on First and Lexington Avenues are now gone too, the latter shuttered to make way for a TD Bank. All were victims of Manhattan's prohibitive rents that make it very difficult for diners like Soup Burg to survive. A 2004 *Time Out New York* article rated the burgers here as the third best in the city. The secret as to why they were so good? Peter's recipe calls for "75 percent meat, 25 percent fat," according to his son, Jimmy.[33]

This Madison Ave. location was featured in an episode in the first season of *Sex and the City,* so it's achieved immortality of a sort.

---

33   Anne Barnard, "Hold the Home Fries. Forever," *The New York Times*, July 3, 2014.

# GEORGE PLIMPTON RESIDENCE

## 541 E. 72ND ST. BETWEEN YORK AVE. AND FDR DRIVE

PLIMPTON WAS THE EDITOR OF *The Paris Review*. His apartment here on the East River became a salon for New York's literary elite in the early 1960s. (Fate would later place Plimpton in the Ambassador Hotel pantry when Bobby was shot; he helped wrestle the gun from the hand of Bobby's accused assassin. Jackie attended a party here while First Lady in 1961 (or 1962) at which she spent a long time chatting with author William Styron. Styron had published his first novel, *Lie Down in Darkness*, in 1951, and helped Plimpton found *The Paris Review* in 1953. Styron's books, *The Confessions of Nat Turner* (1967) and *Sophie's Choice* (1979) would see him acclaimed as one of America's leading writers. Jackie maintained her friendship with Styron for the rest of her life, and in later years often spent time with him and his wife Rose on Martha's Vineyard, where they kept a home.

Jackie was photographed attending a party here in July 1976. Plimpton died at 76 in September 2003.

# ASIA HOUSE/ASIA SOCIETY
## 725 PARK AVE. BETWEEN E. 70TH AND 71ST STS.; FORMER LOCATION AT 112 E. 64TH ST. BETWEEN LEXINGTON AND PARK AVES.

JACKIE ATTENDED THE OPENING OF the "Gods, Thrones and Peacocks" exhibit in this Phillip Johnson-designed building at the 64th St. location on September 22, 1965. She was a donor to the exhibition, as was John Kenneth Galbraith, who, as U.S. Ambassador to India, had escorted Jackie and Lee when they visited in March 1962. Bobby, Ethel, and Secretary of Defense Robert McNamara also attended the preview.

The exhibit featured one hundred Indian paintings from the 15th to the early 19th century. Nearly two years after Dallas, Jackie's appearance here marked one of her first public appearances as she gradually emerged from grieving and resumed her social life. This included a party at the Sign of the Dove restaurant that she threw for Galbraith around this time.

Founded in New York by John D. Rockefeller III in 1956, the Asia Society seeks to foster cooperation, knowledge, and understanding between Asia and the United States. The Society presented Ravi Shankar's first U.S. concert appearance at Carnegie Hall in 1957. The museum's collection includes the many Asian masterpieces collected by Rockefeller and his wife Blanchette, later donated by Rockefeller.

www.asiasociety.org

## JOHN VERNOU BOUVIER RESIDENCE
### 765 PARK AVE. @ E. 72ND ST.

THIS CLASSY BRICK AND LIMESTONE building was built in 1927 from a design by Rosario Candela. Jackie's paternal grandfather, John Vernou Bouvier (1865-1948), owned an apartment here, dividing his time between the city and his Lasata estate in East Hampton. This Bouvier was a Columbia graduate and renowned as one of New York's finest trial lawyers. He was often asked to speak at public events, including the 1931 dedication of the George Washington Bridge, from which his address was broadcast nationwide. Jackie visited her "Gampy Jack" here regularly as a child. He died here on January 15, 1948, at the age of 83.

# JACQUELINE BOUVIER RESIDENCE

## 740 PARK AVE. @ E. 71ST ST.

THIS IS PERHAPS THE MOST famous and prestigious address in New York. It even has a book dedicated to its history.[34] Jackie's maternal grandfather, James T. Lee, developed this site, and Rosario Candela designed this understated (on the outside, anyway) Park Avenue landmark in 1929. Inside, the apartments are like palaces. Some of the wealthiest people in the world call 740 home.

Jackie lived here as a child from age two to seven. Short on funds after losing money in the stock market crash, Black Jack had no choice but to turn to his father-in-law for assistance. Lee offered Black Jack apartment 6/7A (it was a duplex), but not without strings attached, including a monthly accounting of Black Jack's spending and a demand that he sell three of his four cars. Despite a story in the *New York Times* claiming that he'd purchased an apartment here, Black Jack never paid rent or maintenance fees on his new home.

The Bouvier family's apartment boasted eleven rooms, including two nurseries for the girls — Caroline Lee Bouvier was born on March 3, 1933 — and a gym for their father. Jackie's lifelong love of Central Park no doubt began at this time, as it is only a two-block

---

34    Michael Gross's informative *740 Park*, New York: Broadway Books, 2005.

walk from here. It's interesting to note that she spent most of her life at another Candela-designed building at 1040 Park Ave.

Jackie was named after her father, and despite his shortcomings as a husband (in addition to gambling and boozing, he was a world-class skirt chaser), she remained close to him even after her mother, Janet, divorced him in 1940. Perhaps because Janet was so often critical of her children while Black Jack lavished praise on them, Jackie and her sister Lee preferred their father's company to their mother's.

Black Jack lost money in the stock market in 1935 and 1936,[35] and after years of relentless marital strife, moved out of 740 on October 1, 1936.

Lee recalled her father in an interview six years before she died in 2019, taking issue with the way Kennedy biographers had portrayed her father:

> "He was a wonderful man. One thing that infuriates me is how he's always labeled the drunken black prince. He was never drunk with me, though I'm sure he sometimes drank, due to my mother's constant nagging. You would, and I would!"[36]

Upon Janet's marriage to Standard Oil heir Hugh D. "Hughdie" Auchincloss Jr. on June 21, 1942, she, Jackie, and Lee moved to his Merrywood Estate in McLean, Virginia. From then on, they would

---

35  Due partly to trading restrictions on specialist brokers imposed by the Securities and Exchange Commission under its new chairman, one Joseph P. Kennedy.

36  https://www.houseandgarden.co.uk/article/nicky-haslam-on-lee-radziwill

divide their time between there and Newport, Rhode Island, where Auchincloss owned another estate. Jackie never forgave Janet for scheming to have Auchincloss — rather than Black Jack — walk her down the aisle when she married JFK in Newport in 1953. In 1968, when Jackie married Ari over her mother's strenuous objections, Janet told a friend: "She's finally getting even with me for divorcing her father!"

Psychiatrists would no doubt have a field day with how many important men in Jackie's life were called "Jack." In addition to her father and grandfather, the list includes her boyfriend John P. "Jack" Marquand, the son of a renowned novelist who reportedly took her virginity (in a Paris elevator, no less!); JFK, who was always called Jack, not John, by friends and family; and architect John Carl "Jack" Warnecke, whom Jackie met in 1962 when both were involved in the saving and restoration of Washington's Lafayette Square. She later selected Warnecke to design JFK's grave at Arlington Cemetery, had a serious relationship with him in the mid-1960s, and a close friendship after that. Speaking of recurring names, we should also note that John Jr. had an aunt named Caroline (Lee's actual first name), a sister named Caroline and married a woman named Carolyn.

The duplex that Jackie lived in here was sold for $25.25 million in 2017. John D. Rockefeller's triplex here took up an astonishing 20,000 square feet and had 37 rooms. Today, prospective buyers are said to be required to have $100 million *cash on hand*.

740 Park and James T. Lee surely left their mark on Jackie. Her friend Brendan Gill, the chairman of the Municipal Art Society who worked with her to save Grand Central Station and other New York City landmarks, claimed a love of buildings had been instilled in her by her builder grandfather. On the flip side, James left much to be desired in the human being department, with his granddaughter Lee

later describing him as "a very severe man; a miser. He didn't have much warmth or charm." Lee claimed that both she and Jackie disliked him. In later years, Jackie sometimes returned here and asked to walk the long hallway to the 71$^{st}$ St. entrance.

# NEW YORK HOSPITAL –
## WEILL CORNELL MEDICAL CENTER
1414 YORK AVE. BETWEEN E. 68TH AND E. 71ST STS. TO FDR DRIVE

UNBEKNOWNST TO THE PUBLIC, DR. Janet Travell later confirmed that JFK was a patient here on seven or eight occasions for two or three nights at a time between May 1955 and October 1957 while she treated his back issues. JFK didn't tell anyone he would be here, and Travell put a fictitious name on the door to his room and hid his medical chart. This scheme was part of a largely successful effort to hide JFK's extensive health problems and project an image of youth and vigor in the run-up to the 1960 Presidential campaign. It wasn't until decades after his death that the full extent of JFK's maladies and the pain they caused him became known to the public. His undercover hospitalizations here did not become public knowledge until 2002, when author Robert Dallek was granted access to JFK's private medical records.

Caroline was born here on November 27, 1957. Her father was there to welcome her and asked the nurses, "She's easily the prettiest baby in the room, don't you think?" The hospital complex has expanded dramatically in the ensuing decades.

Jackie underwent chemotherapy treatments for her non-Hodgkins lymphoma here in April 1994.

Jackie was here on May 18, 1994, the day before her death.

Doctors informed her that her cancer had spread to her liver and there was nothing more they could do for her. Jackie suffered from anaplastic large cell lymphoma, a rare form of the disease that, in her case, spread rapidly.

The following year, John Jr. — after losing weight and feeling lethargic — was treated here for Graves' disease, an immune system disorder that can cause the overproduction of thyroid hormones and hyperthyroidism, a condition his father also suffered from along with Addison's disease.

## HOSPITAL FOR SPECIAL SURGERY

### (SINCE MID-1955) 535 E. 70TH ST.
### FORMERLY LOCATED AT 320 E. 43RD ST. AT THE SITE OF
### THE PRESENT-DAY FORD FOUNDATION BUILDING

*NOTE:* SINCE HSS MOVED TO its present location in May 1955, only JFK's 1957 operation took place at the new location.

Founded in 1863, HSS is widely regarded as among the top orthopedic hospitals in the United States. JFK underwent spinal fusion surgery here on October 21, 1954. Doctors told him that the procedure — at the site of his first back surgery – would strengthen his lower spine and that he might soon lose the ability to walk without undergoing it. JFK knew going in that the surgery was dangerous. Rose recalled:

> "He told his father that even if the risks were fifty-fifty, he would rather be dead than spend the rest of his life hobbling on crutches and paralyzed by pain."[37]

The steroids used to combat Addison's weakened the immune system, thus making an already dangerous operation life-threatening. As might have been predicted, JFK developed a severe urinary tract

---

37    https://www.cnn.com/2017/11/22/health/jfk-assassination-back-pain/index.html

The Hospital for Special Surgery as photographed in 2023.

infection while recuperating. At one point, he lapsed into a coma and was administered the Last Rites sacrament[38] of the Catholic Church by a priest. His family confronted the very real possibility that he might die. His face was ashen and swollen, and his breathing was labored.

A 1955 article in the *Journal of the American Medical Association* described an anonymous patient JFK's age with Addison's Disease who underwent the same operation as JFK. When discovered years later, this confirmed what the Kennedys had long denied, that JFK had Addison's, which meant his adrenal glands were not producing the required amounts of cortisol and aldosterone.

His grueling recovery was undoubtedly eased when Jackie convinced actress Grace Kelly to dress up as one of JFK's nurses.

---

38   Now known as the Anointing of the Sick.

JFK spent more than two months at HSS before being discharged on December 21 with an open wound at the site of the surgery. The famous photos of JFK under a checked blanket on a stretcher as he rides in an ambulance with Jackie were taken that day. When the wound became infected in early 1955, JFK returned here on February 11 to have a third surgery to clean the area and remove the metal plates. He was discharged on February 25 when he walked out on his own on his way to begin recuperating in Palm Beach. He was back in April for what was described as a "routine checkup," after which he returned to Palm Beach.

In 1955, JFK was examined by Dr. Janet Travell, who concluded that his back problems were the consequence of having been born with his left side a bit lower than the right and the fact that his lower spine had been damaged in trying to correct this imbalance. According to Travell, JFK resented the fact that he'd been advised to undergo the surgeries on his back, the first of which[39] took place on June 23, 1944, at the Lahey Clinic in Boston. She would go on to be his official White House physician.

JFK was again operated on here in September 1957 for a recurrent abscess of the lumbar spine that was very painful and caused him to have a high fever. He was laid up here for two weeks, during which time he obfuscated to the press about his condition. He asked Travell not to mention the abscess, which he called "a very ugly word." Instead, the reason for his hospitalization was given as "a virus infection."

The East River Drive extension was added in the 1990s.

---

39 Doctors at the Mayo Clinic advised against this surgery, and the operation proved unsuccessful, causing JFK back spasms and doing little to relieve his pain and discomfort.

## THE WESTBURY CONDOMINIUMS; FORMERLY THE WESTBURY HOTEL
### 15 E. 69TH ST. @ MADISON AVE.

THIS DISTINGUISHED BUILDING WAS BUILT in 1929. Black Jack Bouvier took a room here in the mid-1930s after leaving the family apartment at 740 Park Ave. The hotel's Polo Bar was Black Jack's favorite watering hole, so he must have felt right at home. It was here in December 1951 that Jackie became engaged to John Husted inside the Polo Bar following a one-month courtship. Upon their engagement, they went to tell Black Jack so John could ask him for his daughter's hand. "Sure — but it will never work,"[40] came the response from a man who knew something about ill-suited couples thrown together by marriage. Husted was a Yale man, but his bankbook and future prospects were deemed insufficient by Janet. Husted was soon given the boot while visiting Jackie in Virginia. It seems Husted's unsuitability for Jackie was about the only thing Jackie's parents could agree on. The hotel was converted to condos in 1998, but it retains its impeccable reputation for the luxurious amenities offered to residents.

---

40   Carl Sferrazza Anthony, *Camera Girl: The Coming of Age of Jackie Bouvier Kennedy*, New York: Gallery Books, 2023.

# RIGHT BANK RESTAURANT

## 822 MADISON AVE. NEAR E 69TH ST.; CLOSED

JACKIE WAS LONGTIME FRIENDS[41] WITH director Mike Nichols, and the pair dined here on March 29, 1968. We know this because a photographer snapped a photo of the gentlemanly Nichols lighting Jackie's cigarette. Jackie never kicked smoking, a lifelong habit, but she usually succeeded in keeping it hidden from the public.

Right Bank was a cozy place located four feet below street level. Nichols was on top of the world at this time, just two weeks away from winning the Academy Award for Best Director for his smash-hit film, *The Graduate*, which was released in December 1967 and was on its way to being the highest-grossing film of the year in the U.S. in 1968. This followed his success directing Elizabeth Taylor and Richard Burton in the 1966 film adaptation of Edward Albee's *Who's Afraid of Virginia Woolf?*[42] in 1966, for which Taylor won an Oscar for Best Actress. With Dustin Hoffman as the unlikely leading man and a soundtrack by Simon and Garfunkel, *The Graduate* was

---

41  ...and nothing more than friends, according to Mark Harris's book *Mike Nichols: A Life*, New York: Penguin Press, 2021.

42  Former *New York Times* theater critic Frank Rich named Nichols' Virginia Wolff one of the three best screen adaptations ever made of Broadway plays. The others he selected were Elia Kazan's *A Streetcar Named Desire* and Nichols' production of Tony Kushner's *Angels in America*, which was broadcast on HBO in 2003.

one of the first mainstream Hollywood movies to be sympathetic to the emerging counterculture's critique of the older generation's middle-class values. Along with *Bonnie and Clyde*, it was in the vanguard of what would soon be called "The New Hollywood."

Nichols met JFK when Nichols and Elaine May performed their comedy at JFK's Madison Square Garden birthday show in 1962. The duo was photographed chatting with JFK at the after-party at Arthur Krim's East Side townhouse. In singer Carly Simon's memoir *Touched by the Sun: My Friendship with Jackie*[43] she writes that Nicols was a regular topic of conversation between the two women. Caroline and John Jr. chose Nichols to do a Bible reading at Jackie's funeral in 1994.

Al Pacino was a regular here in later years. Right Bank closed in July 2000 after 41 years in business.

---

43   New York: Farrar, Straus and Giroux, 2010.

## ARTHUR B. AND DR. MATHILDE KRIM RESIDENCE
### 33 E. 69TH ST. BETWEEN MADISON AND PARK AVES.

ONLY ONE PHOTO EXISTS OF JFK or Bobby with Marilyn Monroe, and it was taken here at a party following JFK's birthday cel-ebration held on May 19, 1962, at the old Madison Square Garden. Arthur Krim was the chairman of United Artists studios at the time, and he and his wife Mathilde were long-time Democratic Party donors. Dr. Krim was instrumental in the fight against AIDS as chair-man of amfAR (American Foundation for AIDS Research) from 1985 to 2004. Singer Diahann Carroll performed at the party, singing songs from the Richard Rodgers'

JFK outside the Krims' townhouse on the afternoon of May 19, 1962. Cecil Stoughton, White House Photographs, JFK Library and Museum, Boston.

musical *No Strings*, in which she was starring on Broadway. Guests seen speaking with JFK included Mike Nichols and Elaine May, Jimmy Durante, and Harry Belafonte.

Arthur Krim served as a trusted advisor to LBJ and President Jimmy Carter. Mathilde Krim was a medical researcher and a prominent advocate for AIDS (Acquired Immune Deficiency Syndrome) education and research in the 1980s. Her work in the fight against AIDS was cited by President Bill Clinton in awarding her the Presidential Medal of Freedom in 2000.

This building dates back to 1914, when it was known as the James Harper Poor Mansion. Today it looks pretty much like it did in 1962.

Stephen Smith and Marilyn Monroe at the Krims' townhouse.
Cecil Stoughton. White House Photographs. John F. Kennedy
Presidential Library and Museum, Boston

# VENEZIANO

## 823 MADISON AVE. NEAR 68TH ST.; CLOSED

FOUNDED IN 1958, VENEZIANO SPECIALIZED in exclusive merchandise made in Italy. Though "not much bigger than a doll's house," according to a 1969 article in the *New York Times*, the store attracted rich and famous ladies such as Barbara "Babe" Paley and Jackie's pal Rachel "Bunny" Mellon. Jackie was said to buy her pant-suits here. The *Times* story noted her purchase of "the churidar or tight silk pants with the choli or matching top that bares the midriff." I wonder if the outfit ended up at Encore Consignment?

# THE PARK AVENUE ARMORY AKA
# THE SEVENTH REGIMENT ARMORY
## 643 PARK AVE. BETWEEN 66TH AND 67TH STS.

THIS UNLIKELY VENUE WAS WHERE Bobby won the Democratic nomination for the U.S. Senate on September 1, 1964, at the state party convention, soundly defeating Rep. Samuel S. Stratton. Democratic leaders in New York had urged Bobby to run, believing that no other prospective candidate could unseat incumbent Republican Sen. Kenneth Keating. Bobby then addressed 6,000 delegates inside the "sweltering" armory. He sought to address the carpetbagger issue by reminding them that half of New York residents had been born somewhere else and that the state's first U.S. senator — one Rufus King —had been born in Massachusetts. New York was hardly the reliably Democratic state it is today back in 1964. Both U.S. senators (Keating and Jacob Javits) and the governor (Nelson Rockefeller) were "moderate" Republicans, and no Democrat had been elected to the Senate in fourteen years.

The building, dating back to 1879, was designed by Charles W. Clinton and features a Victorian crenelated fortress. Stanford White was one of the designers who worked on the interior. Today, the Armory—featuring its huge Drill Hall, where Bobby spoke—provides a unique space for cutting-edge works in the performing and visual arts.

www.parkavenuearmory.org

# PARAPHERNALIA

795 MADISON AVE. NORTHEAST CORNER @ E. 67TH ST.; CLOSED

THIS PLACE SOUNDS LIKE THE epitome of the Swinging '60s: go-go dancers in the front windows, rock music blasting from the speakers, clothes for sale designed by a young Betsey Johnson, who designed micro miniskirts and was outfitting the Velvet Underground at the time...Let's go! How cool was this place? The Velvet Underground and Nico performed at their opening reception, where they were filmed by Andy Warhol and watched by Rolling Stones founder Brian Jones. Proprietor Paul Young had a fashion philosophy: "Clothes should be fun. Nothing about them should be taken too seriously." Featuring a very cool minimalist design by Ulrich Franzen, Paraphernalia celebrated the emerging youth culture of the '60s.

A March 1967 *Look* magazine article listed this boutique as among Jackie's favorites. Although Paraphernalia opened a branch downtown and in some forty other U.S. cities, the boutiques went out of business in the 1970s.

## FRED LEIGHTON JEWELERS;
## FORMERLY LARIMORE CHEMISTS; CLOSED
### 773 MADISON AVE.@ E. 66TH ST., NORTHEAST CORNER

LARIMORE WAS JACKIE'S DRUGSTORE DURING the 1960s and early 70s. The employees here were very protective of her privacy and reportedly sometimes chased out curious reporters. Want to see what it looked like back in the day? Check out this excellent website: https://www.scoutingny.com/the-filming-locations-of-the-naked-city-part-3-the-upper-west-side-and-upper-east-side/

# THOMAS MORRISSEY HAIR SALON

## 787 MADISON AVE. BETWEEN E. 66TH AND E. 67TH STS.

IN HER BOOK *Country Girl: A Memoir*,[44] Jackie's friend, the Irish novelist Edna O'Brien, wrote of her amazement at how Jackie would go alone to places like this with no entourage whatsoever. Morrissey worked as an expert colorist at Mr. Kenneth's for years before opening his own place here in 1985. Jackie apparently moved her patronage from Kenneth when Morrissey left. Stylist Edgar Montalvo later recalled that he would trim Jackie's hair once or twice a week and add a sheen to it, often at her apartment. He said Jackie called him when she needed wigs while undergoing chemotherapy during the final months of her life. Morrissey was in business at this location for 25 years before being forced to close due to a rent hike. He later worked at the John D'Orazio Salon on Madison

---

44    Edna O'Brien, *Country Girl: A Memoir*, New York: Little, Brown and Company, 2013.

# TEMPLE EMANU-EL OF NEW YORK
## 1 E. 65TH ST. @ FIFTH AVE.

COMPLETED IN 1930, THIS IS one of the largest synagogues in the world, seating more than 2,500 people. The congregation was founded as the original branch of Reform Judaism in New York in the mid-19th century. JFK spoke here on November 19, 1957, just a month after the Soviets' Sputnik satellite launch caught Americans off-guard. He recalled the Johann Wolfgang von Goethe quote: "He only earns his freedom and existence who daily conquers them anew." The JFK-inspired U.S. moon landing twelve years hence had its roots in the nation's response to the Sputnik launch as the start of the "space race."

On December 8, 1963, Bobby attended the memorial services held here for former New York Democratic governor and senator Herbert H. Lehman. Lehman — New York's first Jewish governor and, for much of his time in the Senate, the only Jewish senator — had died at 85 three days earlier. This service was among Bobby's first public appearances after JFK's funeral. LBJ also attended, guarded by 2,000 police officers and detectives during his two-hour stay in New York, the result of heightened security just two weeks after Dallas.

Bobby returned to the Lowenstein Auditorium here on October

26, 1967, discussing the difficulties the U.S. faced in Vietnam. This was when speculation about his possible 1968 candidacy was at a fever pitch. Bobby asked the audience if he could pose four questions to them. When they agreed, he laid out four alternative courses of action in Vietnam, ranging from immediate withdrawal to escalation. Via a show of hands, a good number of audience members supported each of the options. Bobby said, "As you can see, there are no easy answers, but we should be able to talk about it in a reasonable way." He added that violent protests would only set back the anti-war cause. Unfortunately, the bitterness and division regarding Vietnam only increased during the coming months, with Bobby — who had evolved from hawk to dove on Vietnam — catching criticism from people on both sides of the issue.

# SIGN OF THE DOVE RESTAURANT

## 1110 THIRD AVE. @ 65TH ST.; RAZED

DENTIST (!) JOSEPH SANTO OPENED Sign of the Dove in 1962, and its lush, elegant décor, which Santo designed, quickly earned it a reputation as one of New York's most romantic places to dine. The food and service were another matter, with an early *New York Times* review claiming that the former ranged from "mediocre to very good" while the latter was described as "at worst lamentable." Sign of the Dove lasted for three-and-a-half decades before closing in 1998. Later reviews were far more laudatory, with a *Times* post-mortem calling it "one of New York's most beloved dining spots."

In September 1965, Jackie and RFK aide William vanden Heuvel threw a midnight dinner dance party here for John Kenneth Galbraith, the economist who'd escorted Jackie on her trip to India in 1962 when he served as U.S. ambassador there. The event marked Jackie's return to nightlife following JFK's death, and she celebrated by dancing until 1:30 a.m. The guest list mixed uptown and downtown and included artist Andy Warhol and his "it girl," the ill-fated Edie Sedgwick, along with Italian industrialist Gianni Agnelli, whose family founded Fiat. Jackie was accompanied by architect John Carl Warnecke, whom she described as her "very, *very* special friend." Bobby and Jackie had selected "Jack" Warnecke to design JFK's permanent gravesite at Arlington, so Jackie saw a lot of Warnecke around this time, and he became Jackie's first serious romance after she became a widow.

# PARADE REVIEWING STAND
## E. 64TH ST. @ FIFTH AVE.

AS PRESIDENT, JFK SAT IN the temporary stand constructed
here to review the Columbus Day Parade on October 12, 1962. With

JFK with (from left) NY Attorney General Louis Lefkowitz, Lieutenant (and future)
Governor Malcolm Wilson, Gov. Nelson Rockefeller, Italian Ambassador Sergio
Fenoaltea, Robert Morgenthau, and Mayor Robert Wagner. *Stoughton, JFK Library.*

him was Robert Morgenthau, then on leave from his post as U.S. Attorney for the Southern District of New York. Morgenthau was running as the Democratic candidate against Republican Gov. Nelson Rockefeller, who was also on hand that day. JFK was grateful that the Republicans had not nominated the moderate Rockefeller to run against him in 1960, and he believed "Rocky" to be his strongest potential challenger in 1964. In a March 1963 conversation between Bobby and JFK recorded on the White House taping system, Bobby informed his brother that Manhattan bartenders were now serving an expensive "Rockefeller cocktail" to voice their displeasure with high costs, as evidence of the governor's supposed dip in popularity in New York.

Fate placed Morgenthau at Bobby's Hickory Hill home for a luncheon the afternoon of November 22, 1963, when word came that JFK had been assassinated. Morgenthau served as Manhattan District Attorney from 1975 to 2009. John Jr. went to work in Morgenthau's office upon his graduation from law school in 1989.

JFK, visible on the lower right, awaits the start of the parade. 828 and 825 Fifth Ave. are visible across the street. *Cecil Stoughton. White House Photographs. John F. Kennedy Presidential Library and Museum, Boston.*

# CENTRAL PARK

JACKIE LOVED TO SPEED-WALK AROUND the reservoir here that now bears her name. Even in the 1970s, when the park was widely regarded as a dangerous place to be at night, Jackie still walked here at dusk every day even though friends like Nancy Tuckerman warned she could be a target for muggers.

John Jr. and Caroline played at the William Church Osborne playground near E. 84th St when they were kids. Jackie attended a performance of the Public Theater's hit production of Gilbert and Sullivan's *The Pirates of Penzance* at the Delacorte Theater here in July 1980. The show starred a young Kevin Kline as the Pirate King and featured pop singers Rex Smith and Linda Ronstadt. After the show, Jackie was photographed with Mike Nichols and Public Theater founder Joseph Papp.

On September 13 of that year, John Jr. was photographed after attending Elton John's free concert in the park, which drew an estimated 500,000 people. John loved the park. He was often photographed here roller skating or tossing a football or frisbee with his friends.

In her book *The Nine of Us,* Jean told an amusing story of how an elderly Rose insisted on walking through the park at night and then reprimanded a would-be mugger on the evils of smoking before she and Jean made a hasty getaway.

On May 15, 1994, just five days before her death, a visibly ailing Jackie was photographed walking here with Maurice Tempelsman.

## GEMINI TWIN CINEMAS I AND II

1210 SECOND AVE. BETWEEN E. 63ᴿᴰ AND 64ᵀᴴ STS.; CLOSED

THESE THEATERS WERE CALLED THE Columbia I and II when United Artists opened them in 1971. Renamed the Gemini in 1978 and United Artists 64ᵗʰ St. and Second Avenue in 1996, the complex was closed for good in October 2012.[45]

In her memoir *Touched by the Sun*, Carly Simon recalls going to see a sparsely attended Thursday afternoon matinee of the movie *Bugsy* starring Warren Beatty here with Jackie in early 1992. Oliver Stone's movie *JFK* had just been released in December 1991, and in selecting a movie to see with Jackie, Carly writes that she went out of her way to ensure that Stone's movie wasn't playing in the same theater complex as the flick she would select. Therefore, she was mortified when Jackie (quite understandably) freaked out when Carly — filling an awkward moment of silence — inexplicably asked Jackie if she'd seen *JFK*. Releasing what she'd done, Carly immediately tearfully apologized. Carly noted that Jackie — apparently still traumatized by JFK's murder — reacted physically every time gunshots rang out in *Bugsy*.

---

45  https://cinematreasures.org/theaters/6121

# CLUB MACANUDO CIGAR BAR;
## FORMERLY QUO VADIS RESTAURANT
### 26 E. 63ᴿᴰ ST. BETWEEN MADISON AND PARK AVES.

IN 1972 QUO VADIS WAS included as one of "Le Six" of the last bastions of fine luxury dining in New York by *W* magazine. Opened by Bruno Caravaggi and Gino Robusti in 1946, Quo Vadis specialized in "Continental," rather than French or Italian cuisine. The food was less expensive, and the vibe was much more casual than its more sophisticated competitors. Even so, in 1968, it received a coveted four-star rating from famed restaurant critic Craig Claiborne in the *New York Times*.

Quo Vadis was said to be a favorite of Jackie's. Andy Warhol sometimes conducted his *Interview* interviews at the bar, including one with Truman Capote and another with Mick Jagger. Former Beatle John Lennon had lunch here with his wife, Yoko Ono, just a week before his assassination. After the new owners they'd sold to went bankrupt, Caravaggi and Robusti repurchased their old place, but Quo Vadis closed for good in 1984.

# VOISIN RESTAURANT

575 PARK AVE. BETWEEN 62ND AND 63RD STS.; CLOSED

A LANDMARK FRENCH RESTAURANT IN New York, Voisin opened in 1913 and had a nearly sixty-year run at several locations in the city before closing in 1969. JFK and Jackie had lunch here in February 1963, just before Voisin moved to the Colony House at 30 E. 65th St. Secret Service agent Clint Hill later recalled that he and other agents assigned to the couple were frantic when JFK and Jackie — noting that it was a beautiful Sunday in New York — exited their limo at 67th and Park Ave. and decided to walk the remaining four blocks to Voisin.

# THE COLONY RESTAURANT
## 30 E. 61ST ST. @ MADISON AVE. CLOSED

FOR MANY YEARS, THIS WAS thought by many to be New York's most fashionable restaurant. The Colony opened in 1919 and was known for having the best booze during the Depression years. Soon, people with names like Astor and Vanderbilt became regulars. The Colony was among the first air-conditioned establishments in the United States.

Maître d' Sirio Maccioni later recalled:

> *"We had all the ladies who counted, including Rose Kennedy, her daughters, and Jacqueline Kennedy.... In those days, the Kennedys were very close to the Colony and to me. I had a fabulous rapport with Jacqueline — as Mrs. Kennedy and Mrs. Onassis. Jacqueline was the only lady in New York who had my home number."*[46]

In a 1983 interview with Frank Gannon, former President Richard M. Nixon recalled the first time he met Joe Sr., who was

---

46   Colacello, Bob "Here's to the Ladies Who Lunched!" *Vanity Fair*, February 2012.

with Teddy outside the Colony:

> *"...it was in 1960. This was before (JFK's)*
> *nomination and Joe Kennedy and Teddy Kennedy*
> *were standing outside the Colony restaurant in*
> *New York City. I shook hands with them... and (Joe)*
> *said, 'I just want you to know how much I admire*
> *you for what you've done in the Hiss case and this*
> *anti-communist activity of yours. ... If Jack doesn't*
> *get (the Democratic nomination), I'll be for you.'*
> *Teddy didn't say anything, but I hope that he felt the*
> *same way."*[47]

Joe was less complimentary of Nixon in a February 1960 note to JFK's aide Ted Sorenson:

> *"I continuously hear about Nixon's experience,*
> *and I certainly think for the most part 'experience'*
> *is a term usually used to describe a lifetime of*
> *mistakes."*[48]

By early 1971, a *New York Magazine* review by Gael Greene noted that the Colony had seen better days and that it now resembled "Forest Lawn," meaning a cemetery. She also wasn't crazy about the food. Owner Gene Cavallero Jr. claimed to be the first to predict Jackie's marriage to Ari Onassis after observing the couple dining here on two occasions. Speaking of Ari, U.S. Marshals once suppos-

---

47   https://www.c-span.org/video/?153806-1/president-richard-nixon-interview

48   Smith, Ed. *Hostage to Fortune*, page 686.

edly apprehended him on the Colony's doorstep for "alleged commercial skullduggery." Labor disputes finally caused the Colony to close in December 1971.

# BLOOMINGDALE'S

## 1000 THIRD AVE. BETWEEN E. 59TH AND 60TH STS.

IT SHOULD COME AS NO surprise to know that Jackie shopped at this store, the flagship of the Bloomingdale's chain. During the 1960 campaign, her friend, newspaper columnist Joseph Alsop, told her it would be a good idea to get her maternity clothes here, as the press was starting to write about her taste for European haute couture.

John Jr. was the cause of "mass hysteria" when he appeared here with Jean and his cousins William Kennedy Smith and Ted Kennedy Jr. in November 1988 to promote the sale of Christmas ornaments to benefit a family charity Very Special Arts. John was greeted by "screaming women and pushing paparazzi," according to one account.[49] One of the organizers later said, "It was obnoxious from the second he walked in.

---

49    Michael Gross, "Favorite Son," *New York Magazine*, March 20, 1989.

John was hoping for something more substantive."

This event occurred weeks after the "Sexiest Man" *People magazine* cover which precipitated a ramping up of media attention on John that would never diminish in the coming years.

After breaking his ankle over Memorial Day weekend, John Jr. was on crutches as he attended a *George* party at the Le Train Bleu rooftop restaurant here on June 10, 1999. The party was to promote the publication of the *George* book *250 Ways to Make America Better.* Upon arrival, John explained to reporters that he had broken his ankle hang-gliding. Richard Blow accompanied John to the event and later wrote[50] that his boss looked "pale and drawn... exhausted" and that John was unable to give even the short speech normally expected of him.

Le Train Bleu was a peculiar place. Opened in 1979, the restaurant was modeled on the 19th-century dining car of the luxury Calais-Méditerranée Express "Blue Train" overnight train that shuttled passengers from the north of France to the Riviera,[51] and its namesake Parisian restaurant. It was also the setting of an Agatha Christie mystery bearing its name. Wider than a train car, Le Train Bleu had mahogany paneling, velvet walls, and an overhead rack where diners could stash their belongings. It offered a spectacular view of the Upper East Side. This Le Train Bleu closed in 2016. Happily, the one in Paris is still going strong.

---

50    Richard Blow, *American Son*, New York: Henry Holt, 2002.

51    The train was the setting for Agatha Christie's 1928 novel *The Mystery of the Blue Train*, which preceded her more renowned *Murder on the Orient Express* by six years.

## SERENDIPITY 3

225 E. 60TH ST. BETWEEN SECOND AND THIRD AVES.

THIS IS A CAFÉ AND boutique founded in 1954 and best known for its ice cream and desserts, especially the famous "Frozen Hot Chocolate." It also lent its name to the 2001 romcom starring John Cusack and Kate Beckinsale. Serendipity moved from E. 58th St. to its current location in 1960. Jackie was a regular here, and legend has it that she once attempted to purchase the secret recipe for the Frozen Hot Chocolate for a party she was giving. In an attempt to bond with his new stepson, Ari Onassis sometimes treated John Jr. to hot fudge sundaes here. His efforts paid off because even in later years, John only ever had nice things to say about Ari, at least in public.

# CORONET THEATER
## 993 THIRD AVE. @ E. 59ᵀᴴ ST. RAZED

BOBBY AND PAT WERE HERE on the evening of Wednesday, March 8, 1967 to attend the U.S. premiere of director Franco Zeffirelli's screen adaptation of Shakespeare's *The Taming of the Shrew*, starring Elizabeth Taylor as Katharina and Richard Burton as Petruchio. The event was a benefit to raise funds for the Society for the Facially Disfigured at New York Medical Center. This was the first of three Shakespeare works filmed by Zeffirelli, the others being the highly successful *Romeo and Juliet* (1968), which received Oscar nominations for Best Picture and Best Director, and Hamlet (1990). He also gave the world the 1981 schlockfest *Endless Love*.

Crowds outside the theater were excited to see genuine British royalty with the presence of the Duke and Dutchess of Windsor. The former King Edward VIII was said to be "visibly moved" by the "ecstatic shrieks and cheers"[52] they elicited from the crowd outside the theater, and he took time to shake hands with well-wishers.

Bobby told reporters that he liked Shakespeare. This was no doubt true as Bobby an Burton were said to try to one up each other

---

52 "Windsors Assure Social Success of 'Taming of the Shrew' Premiere," by Enid Nemy' *The New York Times*, March 9, 1967.

quoting the Bard's sonnets when they got together. Recall that Bobby famously quoted Shakespeare's *Romeo and Juliet* in his tribute to JFK at the 1964 Democratic Convention in Atlantic City:

*"When he shall die take him and cut him out into*
*stars and he shall make the face of heaven so fine*
*that all the world will be in love with night and pay*
*no worship to the garish sun.*

After the movie, guests – including Bobby and Pat - adjourned to the El Morocco nightclub on East 54th St.

During its heyay in the 1960s and '70s, the Coronet (along with the Baronet Theater at the same site) was one of the most prestigious movie houses in the city and the host to many notable premieres. Both closed in 2001 and later met the wrecking ball.

# TRUMP PARK AVENUE;
## FORMERLY DELMONICO HOTEL
502 PARK AVE., NORTHWEST CORNER OF PARK @ 59TH ST.

ACCORDING TO A MARCH 1964 *New York Times* article,[53] the restaurant in Delmonico Hotel had seen a "takeover" by "the socially prominent as well as the rich and famous." Bobby, along with friends and family, convened here in the early morning hours of November 4, 1964, to celebrate his election to the U.S. Senate. They were entertained by Tony Bennett and Sammy Davis Jr. Bobby left at 3:30 a.m. to return to the Fulton Fish Market, where he'd started his campaign in September with a promise to return after the election, win or lose. Bobby was back here a few months later to speak to the Lexington Democratic Club on February 4, 1965.

Delmonico's has earned a place in pop culture immortality for two reasons: on the night of August 28, 1964, Bob Dylan turned the Beatles on to marijuana while the band stayed here. Then, on January 13, 1966, the Velvet Underground and Nico — accompanied by Edie Sedgwick and Andy Warhol (who showed his films) — performed at the annual dinner of (of all things) the New York Society for Clinical Psychiatry. The hotel housed the famed Regine's

---

53   Charlotte Curtis, "Delmonico's Hotel Turns into Haven for Social Elite" *New York Times*, March 22, 1964.

nightclub during the 1970s.

The Delmonico was built in 1929 and converted into condos in 1975. Donald Trump purchased the building for $115 million in 2002.

# MIDTOWN EAST 59TH ST.
# TO E. 14TH ST.

## CHEZ NINON

487 PARK AVE. BETWEEN E. 58<sup>TH</sup> AND 59<sup>TH</sup> STS.; CLOSED

THIS STORE WAS KNOWN FOR selling precise knockoffs of the latest Paris fashions at prices similar to what the originals would have cost. This was ideal for Jackie when she served as First Lady because it allowed her to wear the chicest designs while still buying from an American label. Chez Ninon was founded in 1929, and owners Nona Park and Sophie Shonnard traveled abroad twice a year in search of the latest trends. They catered to the high-society women of the Upper East Side, including Mrs. William S. "Babe" Paley. Among the designers they featured were Balenciaga, Givenchy, and Dior. A June 1, 1961, *New York Times* article noted that Jackie had recently purchased eight ensembles from this store, two of which she'd taken to Paris for her state visit with JFK. The report noted that Jackie and other members of the Kennedy family had shopped here "for years." After moving to the Ritz Towers in 1970, Chez Ninon closed in 1996.

Jackie's most iconic outfit, the pink suit she wore in Dallas, carried a Chez Ninon label. It was a "line by line" authorized copy of a Coco Chanel design that appeared in her autumn/winter collection of 1961. Photographs show Jackie wearing the suit in November 1961 and on several occasions in 1962. Today, Jackie's pink suit is housed at the National Archives in College Park, Maryland. It will be kept under lock and key until at least 2103. A brief March 24, 1966, *Times* article noted that Jackie — accompanied by her Secret Service detail — had shopped in the boutique for an hour the previous day.

# VIKING PRESS

## 625 MADISON AVE. BETWEEN E. 58TH AND 59TH STS.

JACKIE WAS REPORTEDLY AT LOOSE ends by the summer of 1975 following Ari's death in March. Her friend Letitia "Tish" Baldridge suggested that a job in publishing would be an excellent way for Jackie — a passionate lover of books since childhood — to engage with the world and utilize her knowledge and experience. As First Lady, Jackie had written and edited "The White House: An Historic Guide," a room-by-room photographic tour of the building that was sold to tourists to raise funds for its restoration. Jackie was a longtime friend of Viking president Thomas Guinzburg, so his publishing house seemed like a perfect fit for her. Viking was a prestigious outfit that published authors such as D.H. Lawrence, Saul Bellow, and Thomas Pynchon, to name a few.

Jackie started her job as a consulting editor here on September 22, 1975, and she was met by a phalanx of reporters documenting her first day. Her starting salary was $200 a week, and she was to work four days a week. She was starting a new career at 46. She would dedicated herself to her work in publishing until the very end of her life. Her work gave her enjoyment and bolstered her self-confidence by allowing her to use her talents in a productive way. Jackie was given a small office to start, but it had a window. If some coworkers were expecting her to be a dilettante, they were soon convinced otherwise. Jackie made her own coffee and wasn't above crawling around on her hands and knees to examine proofs for a book she was editing.

Jackie resigned from Viking in October 1977 over their publication of the book *Shall We Tell the President?* by Jeffrey Archer. The book was set in 1983 and concerned a plot to assassinate an American president whom Archer had modeled after Ted Kennedy. A *New York Times* review called the book "trashed" and implicitly criticized Jackie for being involved in its publication. Jackie had remained close to Ted, and she didn't like the implication that she'd endorsed the book in any way. For his part, Guinzburg claimed that Jackie *had* been aware of Viking's plans to publish Archer's book and that she hadn't raised any objection. Jackie was said to have been troubled by her ungraceful exit from Viking for the rest of her life. Even so, it was here that she began a long and satisfying career in publishing, during which she would edit 100 books.

Viking published *In the Russian Style* in 1976 and credited Jackie as the editor. The book celebrated the elaborate costumes of the Czarist court and aristocracy. *In the Russian Style* was issued in conjunction with the Met's Costume Institute show of the same name. Along with *The Firebird and Other Russian Fairy Tales*, which Viking published in 1978, this marked the only times Jackie was ever so credited. Among the handful of titles Jackie edited during her brief time at Viking were Barbara Chase-Riboud's *Sally Hemings* and Eugene Kennedy's *Himself! The Life and Times of Mayor Richard J. Daley.*

# MRS. JOHN R. "FIFI" FELL APARTMENT
## 475 PARK AVE. @ E. 58TH ST.

LATE ON THE NIGHT OF December 5, 1961, after addressing the National Football Foundation dinner at the Waldorf, JFK spent about an hour and a half at a small party hosted by Mrs. Josphine "Fifi" Fell here. Her husband, John – scion of the Drexel banking family – and a partner in the Lehman Brothers investment firm, had passed away at 49 the previous April. Eunice and Sarge attended along with Pat and Peter Lawford. A March 1961 *Sports Illustrated* article[54] listed Fifi as a "presidential golfing partner and one noted for her distinctive flair for clothes" on the Palm Beach links.

Several accounts claim that Marilyn Monroe and JFK were present at one of Fifi's parties around this time, although they are often less than clear on the precise timing. If such a meeting occurred it was very likely on this night. Marilyn's presence in New York in December 1961 is documented by photos of her visiting poet and writer Carl Sandburg taken in an apartment in the city that month. Most accounts claim that JFK and Marilyn first met at the Lawford's Santa Monica home on November 19, 1961.

On June 12, 1963, a White House Dictabelt recorded JFK's secre-

---

54 "The Trim New Era of Golf" by Fred R. Smith, *Sports Illustrated*, March 6, 1961.

tary, Evelyn Lincoln, placing a call to Fifi on his behalf.

This 14-story building dates back to 1908, but its white brick façade was part of a 1959 renovation.

# BERGDORF GOODMAN

## 754 FIFTH AVE. BETWEEN W. 57TH AND 58TH STS.

FOUNDED IN 1901, BERGDORF'S IS an old-school, high-end department store known for featuring designers such as Gucci, Chanel, and Oscar de la Renta. This was one of Jackie's favorite places to shop. It's also the place a young Barbra Streisand[55] danced through in a 1965 television special. Jackie was photographed here on several occasions.

In 2023, Howard Stern's sidekick Robin Quivers related a story about once seeing John Jr. here:

> *"There's only two times I've been stunned by how beautiful someone was in person. ... He was perfect. ... Not a hair out of place."*[56]

Bergdorf's is conveniently located next door to Van Cleef & Arpels.

In 2013, a cache of letters that Jackie sent to her Bergdorf's

---

55    John Jr. used to do an impression of Streisand for friends that included a rendition of "People," her hit song from the 1964 musical *Funny Girl*.

56    *The Howard Stern Show*, Sirius XM, April 4, 2023. The other stunner mentioned by Robin was Farrah Fawcett.

personal shopper Marita O'Connor were put up for auction. These letters were written in the weeks following JFK's election and concerned her specifying and selecting the outfits and accessories she'd need for the inaugural festivities in Washington DC. She forwarded detailed instructions and included fabric swatches when she sought to match a hat with a dress.

In a letter dated November 14, 1960, Jackie wrote to O'Connor:

> *"You may not know it yet, but I have decided to get nearly all my clothes through Bergdorf Goodman. Please keep this confidential until I announce it myself."*[57]

---

57   https://www.dailymail.co.uk/femail/article-2493731/Jackie-Kennedy-letters-Bergdorf-personal-shopper-auction.html

# IBM BUILDING
## 590 MADISON AVE. @ 57TH ST.; RAZED.

THE ORIGINAL IBM BUILDING WAS erected here in 1938 and stood twenty stories high. That building was torn down in 1977 to make way for the new IBM Building, which is twice the size of the original. After selling the building to Odyssey Corporation in 1994, IBM remained a tenant here, but in 2022 they announced plans to consolidate their offices at the new One Madison Ave. Bobby and Jackie attended a news conference here on Monday, May 25, 1964, to publicize the exhibit of JFK pictures, papers, and mementos (including his rocking chair) that opened here the following day. The exhibition was open for two weeks here before touring twenty-two other cities in the US. Proceeds went towards the building of the Kennedy Library in Boston. Kennedy family friend and Democratic donor Thomas J. Watson Jr. was the President of IBM at the time, and a connection that no doubt resulted in IBM hosting the event.

Watson recalled[58] meeting with Bobby here in March of 1968. Bobby told Watson that his attempts to form a coalition ticket with McCarthy to serve as vice president had failed. He also spoke of his

58    Thomas J. Watson Jr., JFK Library Oral History Interview. https://www.jfklibrary. org/asset-viewer/archives/RFKOH/Watson%2C%20Thomas%20J/RFKOH-TJW-01/RFKOH-TJW-01

determination to extract the United States from Vietnam despite the criticism such a policy would entail. Watson accompanied Jackie to LA on a private plane on June 5, 1968, upon hearing that Bobby had been shot there during the night.

# VAN CLEEF & ARPELS

## 744 FIFTH AVE. ON THE CORNER OF W. 57TH ST.

IT'S NO SURPRISE THAT JACKIE'S dazzling "Toi et Moi" (You and Me) engagement ring was designed here at a store renowned for refinement and elegance. What is surprising is that the design was selected not by her husband-to-be JFK but by her soon-to-be father-in-law, Joe. Jeweler Louis Arpels' wife knew Jackie and assisted Joe in his selection. It took a while since Jackie still didn't have a ring even after the couple announced their engagement. When finally selected, Jackie's ring consisted of a 2.88-carat diamond and a 2.84-carat emerald, both of which were emerald-cut, on a band of baguette-cut emeralds and diamonds. The design was much admired and helped define Jackie as a woman of taste and elegance. Jackie replaced some of the baguette pieces in early 1962, but she rarely took off her wedding band for the rest of her life.

Hoping to lift Jackie's spirits following the death of their son Patrick that August, JFK came here in the fall of 1963 and selected a ring with a 47-carat pink kunzite stone as Jackie's Christmas gift. After JFK's assassination, the ring was delivered to the White House, and his secretary, Evelyn Lincoln, gave it to Jackie.

Jackie "dashed from the sidelines and kissed"[59] Bobby as he marched down Fifth Ave. in the March 17, 1966, St. Patrick's Day Parade, and a photo shows the pair with Van Cleef & Arpels in the background behind them.

John Jr. wanted to do something special for his mother's 50th birthday in 1979, so he came here to have a special ring designed for her. The ring was dubbed "Star of the Sea" and had two blue-toned sapphires (recalling the family's love of the sea) in the center, symbolizing Jackie and JFK surrounded by four smaller stones representing their children.

Several items from Van Cleef & Arpels were purchased when offered at Jackie's estate auction in 1996. Among them was a pendant necklace that Ari had given her as a wedding gift. It had a heart-shaped cabochon ruby and sold for $288,500, roughly three times its auction estimate.

---

59   Per the UPI telephoto description.

# A LA VIEILLE RUSSIE

## 745 FIFTH AVE., FOURTH FLOOR; FORMERLY LOCATED AT 781 FIFTH AVE. FROM 1961 TO 2017

FOUNDED IN 1851, THIS SPECIALTY antiques dealer specializes in Fabergé and Russian and European jewelry. The story – as told in C. David Heymann's book *Bobby and Jackie* – goes that Jackie and Bobby were here together in February 1967, and Jackie expressed interest in an eighteenth-century decanter. After looking over the piece, Bobby was stunned to learn that it cost $60,000, partly because a Tsar once owned it. He reacted by quickly escorting Jackie to the exit. They soon turned up at Collector's Corner on Madison, where a jade Buddha that Jackie had had her eye on was on sale for the far more reasonable $12,000. Possibly feeling that he was getting off easy, Bobby wrote out a check for $2,000 and arranged for the family office to foot the rest of the bill. Owner Ernest Lowy later stated: "If found out later that Mrs. Kennedy had set him up by first taking him to A La Vieille Russie."

## JEAN KENNEDY SMITH RESIDENCE
### 4 SUTTON PLACE BETWEEN E. 57TH AND 58TH STS.

JEAN BOUGHT A DUPLEX AT this elegant 14-story co-op designed by Rosario Candela in 1997. She moved in the following year after completing her stint as U.S. Ambassador to Ireland, where she helped forge the April 1998 Good Friday Agreement, which ended the thirty-year conflict in Northern Ireland that had killed 3,500 people. She was the last surviving member of Joe and Rose's family when she passed away on June 17, 2020, at the age of 92.

## PATRICIA KENNEDY LAWFORD RESIDENCE
### 1 SUTTON PLACE SOUTH BETWEEN E. 56TH AND 57TH STS.

IN EARLY 1974, PAT MOVED into an 11-room duplex in this elegant Rosario Candela-designed building. Located three blocks south of the Ed Koch Queensboro Bridge, the limestone building has a distinctive triple-arched entrance and offers spectacular East River views. Dating from 1927, the building has long been one of New York's most desirable — and expensive — addresses.

Following Pat's death at age 82 from pneumonia on September 17, 2006, her unit sold for $12 million in 2007. The real estate listing described her apartment as follows:

> *"The soaring ceilings, the stately circular staircase,*
> *the beautiful views, the marble in the hallways,*
> *and the decorative molding throughout make this*
> *apartment unique and reminiscent of a bygone,*
> *more gracious era."*

Upon her death, Ted paid tribute to Pat:

> *"My sister Pat is irreplaceable. Throughout her*
> *life, Pat was constantly inspiring and encouraging*

*others. Whether it was campaigning for her brothers or championing literacy and the arts, her purest gift was her beautiful heart, and it shined brightly in all that she did."*

# LE PAVILLON

## 111 E. 57TH ST.; BETWEEN PARK AND LEXINGTON AVES. CLOSED

IT WAS IN ITS ORIGINAL location at 5 E. 55th St. across the street from the St. Regis Hotel that Henri Soulé (a maître d', not a chef) introduced classic French cuisine to New Yorkers during the 1940s and '50s. The restaurant took its name from the fact that Soulé had operated the restaurant at the French Pavillon at the New York World's Fair in 1939. Artist and gastronome Ludwig Bemelmans once averred that Le Pavillon was the finest restaurant in the United States or France. All of the Kennedys were regulars here, even after Joe fell out with Soulé in 1960.

Visiting New York as president-elect, JFK dined here with his friend Charles Spalding on the evening of December 6, 1960. Around this time, JFK dispatched Clark Clifford to meet with Joe Sr. to try to talk him out of his insistence that Bobby — who'd never practiced law a day in his life — be named attorney general[60] Clifford and Joe discussed the matter over lunch here, but Joe wouldn't be deterred. Given what we've since learned about Bobby's vital role in defusing the Cuban Missile Crisis two years later, we should all be thank-

---

60 "I can't see that it's wrong to give him a little legal experience before he goes out to practice law," quipped JFK.

ful that Clifford failed in his task. Joe was adamant that Bobby be named, finally admonishing JFK:

> *"Goddamn it, Jack, I want to tell you once and for all. Don't be sending these emissaries to me. Bobby spilled his blood for you. He's worked for you. And goddamn it, he wants to be attorney general, and I want him to be attorney general, and that's it."*[61]

Upon getting his wish, Joe only visited the White House once in the year following the inauguration.

JFK and Jackie dined here in February 1962, and again on February 9, 1963, when they were on what the President described as a "completely private and social" weekend visit to Manhattan.

Jackie ate here with Bobby and the Hervé Alphand in early December 1966. When Bobby told the group about the rafting trip that he'd led down Idaho's Salmon River, aka "The River of No Return," the previous summer, Jackie told him, "Oh Bobby, you're *soooo* reckless." She was not the only person close to Bobby to hold this view of him.[62] The restaurant was sold to an investment group a year after Soulé died in January 1967. It finally closed in 1972.

In 2021 chef Daniel Boulud's Le Pavillon opened in the One Vanderbilt Skyscraper. It is named in honor of Soule's restaurant and it opened to rapturous reviews.

---

61    Leamer, *Kennedy Men.*

62    See RFK Jr.'s book *American Values: Lessons I Learned from My Family*, New York: Harper Perennial, 2019.

## FORMER BONWIT TELLER LOCATION
### FIFTH AVE. @ 56TH ST., RAZED.

IN AUGUST 1944, JFK'S SISTER Kathleen returned to the U.S. to join the family in mourning for Joe Jr. On May 6, Joe Jr. had been the only member of her family to attend her London wedding to Billy Cavendish, aka Lord Hartington, the scion of one of Britain's noble families. On September 19, 1944, Joe Sr. was at his suite at the Waldorf when he received a War Department telegram saying that Billy had been killed, the victim of a sniper in Belgium. Kathleen wasn't there, having gone shopping in Manhattan. Eunice eventually found Kick shopping here but could not steel herself to tell her the devastating news. "Something's happened," Kick said, correctly sensing something was wrong. Eunice took Kick to the Waldorf, where Joe read the War Department telegram to her. "Life is so cruel," Kick wrote in her diary. She remained in England following her husband's death and died in a plane crash in France on May 13, 1948.

# ST. REGIS HOTEL
## 2 E. 55TH ST. BETWEEN FIFTH AND MADISON AVES.

THE ST. REGIS HAS LONG been considered one of New York's finest hotels. A fundraiser to raise money for the construction of the JFK Library was held here on June 16, 1964. Jean and Steve Smith hosted the event, which took place on the hotel's roof. Bobby, Jackie, LBJ, Lady Bird, and most of the Kennedys were present, along with Chief Justice Earl Warren and U.N. Ambassador Adlai Stevenson. Actor Fredric March read excerpts from JFK's speeches. March was featured in the John Frankenheimer film *Seven Days in May*, which was released in February. In it, March played a U.S. President fighting off an attempted coup by right-wing military officers. JFK enjoyed the Richard Condon novel and allowed Frankenheimer[63] the rare opportunity to film outside the White House for the movie.

On November 29, 1967, Bobby gathered at the elegant King Cole Bar here with Pierre Salinger and Arthur Schlesinger to discuss LBJ's removal of Robert MacNamara as defense secretary and assignment to the World Bank. Knowing that he'd lost confidence

---

63 Bobby and his family were at Frankenheimer's Malibu home on June 4, 1968, having stayed over the previous night. The director later drove him to the Ambassador Hotel early in the evening. When Frankenheimer missed the downtown exit off the freeway, Bobby told him not to be upset, saying, "Life's too short, John."

in the war, Bobby had been urging MacNamara to quit for months, during which time he spoke to him almost nightly. Bobby had hoped that McNamara —who had long been the public face of the Vietnam War — would use the occasion to call for a reassessment of U.S. policy, but it didn't happen. This was despite the fact that McNamara was now convinced that the U.S. effort was futile.

Early on January 19, 1968, Bobby was at the King Cole Bar with producer George Stevens Jr. and asked him: "Why does everyone think I have to be President? I have ten kids. There are other things for me to do."[64] His belief that he needed to do all he could to stop the war ultimately compelled him to run for President.

Stevens went on to create the American Film Institute. Many decades later, he said of his friend:

> "I think Bobby's murder was, in fact, more
> consequential than John Kennedy's.... I really
> believe Bobby could have led us out of the ...
> difficulties we were in.... I think he could have
> brought America together in that very difficult
> time ... Many people as they get older get more
> fixed in their views. Bobby was the opposite. He
> was more questing. I think he would have been an
> extraordinary leader."[65]

Ted celebrated his 66th birthday at the St. Regis on February 17, 1998, five days prior to his birthday. The event was a $1,000-per-

---

64    Quoted in Evan Thomas *Robert Kennedy: His Life* New York: Simon & Schuster, 2000, page 468 fn.

65    LBJ Library Podcast George Stevens interview 6/13/22.

ticket cocktail party to raise money in advance of Ted's upcoming re-election campaign in 2000. Tom Hanks, Lauren Bacall, and Chevy Chase were in attendance along with John Jr. and Carolyn, Pat Lawford, Caroline, and her husband Ed.

In what would prove to be one of his last New York events, John Jr. attended the Fisher Center Gala Dinner and Auction on April 26, 1999. The organization, which is affiliated with Rockefeller University in New York, advocates for Alzheimer's research.

www.Rockefeller.edu

# LA CÔTE BASQUE

5 E. 55TH ST. BETWEEN FIFTH AND MADISON AVES.; CLOSED.

FOUNDED BY HENRI SOULÉ OF La Pavillon, La Côte Basque took over La Pavillon's old home in 1958 when Soulé moved it to E. 57th St. With its elegant décor and outstanding French and Basque-inspired cuisine, it was a favorite gathering place for New York's rich and famous for 45 years before it closed in 2004. The restaurant was immortalized in the Truman Capote story "La Cote Basque 1965," which first appeared in *Esquire* in 1976.

Bobby and Ethel were photographed outside the restaurant on November 2, 1965. It was one of the few times Bobby was caught with a cigar in his hand. Jackie was photographed here in 1969. In September 1970 and January 1973, she was photographed leaving here with Ari Onassis. Jackie attended a party for the little-remembered Liza Minelli film *Lucky Lady* here in December 1975.

# P.J. CLARKE'S

## 915 THIRD AVE @ 55TH ST.

THIS ESTABLISHMENT IS, "THE ORIGINAL, virtually unchanged since 1884," according to its website. This brick-walled, wood-paneled saloon is known for its excellent burgers. Jackie and the kids sometimes ate lunch here on Saturdays in the early 1970s. A portrait of JFK hangs over the bar.

Bobby came here often, including on October 30, 1966, when he met with Arthur Schlesinger. The historian reported in his diary that when they discussed the Warren Commission Report, Bobby expressed his doubts about its finding that Lee Harvey Oswald had acted alone, and though the commission had done a "poor job." Bobby was nonetheless reluctant to go public with his criticism and "reopen the whole tragic business," as Schlesinger described it.[66] He also wondered how long he could go on avoiding commenting on it. Mark Lane's critique of the Warren Report, *Rush to Judgment*, had been published that August and would spend months on the *New York Times* bestseller list. Also, at this time, Bobby and Jackie were enmeshed in controversy as Jackie sought to prevent the publication of their hand-chosen author William Manchester's account of

66   Schlesinger, *Journals* 1952-2000, page 254.

the assassination, *The Death of a President*, after first objecting to its serialization in *Look* magazine. Eventually, several passages that Jackie objected to were removed from the manuscript — but made public anyway — and the book's publication moved forward. Manchester's book was hugely successful when released in April 1967, selling a million copies by the summer.

In January 1971, Jackie and Ari were photographed having lunch here.

In 1980, Ted came here following his concession speech at Madison Square Garden. It must have been a bittersweet night, marking the end of his prospects as a serious Presidential contender.

P.J. Clarke's doubled as "Nat's Bar" in Billy Wilder's 1945 movie *The Lost Weekend*, and Johnny Mercer was said to have written the words to the ultimate saloon song "One for My Baby" here.

www.pjclarkes.com

# LE CLUB

416 E. 55TH ST. BETWEEN FIRST AVE. AND SUTTON PLACE; RAZED.

FOUNDED BY GAY FRENCH EXPATRIATE Olivier Coquelin in 1960, this was a private club catering to the rich and famous. It laid claim to be New York's first discotheque since it always featured dancing to records rather than a live band. Le Club's first board of governors included Italian automaker Giovanni Agnelli and fashion designer Oleg Cassini, both of whom were friends of Jackie. According to reports, Jackie was sometimes escorted here by Bobby. In 1966, Coquelin founded the vast and elaborate Cheetah club on Broadway and 54th St., which housed the musical *Hair* after it left the Public Theater and before its arrival on Broadway. He later ran the popular club Hippopotamus in the early 1970s.

Jackie held a combined birthday bash for John Jr. (his 18th) and Caroline (her 21st) here on November 25, 1978. When the paparazzi ambushed the group as it exited at 4 a.m., John's pal Billy Noonan got into a shoving match with the lensmen. John somehow got knocked down in the fracas, and photos of the incident soon appeared in newspapers worldwide. Le Club closed in 1995. The one-and-a-half-story building that housed it is long gone, and a high-rise apartment building stands on the site today.

## KENNETH SALON

### 19 E. 54TH ST. BETWEEN FIFTH AND MADISON AVES.

"MR. KENNETH" BATTELLE WAS THE most prominent American hairdresser of the 1960s, primarily because he was responsible for Jackie's iconic tousled bouffant "do" when she was First Lady. Kenneth first did Jackie's hair in 1954, and he soon became her go-to stylist. The now-famous Mr. Kenneth opened his studio here in a granite five-story Renaissance Revival house on March 4, 1963. The house was built in 1897. Noted decorator Billy Baldwin designed the interior that *Glamour* described as "more glorious ornament and detail ... than an entire collection of Matisse paintings." When a client once screamed, "I'm getting out of here. It looks like a brothel!" Kenneth quipped loudly enough for the woman to hear, "Do you suppose she's been in one before?"[67] On the other hand, clients, including Jackie's sister Lee, found the atmosphere surprisingly comforting because they were pampered with finger sandwiches and cups of tea. Kenneth had a reassuring way about him that the ladies appreciated, and he was once described as having "magic hands." Jackie was a regular here after moving to New York in 1964. She was having her hair done here on March 15, 1975, when she received word that

---

67    Amy Fine Collins, "It Had to be Kenneth," *Vanity Fair*, June 2003.

her husband Ari had died at the American Hospital in Paris.

Mr. Kenneth's famous clients included Marilyn Monroe (he did her hair for her "Happy Birthday" performance for JFK at Madison Square Garden), Bunny Mellon, Lauren Bacall, Babe Paley, Judy Garland, Katherine Graham, and Diana Vreeland. Appointments usually required a three-month wait. Sadly, the building burned down in 1990, after which Kenneth relocated operations, first to the Helmsley Palace Hotel, and then to the Waldorf. Mr. Kenneth died in 2013. He is widely recognized as having invented modern American hairdressing.

# EL MOROCCO NIGHTCLUB
154 E. 54TH ST. BETWEEN LEXINGTON AND THRID AVES.
AFTER 1960: TWO BLOCKS EAST TO 307 E. 54TH ST.
BETWEEN FIRST AND SECOND AVES.; CLOSED

THIS CLUB BEGAN LIFE AS a speakeasy in 1931. After the repeal of prohibition in 1933, El Morocco became the most famous nightclub in New York, the place to see and be seen, sort of like the Studio 54 of its day. Like that club, El Morocco offered an exclusivity that made patrons feel special. Here, the rich rubbed elbows with movie stars and politicians, making for a unique and exciting night out. JFK and Jackie came here with their friend, actor David Niven, in 1958. Niven danced with Jackie that night and later recalled:

> *"JFK sat in the back room and when I asked why he wouldn't join us, she laughed and said, 'He doesn't want to be photographed doing something so frivolous.... He wants to be President."*[68]

Considering that a photo of him dancing at a swank Manhattan club would have been a gift to political opponents eager to tag him as a privileged playboy, this was undoubtedly shrewd thinking on JFK's part.

---

68    Quoted in Jay Mulvaney, *Jackie: The Clothes of Camelot* New York: St. Martins, 2001.

A June 1966 item in the *Daily News* mentioned that Jackie had recently been here. On March 8, 1967, Bobby and Pat came here following the premiere of the film *The Taming of the Shrew* at the Coronet Theater. Ari and his girlfriend, opera singer Maria Callas, were spotted here in November 1967. This was said to be Ari's favorite place in New York, even if he sometimes read a newspaper at his table. Jackie and Ari were spotted here while dating in early 1968. They had their fourth wedding anniversary party on October 21, 1972, but by then, the club, like the marriage, had seen better days.

# PALEY PARK; FORMER SITE OF THE STORK CLUB
## 3 E. 53ᴿᴰ ST. BETWEEN FIFTH AND MADISON AVES., RAZED.

BUILT IN 1967, PALEY PARK has a waterfall that helps make it a small but welcome oasis in the midst of Midtown. The Stork Club was located here from 1934 to 1965. The Stork Club was the epitome of café society in New York during its heyday in the 1930s and '40s; something like Studio 54 was in the 1970s, minus the cocaine and disco music. Frank Sinatra, Marilyn Monroe, and Ernest Hemingway were among the regulars. Owner Sherman Billingsley enjoyed schmoozing with his customers and generated publicity for the club by ensuring photographers were on hand to document the nightly festivities. Columnist Walter Winchell once described the Stork as "New York's New Yorkiest place."

Joe Jr. was a regular here, leaving Harvard on Fridays to spend his weekends in New York. On one occasion, he spotted his younger brother JFK chatting up the prettiest girl in the club and decided he wanted her for himself. Joe had JFK paged and escorted the lady out of the club while his brother was distracted. JFK was furious and ready to fight Joe when he returned to their Bronxville home. Although it's sometimes posited that Joe Jr. would have entered politics and perhaps become President had he survived World War II, Joe Jr. confided to a female friend that if either of them was destined to one day become President, it was JFK, whom he conceded was smarter, and with his PT-109 heroics, more accomplished than he was.

While at Harvard in the late 1930s, JFK often met up with Lem Billings (who was attending Princeton) and their dates for dancing here.

Billings later remembered the Stork Club in his Kennedy Library oral history interview:

> "In those days, that was the place to go. They particularly encouraged young models and pretty girls to come there. ... On Sunday nights, they used to have a balloon game. ... Balloons would drop from the ceiling, and you'd grab all of them. Some of them contained hundred-dollar bills ... free meals ... bottles of champagne, etc. Jack wasn't much of a drinker.... He liked to dance very much."

While undergoing naval training near Newport R.I. in 1942, JFK often headed to New York on the weekends and stopped at the Stork. Back from the Pacific during World War II, JFK had a fortuitous meeting here in January 1944 with author John Hersey. Hersey's account of the JFK's PT-109 incident — embellished with novelistic methods for dramatic effect — was rejected by *Life* magazine but was published in *The New Yorker* in June and, more importantly, in condensed form subsequently in the mass circulation *Reader's Digest*. Hersey titled his account "Survival," and he emphasized JFK and his crew's determination to live through their ordeal more than any heroic aspects of the story. When the story appeared in *Reader's Digest*, JFK became known nationwide as a war hero. His campaign widely distributed reprints of the *Reader's Digest* article during his successful run for Congress in 1946. The PT-109 story became a part of JFK's legend and was the subject of a major motion picture starring Cliff Robertson and a Top 10 song by Jimmy Dean during his Presidency.

Apparently retaining fond memories from his youth, JFK — now a senator — was photographed here with Jackie on May 8, 1955. The following year, he was photographed here with Ted and Bobby.

# LA GRENOUILLE RESTAURANT
## 3 E. 52ND ST.

JFK IS AMONG THE MANY Presidents who've dined at this elegant restaurant since it opened in 1962. Renowned for its lavish displays of fresh flowers, it is now the last of the great French restaurants of the 1960s still in business in New York. When founder Charles Masson died in 1975, his *New York Times* obituary noted that La Grenouille was "widely regarded as one of the best French restaurants in the United States." The restaurant earned a rare four-star review from the *Times* critic Mimi Sheraton in 1980, who described it as "extraordinary."

In 2008 Masson's son (also named) Charles told *Vanity Fair*[69] a somewhat incongruous story of Bobby — having consumed one too many — complaining the vichyssoise soup was canned, a claim that the owner Charles Sr. and his wife Giselle quickly and correctly refuted to him in no uncertain terms. The article placed the incident in the "mid-60s," although in his book *Bobby and Jackie: A Love Story*, author C. David Heyman quotes reporter Jack Newfield as saying it occurred on March 16, 1968, the day Bobby announced his Presidential candidacy in Washington DC before marching in the St.

---

69    McGrath, Douglas "An Immovable Feast" *Vanity Fair*, September 2008.

Patrick's Day Parade in New York. Newfield blamed Bobby's condition on having stayed too long at Charley O's Bar.

Following the death of their mother, Charles' younger brother Philipe assumed control of La Grenouille. In January 2024 the restaurant was reported to be for sale. Old-timers hoped a new buyer might return Charles to the fold.[70]

---

70   "The Death of La Grenouille?" by Korby Kummer, *Air Mail*, January 6, 2024.

# LE MISTRAL RESTAURANT
14 E. 52ᴺᴰ ST. BETWEEN FIFTH AND MADISON AVES.; CLOSED

THIS ELEGANT TWO-STORY FRENCH RESTAURANT was a favorite of Jackie's. That's hardly surprising since its owners, Jean Larriaga, Joseph Lemerdy, and Guy Moruzzi, were all veterans of Kennedy family favorite La Caravelle. A December 1964 *New York Times* article by Craig Claiborne noted the new restaurant's "style and charm" and that it traced its culinary lineage back to Henri Soulé and Le Pavillon, like just about all of the prominent French restaurants in New York and beyond.

# THE FOUR SEASONS RESTAURANT

## 99 EAST 52ND ST. BETWEEN PARK AND LEXINGTON AVES.; CLOSED

FROM ITS OPENING IN 1959 until it closed in 2016, this was the favorite gathering spot for New York's rich and powerful. The "power lunch" originated here. Located in Mies van der Rohe's modern "cereal box" Seagram Building, the interior of the Four Seasons was designed, in the main, by another renowned architect, Philip Johnson. Artworks by Pablo Picasso and James Rosenquist adorned the walls.

JFK hosted a dinner for Democratic donors on the evening of May 19, 1962, before heading to Madison Square Garden for his birthday tribute. Jackie and Bobby were here on July 28, 1964, for a board meeting of the Kennedy Library that also served as a 35th birthday party for Jackie. Jackie referred to the Four Seasons as "the cathedral." In later years, she often had lunch here, sometimes with the writers she was editing.

Co-owner Julian Niccolini later remembered that the entire room full of prominent businessmen dining here would stare at Jackie when she walked in. Upon losing its lease in 2016, the Four Seasons was forced to move from the Seagram Building. After briefly relocating to E. 49th St., it closed for good in June 2019.

# ST. PATRICK'S CATHEDRAL
## FIFTH AVE. BETWEEN 50TH AND 51ST STS.

ST. PATRICK'S WAS DESIGNED IN the French Gothic Revival style by James Renwick, Jr. and dedicated in 1879. With seating for 2,400 people, it is the largest Roman Catholic cathedral in North America. It replaced the Mulberry Street St. Patrick's Cathedral downtown when New York's growing and largely immigrant Roman Catholic population had outgrown it.

St. Patrick's was the site of a plethora of Kennedy-related events through the years, the most notable being Bobby's funeral mass on June 8, 1968. An estimated 151,000 lined up to enter the cathedral through the side entrance on 51st St. near Fifth Ave. They filed past the bier during the twenty-three hours of viewing time that was halted with people still in line at 5:30 a.m., hours before the funeral began. The 2,300 attending the funeral included LBJ, Richard Nixon, Cary Grant, and Harry Belafonte. The Requiem Mass was televised nationally on all three networks and was notable for Teddy's moving eulogy[71] in which he said:

---

71  A profound remembrance of Bobby was given by the Kennedys' friend Lord Harlech, who said of him: "Violence in the United States has become a world scandal. Bobby Kennedy's assassination is horrible and tragic. Contrary to some people's idea of him, he was the most kind, generous, and compassionate of men. His courage was supreme and he really cared about people in every land and in every walk of

*"My brother need not be idealized or enlarged
in death beyond what he was in life, to be
remembered simply as a good and decent man who
saw wrong and tried to right it, saw suffering and
tried to heal it, saw war and tried to stop it. Those
of us who loved him and who take him to his rest
today, pray that what he was to us and what he
wished for others may someday come to pass for
all the world."*

Although secular music was prohibited during Roman Catholic masses, Bobby's friend Andy Williams turned in a memorable rendition of " Battle Hymn of the Republic," a song Bobby liked and that seemed to resonate with the way he lived his life.

Jackie's friend Leonard Bernstein conducted the New York Philharmonic through a moving performance of the "Adagietto" from Gustav Mahler's *Symphony No. 5*. After arriving in Washington DC following a long train ride from New York and Bobby's nighttime burial near JFK's gravesite in Arlington National Cemetery, Jackie — who was spending the night at her mother Janet's Georgetown home — composed a thirteen-paragraph letter to Bernstein at 4 a.m. in which she wrote:

*"When your Mahler started to fill (but that is the
wrong word — because it was more this sensitive
trembling) the Cathedral today — I thought it the
most beautiful music I had ever heard. I am so*

---

life. With all these rare qualities, America and the world needed him disparately. Unbridled hate has now killed him."

*glad I didn't know it — it was this strange music of all the gods who were crying. ... Your music was everything in my heart, of peace and pain and such drowning beauty. You could just close your eyes and be lost in it forever. ... Thank you, dear Lennie."*[72]

The fact that she could write such a lengthy and heartfelt letter after such an emotionally exhausting day at the end of an unimaginably brutal week is a testament to how highly Jackie regarded Bernstein and how moved she was by the music he played at the funeral.

On May 23, 1953, Eunice Kennedy married R. Sargent Shriver here at a ceremony presided over by Francis Cardinal Spellman. "Sarge" would go on to head the newly founded Peace Corps under JFK and the "War on Poverty" programs instigated by LBJ. He later served as U.S. ambassador to France. Following the withdrawal of Missouri senator Thomas Eagleton, he was the 1972 Democratic Party's Vice Presidential nominee on the George McGovern ticket, which managed to lose forty-nine states to the Republican ticket of President Richard Nixon and Vice President Spiro Agnew.

Inspired by the plight of her developmentally disabled sister Rosemary, Eunice started Camp Shriver for special needs kids at their Maryland home in 1962. That would develop into her founding of the Special Olympics in 1968. Today, it is the largest organization in the world serving children and adults with special needs. With the Shriver's son Timothy serving as CEO, Special Olympics oper-

---

72  Nigel Simione, Ed., *The Leonard Bernstein Letters*, New Haven and London: Yale University Press, 2014.

ates in 172 countries and has more than five million participating athletes. Eunice once said about her work: "As we hope for the best in them, hope is reborn in us."

www.specialolympics.org

Jean Kennedy and Stephen Smith were married here on May 19, 1956, with Cardinal Spellman officiating. This time, the ceremony was held at Lady Chapel behind the main altar. Steve was close to all of his new brothers-in-law, serving as a wise and trusted advisor to each of them through the years. He also ran the family business once Joe Sr. could no longer do so. Jean was the second youngest in the family, and she introduced JFK, Bobby, and Ted to their future wives. Jean was especially close to Bobby; she and Steve were at the Ambassador Hotel in Los Angeles when he was shot on June 5, 1968. Steve, calm in the face of shock and pandemonium, took to the podium to ask, "Is there a doctor in the house?" Jean became the only Kennedy sister of her generation to hold a format political position when, in 1993, President Bill Clinton appointed her as U.S. ambassador to Ireland, a land where JFK was regarded as a secular saint.

Caroline was baptized here on December 13, 1957, with Lee and Bobby serving as her godparents.

Bobby and Ethel's ninth child, Maxwell, was baptized here on January 17, 1965. Photographers snapped photos of Bobby carrying his heavily blanketed new son into the building.

The funeral for Francis Cardinal Spellman was held here on December 7, 1967. Spellman had served as Archbishop or Cardinal of the New York Archdiocese since 1939. On a Christmas visit to Vietnam in 1966, the hardline anti-communist made headlines when he said: "Anything less than victory is inconceivable." Bobby was at his funeral (and was photographed wearing his horn-rimmed reading glasses) along with a host of dignitaries, including President Johnson, Vice President Humphrey, Gov. Rockefeller, and Mayor Lindsay. Viewed today, Spellman's funeral looks like a dry run for Bobby's funeral almost exactly six months later, with many of the same people again on hand. The event took place amid the turmoil of the times. Johnson took a helicopter to Central Park to avoid anti-war protesters who tied up streets south of 42$^{nd}$ St. He took the same route to attend Bobby's funeral in June.

Bobby marched in New York's St. Patrick's Day Parade on March 16, 1968, the second event of his Presidential campaign, following his Washington announcement earlier in the day. Jackie and John Jr. watched from their apartment window at 1040 Fifth Ave. "Kennedy Parades to Mixed Chorus," read the *New York Times*[73] headline the following day, noting that Bobby faced scattered boos even from Irish-American New Yorkers. There was anger in the air in the spring of 1968, and Bobby was the target of much of it. Knowing this and fearing for his brother's safety, Ted, like Jackie, had tried to dissuade Bobby from running, but Bobby felt that he needed to do all he could to stop the Vietnam War immediately and not wait to run in 1972. Bobby stopped by St. Patrick's Cathedral during the parade to greet archbishop-designate Terence C. Cooke, who presided over Bobby's funeral here eleven weeks later. Strangely enough, Bobby's 1968 campaign odyssey both began and ended at St. Patrick's Cathedral.

---

[73] Probably due to his work with Senator Joe McCarthy in the early 1950s, Bobby often received less than favorable coverage in the *Times*; this included being lambasted by their editorial board for his break with LBJ over Vietnam. Bobby Jr. remembered his father's reception at the parade as being a warm one.

# VILLARD HOUSES

## 415-457 MADISON AVE. BETWEEN E. 50TH AND E. 51ST STS.

JACKIE ADVOCATED FOR PRESERVING AND restoring these Renaissance Revival houses, dating from 1884. At the behest of financier and New York *Evening Post* publisher Henry Villard, these buildings were designed by two members of the famed architectural firm McKim, Mead & White and erected in 1883. Joseph Wells designed the façades, while Stanford White did the interior. It's striking to see what looks like a 15th-century Italian palazzo in midtown Manhattan. Jackie was photographed touring the site in 1979 when she leased 30,000 square feet in the north wing. The Villard Houses were granted landmark status in 1968 and added to the National Register of Historic Places in 1975. The Municipal Art Society was located here for many years before it moved to 488 Madison Ave. in 2010. The original buildings were incorporated into the fifty-one-story Palace Hotel site that developer Harry Helmsley opened in September 1980. It's now the Lotte New York Palace Hotel.

# LAFAYETTE RESTAURANT
## 202 E. 50TH ST. @ 3RD AVE.; CLOSED

A FRENCH RESTAURANT OPENED IN early 1965 by two former members of Le Pavillon's service staff, Jean Fayet and his wife Jacqueline, Lafayette quickly became known for its excellent food and celebrity clientele. Bobby and Jackie both ate here on numerous occasions. The Fayets imposed a strict dress code forbidding women from wearing miniskirts or slacks. As *Women's Wear Daily* publisher John Fairchild once recalled, Mrs. Fayet wasn't shy about enforcing the dictates, no matter who the customer was:

> *"I was at Lafayette one day, and Jackie Onassis*
> *has her sunglasses up in her hair…. The owner said*
> *she didn't like people who had dark glasses shoved*
> *up in their hair and asked her to remove them."*[74]

In 1972, Fairchild's *W* Magazine named Lafayette among the "Le Six, the last bastions of fine luxe dining in New York." It received a so-so two-star review from the Times in 1973 and closed in the late '70s.

---

74   Colacello, Bob "Here's to the Ladies Who Lunched!" *Vanity Fair*, February, 2012.

# ST. BARTHOLOMEW'S EPISCOPAL CHURCH
## 109 E. 50TH ST. @ PARK AVE.

WHEN THIS HISTORIC CHURCH WANTED to tear down its six-story community house and let a developer build a skyscraper on the site, Jackie was among the celebrities who opposed the plan, claiming that it destroyed the beauty of the church. She felt so strongly that in February 1984, she testified in Albany against a proposed state law that would have allowed religious institutions to skirt landmark preservation efforts. The present building — the third to house the church — was designed by Bertram Goodhue in the Byzantine Revival style and erected in 1918. The church had been designated as a landmark by the city in 1967. Episcopal Bishop Paul Moore Jr. said the revenue from the proposed tower would fund their church building maintenance and assist St. Bart's in its charitable mission. Other religious leaders supported his contention that their buildings should be exempt from landmark presentation laws. After losing in the lower courts, St. Bart's appealed all the way to the U.S. Supreme Court, which declined to hear a further appeal in 1991.

## PALACE HOTEL, FORMER HOME OF LE CIRQUE 2000
### 455 MADISON AVE. @ 50TH ST.

IN EARLY 1997 LE CIRQUE (that's "The Circus" in French...you're welcome) moved here from its original location at 58 E. 65th St. Renowned chef Daniel Boulud was the executive chef there from 1986 to 1992.

Jackie knew owner Sirio Maccioni from his days at the Colony, and she occasionally held business lunches at the E. 65th St. location. John Jr. was photographed following a lunch here with *George* executive editor Elizabeth "Biz" Mitchell in 1997.

John held a press conference here on March 2, 1999 — a time when speculation was rampant about his possible candidacy to replace retiring New York Senator Daniel Moynihan. (First Lady Hillary Clinton had yet to announce her candidacy, although she was known to be considering the race.) The "very special announcement" John teased that day was somewhat less than earth-shattering: He informed the crush of reporters that former New York senator Al D'Amato would be writing a column for *George*. It showed that John was adept at exploiting his celebrity to his advantage. In his remarks, D'Amato mused about the possibility of John running for mayor of New York in 2001 — "I mean, a Kennedy leading the city? Pretty good!" "Not today,"[75] John replied.

After moving to the Bloomberg Tower Building on E. 58th St. in 2006, Le Cirque closed in 2018.

---

75   Richard Blow *American Son*, New York, St. Martin's Paperbacks, 2002.

## SAKS FIFTH AVENUE

611 FIFTH AVE. BETWEEN E 49TH AND 50TH STS.

JEAN RECALLED THAT WHEN THEY lived in Bronxville, the entire family often came here on Sundays during their excursions into Manhattan.

*Time* magazine reported that Carolyn spent part of July 16, 1999, here, shopping for a dress to wear to Rory Kennedy's wedding at Hyannis Port that weekend. After looking through numerous dresses in the boutiques on the third floor, she settled on a $1,630 black silk crepe evening dress from the fall/winter collection of Rive Gauche, the ready-to-wear line by Yves Saint Laurent. The off-the-shoulder dress went below the knee and featured a gathered bodice cinched with a satin bow in the back of the neck. It was an appropriate choice since the designer of the dress, Alber Elbaz, considered Carolyn to be one of his muses and "really admired her style," although he had never met her.[76]

When a salesperson wished her luck on her flight to the Cape, Carolyn — who'd shared her apprehension about John flying with his injured leg — reportedly replied, "Thanks, I'm going to need it."

---

76  "Carolyn's Terrible Premonition..." by Libby Callaway, *The New York Post*, July 22, 1999.

# LONGCHAMPS RESTAURANT

### 423 MADISON AVE. BETWEEN E. 49TH AND 50TH STS.; CLOSED

BOTH TED AND JOAN PENNED memoirs in the twilight of their lives, and both wrote of Sunday dinners at Longchamps as a happy memory from their childhood when the family was still intact. When they lived in Bronxville, the family would get into two cars after mass on Sunday mornings and head into the city. They often shopped at nearby Saks Fifth Ave. before coming here to eat. Jean recalled that Joe Sr. always ordered roast beef for everyone and that it was very good. Barely remembered today, Longchamps was

Courtesy NYPL.

a big deal in the 1930s and '40s, and this was the first of more than ten locations in the city. They were highly regarded for their excellent cuisine. This was the first location, but later iterations featured very cool Art Deco interiors.

The building that housed this Longchamps is still here. If you look carefully, you'll see a crack in the cornice where the upright Longchamps sign used to sit.

# WALDORF-ASTORIA HOTEL

## 301 PARK AVE. BETWEEN 49TH AND 50TH STS.

RISING 47 STORIES, THIS WAS the world's tallest and most expensive hotel when it was built in 1931 and remained so until 1963, when Moscow's Hotel Ukraina was erected. A name synonymous with style and luxury — beginning with the marble stairs at the Park Avenue entrance that led you to the wood-paneled lobby — the Waldorf is one of the most iconic hotels in the world, if not *the* most. Among other innovations, the Waldorf was the first hotel to offer room service. It has hosted countless events involving the Kennedys through the years for both business and pleasure.

Joe maintained a suite here during the 1940s, while Rose often stayed at the Plaza. It was in Joe's suite here on September 19, 1944, that Joe gave Kathleen the devastating news that her husband, Billy Cavendish, had been killed in action in Belgium.

JFK and Jackie spent their wedding night here on September 12, 1953, having married in Newport, Rhode Island, earlier in the day. The following day, they flew off to begin their honeymoon in Acapulco, Mexico.

JFK and Jackie attended the April in Paris ball here on April 11, 1957 (along with Sarge and Eunice Shriver) and again on April 10, 1958. Marilyn Monroe was on hand with her then-husband, playwright Arthur Miller, at the 1957 ball, but it is unlikely JFK spoke to her that night. JFK and Jackie attended for the last time in 1959. The society fundraising event celebrated French and U.S. ties and was first held at the Waldorf in 1951.

JFK gave a speech here entitled "Foreign Policy in a Democracy" for the New York Herald Tribune forum for High Schools. The event was held in the Grand Ballroom on March 23, 1957, and broadcast over WNYC. In his talk, JFK discussed his belief that leaders in a democracy would ultimately benefit by being open and honest with the public in formulating foreign policy. It makes interesting reading in light of what we now know about the Kennedy and Johnson administrations' failure to adhere to this advice regarding Vietnam.

On December 7, 1959, JFK and all the other Democratic Presidential hopefuls gathered here to honor Eleanor Roosevelt. Even at this early stage of the campaign, JFK was considered the front-runner for the party's presidential nomination. His official announcement was still a few weeks away. At the dinner, JFK was photographed conferring with former President Harry S. Truman.

The following night, JFK and Jackie were back at the Waldorf's Grand Ballroom to attend the "Wild West Ball." This was a benefit organized by Jean to aid the Kennedy Child Study Center for Retarded Children, a non-denominational school operated under the auspices of the Archdiocese of New York. The school was started with a grant from the Joseph P. Kennedy Jr. Foundation.

JFK spoke at the annual Al Smith Dinner here on October 22, 1959, an event hosted by the diminutive Cardinal Francis Spellman, the most powerful American Catholic clergyman of the time. JFK and his Republican rival Vice President Richard Nixon spoke at the Smith Dinner here on October 19, 1960, just two weeks before election day. According to the *New York Times* account, JFK got more laughs but Nixon got louder applause. JFK said he was confident voters would make their choice without regard to his religion. (The dinner's namesake had dealt with anti-Catholicism when he was the Democratic presidential nominee facing Herbert Hoover in 1928.) Before the dinner, JFK took time to meet with fifty New York Board of Rabbis members. A photo of the candidates and Spellman taken at the dinner appeared on the front page of the following day's *New York Times*. Joe was not happy with the lukewarm reception Spellman gave JFK at the dinner. He would soon sour on Spellman completely, writing a mutual friend in January 1961 that he was "very unhappy" with the cardinal:

> *"I have never asked for many things, but I needed all the help I could get in this campaign. I don't think he gave the help he should have, and I think we did as badly in New York amongst the Catholics as we did anywhere in the country. He was asked to do two or three things, and he just didn't deliver.... I am not the slightest bit interested in him in the future."*[77]

JFK spoke at the Waldorf on numerous occasions while President. Among these was his December 5, 1961, address to the National Football Foundation and Hall of Fame dinner in which he lamented that "The sad fact is ... that our national sport is not playing at all but watching. We have become more and more not a nation of athletes but a nation of spectators." He emphasized the role of sports in pre-

---

77    Joe Kennedy letters to Enrico Galeazzi 1/6/61 in Amanda Smith, ed. *Hostage to Fortune: The Letters of Joseph P. Kennedy.*

venting the country from getting collectively further out of shape.

JFK called on ex-President Herbert Hoover at Hoover's home here on April 28, 1961. Hoover lived at the Waldorf in Suite A on the 31st Floor from 1940 until he died there on October 20, 1964.

JFK met for more than an hour on the same day with retired Gen. Douglas MacArthur in the latter's 37th-floor home here. During this meeting, the general famously cautioned JFK of the inadvisability of involving the U.S. in a ground war in Southeast Asia. JFK dictated a memo of the meeting, in which he stated:

> *"MacArthur believes it would be a mistake to fight in Laos (and that) anyone wanting to commit ground troops to Asia should have his head examined."*[78]

JFK took the general's advice concerning Laos, which was a front-burner issue at the time of the meeting. In a subsequent meeting with JFK in Washington DC, MacArthur reinforced his advice about Vietnam.

The "President's Club"[79] birthday celebration for JFK was held here on May 23, 1963. Despite the presence of a good number of Hollywood stars, this event might be called, "The Unknown Birthday Show", as it has been largely lost to history. This is no doubt because it lacked an iconic moment such as the (since deceased) Marilyn Monroe's serenading the birthday boy at Madison Square

---

78  Francis P. Sempa, "A New Take on General MacArthur's Warning to JFK to Avoid a Ground War in Asia," *The Diplomat*, October 8, 2018. https://thediplomat. com/2018/10/a-new-take-on-general-macarthurs-warning-to-jfk-to-avoid-a-land-war-in-asia/

79  A group of elite Democratic donors.

Garden the previous year. It did, however, feature young starlet Ann-Margret — then starring in the film *Bye Bye Birdie* — crooning a sexy rendition of "Baby Won't You Please Come Home" that, she later wrote, brought a smile to JFK's face. The "Happy Birthday" honors this year were handled by Audrey Hepburn, whose rendition was unfortunately not filmed, thus failing to become the emblematic moment it might have been. Bobby Darin (who also performed at the MSG show the previous year) sang his hit "Won't You Come Home Bill Bailey," which JFK's secretary Evelyn Lincoln later reckoned to be her boss's favorite song.[80] Louis Armstrong closed the show with "When the Saints Go Marching In" as people did the Twist on stage.

Bobby, already distancing himself from LBJ on Vietnam at this early date with his call for a coalition government that would include communists, attended LBJ's speech here defending his administration's conduct of the war on February 23, 1966. A demonstrator interrupted LBJ's speech, shouting, "Mr. President, peace in Vietnam!" and was quickly escorted out. In a preview of coming attractions, some 4000 antiwar demonstrators filled the west side of Park Avenue behind police barricades protesting LBJ's visit.

Bobby and LBJ attended another Democratic fundraiser here on June 3, 1967. Although they were photographed laughing together, tensions between them were high following Bobby's call for a bombing halt a few months earlier.

At Jackie's request, Sonny and Cher performed at a private dinner in Jackie's honor thrown by mining tycoon Charles Engelhard Jr. and held at his penthouse apartment here. The event took place late in 1965. Jackie told Cher that "I Got You Babe" was one of her and

---

80   For a comprehensive examination of JFK and Bobby's musical tastes and how the music of the 1960s impacted their lives, see the author's book *Popology: The Music of the Era in the Lives of Four Icons of the 1960s.*

her children's favorite songs,

Rose attended the April in Paris Ball here on October 29, 1965, October 28, 1966, and again on October 31, 1969. On April 27, 1977, Jackie attended a party for Frank Sinatra here, celebrating his charity concert held at Carnegie Hall for the benefit of Lenox Hill Hospital.

John Jr. attended the Museum of the Moving Image's tribute to Robert DeNiro here on March 9, 1991. John became friendly with the actor when they lived near each other in Tribeca. John Jr. and Carolyn were here on October 20, 1998, to attend the New York Breast Cancer Foundation luncheon. On March 8, 1999, John Jr. spoke at the Jackie Robinson Foundation Awards Dinner here, an event he attended with Caroline.

As of 2023, the Waldorf was in the midst of an extensive renovation that closed the hotel in 2017. Plans call for some of the lower eighteen floors to be used as hotel rooms while the upper floors are being converted into luxury condominiums, with a prospective reopening planned for 2024.

www.waldorftowers.nyc

# WMCA STUDIOS
## 415 MADISON AVE. BETWEEN 48TH AND 49TH STS.; RAZED

THE ONLY DEBATE OF BOBBY'S 1964 Senate campaign was held here from October 30-31, 1964. After being unable to agree on terms for a televised debate, Bobby and incumbent Sen. Kenneth Keating agreed to this radio debate, moderated by New York main-stay Barry Gray. The debate started at 11:05 p.m. Friday and ended at 12:20 a.m. Saturday. Since this was not exactly primetime, and the election was only a few days away, the debate had little impact on the course of the campaign. Given GOP presidential nominee Barry Goldwater's unpopularity in the state, the liberal Republican Keating had his work cut out for him, disassociating himself from him while not alienating hardcore conservatives.

Bobby only participated in two more formal debates during his lifetime: one (in separate television studios) with California Gov. Ronald Reagan on May 15, 1967, and the last in ABC's San Francisco studios with Sen. Eugene McCarthy on June 2, 1968. To the surprise of many, Reagan bested Bobby in their matchup, with Bobby asking an aide after it was over, "Who the fuck got me into this?" Liberal and sometimes abrasive, Gray was in the midst of a thirty-nine-year career at WMCA, where he pioneered the talk-radio format. He would later recall walking the streets of New York with Bobby and the friendly and casual way the locals greeted their new senator.

WMCA was and is located down your AM dial at 570. The station was at the height of its popularity in 1964 with its "Good Guys" deejays. The station is credited with being the first to play a Beatles record on New York radio. WMCA moved its studios from Madison Ave. years ago. It became a Christian talk station in 1989.

# NEW YORK THEOLOGICAL SEMINARY

## 235 E. 49TH ST. BETWEEN SECOND AND THIRD AVES.

BOBBY CAST HIS FINAL BALLOT here on November 7, 1967, voting in favor of a referendum to overhaul the New York State Constitution. The new charter failed to pass, losing in a 2½ to 1 landslide.

# ROBERT KENNEDY RESIDENCE
## 870 UNITED NATIONS PLAZA BETWEEN E. 48TH AND E. 49TH STS.

THIS BUILDING'S TWIN GLASS TOWERS are located just north of the UN Headquarters and are an easily spotted feature of the Manhattan skyline. Architects Wallace Harrison and Max Abramovitz had earlier designed the modernist United Nations complex and Time-Life Building in addition to working on the plans for Lincoln Center. A June 1965 *New York Times* article[81] noted that Bobby had purchased an apartment here for $68,000 (plus yearly maintenance of $6,500), which was in the middle range of what the units were selling for. Bobby moved in when the building — featuring state-of-the-art luxury amenities including floor-to-ceiling views of the city — opened in 1966. It has 336 apartments and a huge lobby with the main entrance via a long private driveway on E. 49th St.

Bobby owned a six-room, three-bedroom apartment on the 14th floor of the east tower. Its yellow walls, "grass green carpeting," and "contemporary paintings" made for a "warm" atmosphere, according to a March 1968 *New York Times* story that focused on the New York residences of three Presidential candidates that year, the other

---

81   https://timesmachine.nytimes.com/timesmachine/1968/03/18/79937427.
html?pageNumber=47

two being Richard Nixon and Gov. Nelson Rockefeller. The corner apartment looked out on the East River, the famous neon Pepsi-Cola sign on the other side and FDR Drive to the east, and the UN looking south. *Tonight Show* host Johnny Carson and writer Truman Capote lived here at the same time as Bobby. *Washington Post* publisher Katharine Graham, *CBS Evening News* anchorman Walter Cronkite, and Bobby's predecessor as U.S. Attorney General and future Secretary of State William P. Rogers also owned apartments here. Capote told an amusing story of Bobby confronting a teenager smoking near their building and proceeding to give the kid hell over his bad habit.

While serving as senator, Bobby commuted between New York and Washington DC several times a week. He usually did so on the

The UN Plaza Apartments as photographed in 2023. Bobby's apartment was on the 14th Floor facing the East River.

Eastern Air Lines Shuttle out of LaGuardia Airport, which did not require reservations and always had a new plane at the ready if the first one was full. Although he maintained a Senate office in Manhattan, Bobby was rarely there, preferring to conduct business in his living room here. He used the downstairs lobby as a kind of waiting room, sending down an aide to escort his visitors upstairs.

The UN Plaza apartment turns up in RFK biographies

describing the night of March 31, 1968, the night LBJ shocked the political world by announcing that he would not be a candidate in 1968. Bobby was on a plane from the West Coast when Johnson dropped the bombshell. When he got to his apartment, supporters gathered there were already celebrating. Ending Johnson's war in Vietnam was the reason Bobby had announced his candidacy two weeks earlier, so it was no surprise that people were in a celebratory mood. Bobby, however, was more cautious. He called the celebration "premature" and told Ethel to serve scotch rather than champagne, lest reporters pick up the sounds of corks popping. Bobby's instincts proved correct as that night and the coming days would bring a mere trickle of endorsements from elected Democratic officials around the country, many of whom would coalesce behind Vice President Hubert Humphrey. LBJ's withdrawal took away Bobby's main campaign focus and muddled its most prominent issue, LBJ's conduct of the war in Vietnam. Bobby's friend, journalist Jack Newfield, later perceptively wrote:

> "Johnson's withdrawal appeared to benefit
> Kennedy, but in the long run, it did not....In a
> mysterious way, it made Robert Kennedy the
> magnet for much of the free-flowing venom in the
> country that had previously been directed at the
> President." [82]

Following his victory in the Indiana primary, Bobby returned here for the final time on May 8th. Inn of the Clock was a restaurant located in the west tower, and it was there that Bobby spoke

---

82    Jack Newfield, Robert Kennedy: *A Memoir*, New York: Dutton, 1969.

to a group of about two hundred New York Democrats. New York would hold its primary on June 18, and both Humphrey and McCarthy had strong campaign organizations in the state, making a Kennedy victory far from certain even in his home state, or one of them anyway. (On May 19, McCarthy drew 19,000 people to hear him speak at Madison Square Garden.) In his talk, Bobby pledged to make an all-out effort in New York in the two weeks following the June 4 California primary. A sad document at the JFK Library lists Bobby's scheduled New York Primary campaign events — including an extensive motorcade through New York City — that never occurred.

## HOLY FAMILY ROMAN CATHOLIC CHURCH
### 315 E. 47TH ST. BETWEEN FIRST AND SECOND AVES.

UNUSUALLY MODERNIST FOR A AMERICAN Catholic church, Holy Family was designed by George J. Sole and completed in 1965. The old church was razed to make room for the United Nations complex. Located on Dag Hammarskjold Plaza, the church is a short walk from Bobby's UN Plaza apartment, and he attended mass here when he was in town during his Senate years. Bobby and Ethel met with Pope Paul VI here in 1965, when Holy Family became the first church in the Western Hemisphere to be visited by a Pope. Ethel and Bobby's family attended a private requiem mass for him here on the morning of June 8, 1968, before the St. Patrick's Cathedral funeral.

## KENNEDY FAMILY APARTMENTS

277 PARK AVE.; EAST SIDE OF PARK BETWEEN 47TH
AND 48TH STS.; RAZED

THIS BUILDING WAS REPLACED BY a present-day office building in July 1964, some of which currently houses J.P. Morgan offices.
The original buildings were designed by McKim, Mead & White,
noted architects who were hugely influential in modern American

277 Park Ave. as it looked in the 1950s. NYPL

architecture. The firm designed Penn Station, Madison Square Garden, the Brooklyn Museum, and the Columbia campus, to name a few. This building took up an entire block, extending back to Madison Ave. It featured a vast courtyard and more than 300 apartments, including the one JFK stayed in, on the eighth floor of House 10. According to a 1956 FBI background check, Joe rented an apartment here around 1949, and Jean lived in it in 1956.

JFK got Jackie a dog for Christmas 1956 while the couple was staying here. Unfortunately, the dog caused JFK to have a severe asthma attack that recurred on subsequent visits to the apartment. They eventually had to give the dog away.

JFK and Bobby began organizing his presidential campaign office here following JFK's re-election to the Senate in 1958. JFK's campaign rented 25 offices here during the 1960 campaign. On August 5, 1960, JFK — having secured the Democratic Presidential nomination — met with state Democratic leaders. All of the tenants moved out by January 1962.

## DOUBLEDAY OFFICES

245 PARK AVE. BETWEEN E. 46TH AND 47TH STS.;
LATER 666 FIFTH AVE. AT 52ND ST. (AND STARTING LATE IN
1992, AT 1540 BROADWAY BETWEEN W. 45TH AND W. 46TH STS.)

JACKIE'S FIRST DOUBLEDAY OFFICE WAS just north of Grand Central Station, which she was at the forefront of trying to save at the time. Doubleday was a much larger company than Viking, with three times as many employees. After her messy exit from Viking a few months earlier, Jackie started working as an associate editor here in February 1978, working three days a week — Tuesday through Thursday — at a salary of $20,000 per year, almost double her Viking salary. Jackie published more than 90 books during her 15-year tenure at Doubleday. Notable among them were her friend Diana Vreeland's *Allure* (1980), Michael Jackson's *Moonwalk* (1988), Edvard Radzinsky's *The Last Tsar: The Life and Death of Nicholas II* (1992), ballerina Gelsey Kirkland's candid memoir *Dancing on My Grave* (1986), and *The Power of Myth* (1988) by Joseph Campbell and Bill Moyers.

Jackie became involved with the Jackson project not because she wanted to, but because Doubleday successfully used her to lure the singer, the biggest star in the world in 1988. Jackson was reluctant to write the revealing book Doubleday hoped for, so the four-year-long experience of editing "The King of Pop" was frustrating for Jackie. Jackie agreed to write a three-paragraph introduction for the book after Jackson threatened to scrap the project unless she did so. *Moonwalk* went on to sell more than half a million copies and topped the *New York Times* bestseller list, making it the most commercially successful of all the books Jackie worked on.

Jackie edited about a dozen books each year at Doubleday. History and the fine arts were of particular interest to her. Still, she edited a broad range of manuscripts, including *The Ballad of John and Yoko*, which compiled *Rolling Stone* magazine's extensive coverage of the ex-Beatle and his wife through the years.[83] Jackie was heard saying she'd "give up food to publish Hunter Thompson," the "gonzo" journalist whose drug-fueled works included *Fear and Loathing in Las Vegas*.

Perhaps due to its convenience, Jackie enjoyed dining at the iconic Top of the Sixes restaurant at 666 Fifth Ave., even though she accurately described the cuisine as "airport food." Largely thanks to its breathtaking view of the Manhattan skyline, the restaurant thrived from 1958 to 1996.

During her last two years, Jackie had a small office on the 20th floor at Doubleday's offices at Broadway and 45th Street. She was

---

83    Jackie was friends with *Rolling Stone* publisher Jann Wenner. She was said to have been greatly affected by Lennon's assassination on December 8, 1980, which occurred at his Dakota apartment building across the street from Central Park on the Upper West Side, about a mile from "1040." Perhaps Lennon's seemingly senseless murder brought back memories of JFK's assassination. Lennon and JFK had more in common than might have been initially apparent. In addition to having the same first name and very similar last names, both came to worldwide fame in the early 1960s and became among the decade's most admired figures – especially among young people — forever to be associated with those years. Both were of Irish extraction (Lennon's paternal grandparents were Catholics born in Dublin), and both were (allegedly) murdered by discontented young men raised in the American South. The Beatles' *Ed Sullivan* appearance on February 9, 1964, which skyrocketed the band to fame in the U.S., came just eleven weeks after JFK's assassination. For many, the Beatles' arrival helped end the long period of national mourning for JFK. Jackie was photographed with Paul and Linda McCartney following a Wings concert at Madison Square Garden in 1976, so she was a Beatles fan.

involved in every aspect of the publishing process, including book cover designs and the development of sales and marketing strategies. She eventually rose to the position of senior editor with a six-figure salary.

Doubleday president and publisher Stephen Rubin said of Jackie:

> *"Every single person on the staff adored her. She was not just accessible, she was genuinely caring. She also had a wicked sense of humor and was a lot of fun. She really connected with the authors, too, once they got over the idea that their editor was Jackie Kennedy Onassis. She was warm, engaging, smart — a friend."*[84]

Although she eventually had issues with the company's cost-cutting after Doubleday was bought out by the German conglomerate Bertelsmann AG in 1986 (when it was renamed Bantam Doubleday Dell) because she thought it affected the quality of the reproductions contained in her books, Jackie had a long and satisfying career at Doubleday. When she became ill in March 1994, she was rushed to the hospital from her Doubleday office. She was said to be still coming into her office in April, by which time her health had further deteriorated, a testament to how much she loved her job.

84   https://www.nytimes.com/1994/05/22/nyregion/jackie-new-yorker-friends-recall-a-fighter-for-her-city.html

# THE HELMSLEY BUILDING; FORMERLY THE NEW YORK CENTRAL BUILDING

## 230 PARK AVE. BETWEEN E. 45TH AND E. 46TH STS.

THIS IS THE BUILDING THROUGH which you enter the Grand Central Station complex if you're driving south down Park Ave. Designed in the Beaux-Arts style by renowned architects Whitney Warren and Charles Wetmore and built in 1929, it dominated the area landscape before the erection of the Pam Am (now the Met Life) Building in 1963. Joe began renting a ninth-floor office here in 1948 when the building was known as the New York Central Building. He used his office here for many years to conduct family business. Joe's use of the office here is noted in a 1956 report in his FBI file.

# THE METLIFE BUILDING; FORMERLY THE PAN AM BUILDING

## 200 PARK AVE. @ E. 45TH ST.

AFTER MOVING TO NEW YORK, Jackie maintained a private office here during the 1960s. When she closed the office in July 1969, her friend and aide Nancy Tuckerman explained: "The mail is no longer as heavy as it was." This was no doubt due in no small part to her marriage to Ari the previous October, which, fairly or not, tarnished her public image in the U.S. The building is just north of and adjacent to Grand Central Station, which Jackie helped save from the wrecking ball in the 1970s.

A 1977 article in the *New York Times* described how Steve Smith oversaw the Kennedy family's business from an office on the 30th floor here. Joe Kennedy wisely set up trusts for his children and grandchildren, thus keeping the beneficiaries' funds away from the clutches of greedy spouses and the IRS. Although a door had the name "Joseph P. Kennedy Enterprises," it was not a registered company. "Park Agency, Inc." (a nod to its earlier home next door at 230 Park Ave.) was the actual name of the family's real estate holding company.

# UNITED NATIONS HEADQUARTERS

## 405 E. 45TH ST. BETWEEN FIRST AVE. AND FDR DRIVE

JFK ADDRESSED THE U.N. ON September 25, 1961. He paid tribute to the late Secretary General Dag Hammarskjöld, who'd been killed in a suspicious plane crash in Northern Rhodesia (now Zambia) only a week earlier. In his talk, JFK vowed to defend West Berlin and keep other Western commitments but also opened the door to reducing tensions with the Soviets via disarmament negotiations. Among those in the audience lending moral support were Pat, Jean, Ethel, Eunice, and Jackie. Dr. Max Jacobson later claimed that JFK was suffering from laryngitis before this address and

JFK before his address to the UN General Assembly on September 25, 1961.
Cecil Stoughton. White House Photographs. John F. Kennedy Presidential Library and Museum, Boston.

that he was called to the Carlyle to minister to him. Dr. Max claimed he gave a hypodermic shot in the neck into the voice box that solved the issue.

JFK addressed the U.N. for the last time on September 20, 1963. Following up on his American University speech in June, he called for the U.S. and Soviet Union to resolve their differences peacefully and even suggested they cooperate in outer space.

Bobby, Ted, and Jackie were on hand when Pope Paul VI made his "War No More" address here on October 5, 1965. They also had a brief private audience with him. Jackie was seen crying when the Pope called JFK a "great man" in his speech and recited his "lucid words": "Mankind must put an end to war, or war will put an end to mankind."

Bobby and Jackie paid a lunchtime visit to Secretary General U Thant here on February 1, 1968. They were accompanied by the U.S. ambassador to the U.N., Arthur Goldberg.

www.un.org

# SENATOR ROBERT KENNEDY'S OFFICE
## 110 E. 45TH ST.; RAZED.

THIS BUILDING WAS LOCATED NEAR the Park Ave Viaduct overpass and was the location of Bobby's New York office while he served as senator from 1965 until his death in June 1968. Senator Kenneth Keating had used the office previously. A meeting of historical importance took place here during the third week of October 1967 when Bobby met with Allard Lowenstein, who was leading a "Dump Johnson" movement in the Democratic Party. Lowenstein was looking for a candidate to challenge LBJ, and he implored Bobby to enter the campaign. Bobby, knowing how difficult it would be to keep an incumbent President from being renominated and skeptical of the political strength of the anti-war movement, turned Lowenstein down. Eugene McCarthy soon announced his candidacy, coalescing anti-war Democrats around him. Many on the left saw Bobby's entry into the race immediately following McCarthy's near defeat of Johnson in the New Hampshire primary as pure opportunism. Bobby ended up having to battle McCarthy in several primaries. Had Bobby entered the race before McCarthy, the left would have been united in seeking to unseat LBJ.

# THE FORD FOUNDATION BUILDING; FORMER SITE OF HOSPITAL FOR SPECIAL SURGERY
320 E. 43RD ST.

SEE ENTRY IN UPPER EAST SIDE SECTION.

## ROBERT KENNEDY 1964 SENATE CAMPAIGN HEADQUARTERS

### 9 E. 42ND ST. BETWEEN FIFTH AND MADISON AVES.

JACKIE AND JOHN JR. VISITED here on September 15, 1964, in a show of support for Bobby's campaign. She carried John as she greeted volunteers. Asked how she would assist the campaign, Jackie said, "I'll do whatever they ask me." Jackie and John Jr. were soon mobbed by a crowd of 500 people — "who nearly swept her off her feet," according to the next day's *Daily News* — as they tried to leave the building to get to their car.

# GRAND CENTRAL STATION

## 89 E. 42ND ST. @ PARK AVE.

BUILT IN 1913, THIS BUILDING symbolized old New York. The Beaux-Arts style of architecture was popular in Europe at the time, and Grand Central was one of many New York buildings built in that style. Bobby was met with enthusiastic crowds when he campaigned here in September 1964.

By 1975, Grand Central had seen better days. Its landmark status had been voided, and plans were announced to build a high-rise tower atop Grand Central. A proposed artist's rendering of the new structure resembled a shoebox top placed on its side. Jackie made a rare public appearance at Grand Central's iconic Oyster Bar to protest the redevelopment. Then she wrote a longhand letter to then-Mayor Abe Beame dated February 24, 1975, in which she asked:

> *"...is it not cruel to let our city die by degrees, stripped of all her proud moments, until there is nothing left of all her history and beauty to inspire our children? If they are not inspired by the past of our city, where will they find the strength to fight for its future?"*

Jackie was photographed chatting with *Rolling Stone* publisher Jann Wenner at a "Save Grand Central Station" party held at the Oyster Bar here on July 20, 1977. Wenner had recently relocated *Rolling Stone*'s operations to New York, and Jackie became a friend.

John, Carolyn, and Lee Radziwill were here in October 1998 for a gala honoring Jackie's work in saving the building.

In March 1994, Jackie attended her last public event here, a party she co-hosted with Brendan Gill to celebrate the one-hundredth anniversary of the Municipal Arts Society." A cameraperson from WPIX-TV in New York filmed her saying, "It's a wonderful evening, isn't it?" It would turn out to be her last public statement.

In 2014, the Grand Central foyer at the Park Avenue and E. 42nd St. entrance was dedicated to Jackie in recognition of her successful efforts to preserve the building. A large plaque with a bronze relief of Jackie outlines her role in saving Grand Central.

# STEPHEN A. SCHWARZMAN BUILDING, NEW YORK PUBLIC LIBRARY, MAIN BRANCH
## 476 FIFTH AVE. BETWEEN W. 40TH AND W. 42ND STS.

CONTRARY TO HER PUBLIC IMAGE, Jackie probably felt more at home in this majestic Beaux-Arts building than at New York's finer clubs and restaurants. She spent long hours here in the Slavonic Room researching the book *The Firebird and Other Russian Fairy*

The Schwarzman Building of the New York Public Library as photographed in 2023

*Tales.* Then-New York Public Library president Vartan Gregorian later brought the library's journal of a soldier in Napoleon's army to Jackie's attention, which resulted in the publication of Jakob Walter's 1991 book *The Diary of a Napoleonic Foot Soldier.* The curator of the library's Slavic and Baltic division, Edward Kasinec, assisted Jackie in the publication of the Walter book and several others, including The *Empire of the Czar,* a 19th-century De Tocqueville-esque study of Russia by Astolphe de Custine. Jackie was also involved with organizing the annual Literary Lions gala here.

She was often allowed to use the library on days it was closed to the public, thus ensuring her privacy. After having spent a long day at the library, Jackie wrote to thank Gregorian, revealing the joy she felt when being surrounded by books:

"I'm deeply grateful for the magnificent day you gave us last week. It was the privilege of a lifetime to be in that beautiful room with all those great stars and the sun. Everything one cares about most was there. The treasures revealed to us warrant spending the next five years in the stacks."[85]

---

85    Lawrence, *Jackie as Editor*, page 198.

# HYATT GRAND CENTRAL NEW YORK; FORMERLY THE COMMODORE HOTEL

## 109 E. 42ND ST. @ LEXINGTON AVE.

NEWLY ELECTED TO THE SENATE and seemingly already with an eye toward 1956 and 1960, JFK addressed the New York County Democratic Dinner here on April 15, 1953. He told the Democrats that Adlai Stevenson's defeat to Dwight Eisenhower the previous fall — making this the first time in twenty years the party didn't occupy the White House — gave them "...an opportunity to regain perspective, to renew our energies and find out where we are going."

On the evening of January 12, 1957, JFK addressed a gathering of the Irish Institute here. The *New York Times* noted that the event was to be held "in honor of Senator John F. Kennedy." JFK spoke of Irish history and the lessons it held for the present-day fight against communism, comparing the struggle of Irish freedom fighters in the 1641 rebellion led by Owen Roe O'Neill to that of Hungarians resisting communism in their recent uprising, stating:

> *"...The education of their children and the preservation of their native language and customs were controlled by a foreign dictator in a manner no less ruthless than that demonstrated by the Soviets in Hungary today."*

O'Neill was assassinated before he could take on Oliver Cromwell, a huge setback for the Irish freedom struggle.

Paul O'Dwyer was among the founders of the Irish Institute in 1950. The younger brother of New York mayor William O'Dwyer, Paul would go on to serve as New York City Council president in the 1970s. He later recalled that on this night, JFK was introduced as "the next president of the United States," showing that the 1960 campaign was already underway at this early date. O'Dwyer wrote[86] that at the time, few present believed JFK would be elected in 1960, with the notable exception of the powerful Bronx congressman Charles A. Buckley,[87] widely described as a political "boss." The Irish Institute is still going strong today.

www.irishinstituteofny.com

The Commodore was the setting for an amusing JFK story. Later in 1957, he gave a speech at the Sheraton-Astor Hotel near Times Square. JFK had recently voiced sympathy for the Algerian rebels seeking independence from France and other nationalist movements, and he arranged to meet foreign correspondent Arnold Beichman, who'd just returned from covering the conflict. As they walked the streets together after the speech, JFK impressed Beichman with his in-depth knowledge of the politics of the Algerian situation. As they arrived at the Commodore, Beichman found himself puzzled that JFK would be staying at such an inferior hotel. As he pushed the elevator button, JFK grinned at the reporter and said: "I've got a very

---

86   https://www.irishinstituteofny.com/history

87   When Buckley was ill with the cancer that would take his life, both Bobby and Jackie made time to visit him; an indication of how much they valued his support and friendship. Bobby flew up from Washington DC to attend Buckley's wake on January 23, 1967, at the Fox Funeral Home on the Grand Concourse.

important date…. Sorry I can't invite you up."[88]

The Commodore closed in 1976, was purchased by Donald Trump, and underwent extensive renovations before emerging as the Grand Hyatt New York in 1980. The Hyatt Grand Central is scheduled to be torn down and replaced with an office tower named Project Commodore in 2024.

---

88    Leamer, *The Kennedy Men.*

## OVERSEAS PRESS CLUB
### 35 E. 39TH ST (1960); CURRENTLY AT 40 W. 45TH ST.

JFK ADDRESSED THE CLUB ON May 6, 1957. On August 5, 1960, he held the first formal press conference of the 1960 general election campaign here. On the first day of his Senate campaign, Bobby spoke to political reporters here on September 2, 1964. SEE ALSO: West Side Location.

www.opcofamerica.org

# ROBERT KENNEDY 1968 NEW YORK CAMPAIGN
# HEADQUARTERS

244 MADISON AVE. BETWEEN E. 37TH AND E. 38TH ST.

JACKIE CAME HERE DURING BOBBY'S presidential campaign, escorted by Roswell Gilpatric. "Ros" served as Deputy Secretary of Defense under JFK and LBJ. He'd accompanied Jackie on her trip to Mexico in March, a visit that prompted speculation about whether a marriage was in the couple's future. You won't be surprised to learn that Gilpatric was served divorce papers from his wife upon his return to the U.S.

This visit likely occurred on May 7, the day of the Indiana Primary (the first one Bobby contested), although at least one source dates it to June 4, the day of the California Primary. On June 4 the *Daily News* carried the front-page headline "Actress Shoots Andy Warhol." In a telephone conversation the night before, Jackie had informed Bobby of the Warhol shooting. Speaking of the shooting with director John Frankenheimer — at whose Malibu home he was staying, Bobby shook his head and said, "This country's gone mad. Absolutely mad." He was dead 48 hours after he spoke those words. Ironically, Warhol's "Jackie" paintings are among his most renowned works. Gilpatric came to 1040 Fifth the following morning to escort Jackie to Los Angeles, where she saw Bobby a final time before he died.

# NO. 237 APARTMENTS;
## FORMERLY ASIA DE CUBA RESTAURANT
### 237 MADISON AVE. BETWEEN E. 37TH AND E. 38TH STS.

*GEORGE* HELD ITS SECOND-ANNIVERSARY PARTY here in November 1997. John Jr. and Carolyn welcomed guests Ellen DeGeneres,[89] Anne Heche, Donald Trump, singer Sheryl Crow, Rev. Al Sharpton, and Detroit's "Motor City Madman," rocker Ted Nugent, among others. Now there's an eclectic guest list for you! Noting that Nugent was wearing a Ducks Unlimited cap, Carolyn teased him, saying, "Don't be too hard on those ducks."

At one point John was overheard asking his wife, "How're you doing honey-bunny?"

This Asian-fusion hot spot helmed by Jeffrey Chodorow had just opened in October but was already something of a sensation at the time. French designer Philippe Starck did the restaurant's interior, which, in addition to a rum bar, featured a long communal marble table, and a giant two-story mural of a waterfall that seemed to move. "Kate Moss meets Carmine Miranda" is how the *New York Times* described the vibe in early 1998.

Asia de Cuba was located in Ian Schrager's Morgans Hotel and

---

89   DeGeneres had recently famously come out as gay, and she and Heche were a couple at the time.

was once featured on an episode of the era-defining HBO show *Sex and the City.* This location closed in 2011. A new Asia de Cuba opened on Lafayette St. in 2015 but closed two years later. The Morgans Hotel was sold a few years ago and converted into luxury condos named No. 237.

## THE RUSK INSTITUTE OF REHABILITATION MEDICINE; FORMERLY NYU MEDICAL CENTER INSTITUTE OF PHYSICAL MEDICINE AND REHABILITATION

### 400 E. 34TH ST. BETWEEN FIRST AVE. AND FDR DRIVE

JOE SR. UNDERWENT REHAB HERE after suffering a stroke in Palm Beach on December 19, 1961, that left him paralyzed on his right side and almost unable to speak. Perhaps sadly, he was still mentally aware and was able to fully comprehend the series of tragedies his family would soon endure. The rehab here seemed to help him somewhat. Joe was staying at Horizon House, a model ranch house located in the garden of the Institute of which he was the first resident. JFK visited him there on May 20, 1962, (the day after his birthday bash at MSG) and attended a private mass there. He stayed for a half-hour afterward to chat with Joe in the garden. On June 10, 1962, JFK was photographed greeting patients here when he again came to visit with his father. One can imagine how wrenching these visits must have been for the son, who knew he owed so much to his now-incapacitated father. Joe's physician, Henry Betts, later recalled the toll Joe's condition took on the family when they visited him here:

> "For a group of people who don't want to face
> bad things, it was hard. It was harder than death
> because with death, they always went on.... How

*could you repress this? It was around all the time.
So, it was just terrible on all of them."*[90]

Rose stayed here with Joe for a while, spending quality time together for the first time in years. Although doctors hoped she'd stick around, Rose — unable to deal with the situation any longer — went home, and Kennedy cousin Ann Gargan became Joe's chief caregiver.

In the fall of 1967, Joe was well enough to attend a World Series game at Boston's Fenway Park with Bobby and Ted.

JFK greets patients outside New York University Medical Center, June 10, 1962.
*Cecil Stoughton (Harold Sellers) JFK Library, Boston.*

90   Leamer, *Kennedy Men.*

# UPPER WEST SIDE
# ABOVE 59ᵀᴴ ST.

# YESHIVA UNIVERSITY
## AMSTERDAM AVE. @ 186TH ST.

THE KENNEDYS HAD A LONG history with this private Orthodox Jewish school, starting with JFK receiving the University's Charter Award for having "contributed nobly to the advancement of democracy" on October 27, 1957. In his acceptance speech at the Waldorf, JFK defended Jewish Americans against "dual loyalty" accusations, asserting that having an interest in one's homeland was in no way inconsistent with being a loyal American citizen.

Bobby, Rose, and Peace Corps director Sargent Shriver held a news conference at the Albert Einstein College on March 18, 1965, to announce the Joseph P. Kennedy Jr. Foundation's $1 million grant to Yeshiva to build a center to aid the developmentally disabled.

On May 1, 1966, Rose and Bobby joined Yeshiva president Samuel Belkin in breaking ground on the Rose Kennedy Center for Mental Retardation and Human Development in the Bronx. The center would be part of Yeshiva's Albert Einstein College, which Yeshiva fully owned at the time.

Yeshiva awarded an honorary degree to Bobby in 1967 and to Ted in 1973.

## NEW YORK PRESBYTERIAN/
## COLUMBIA UNIVERSITY IRVING MEDICAL CENTER
662 W. 168TH ST. BETWEEN W. 165 AND W. 169TH STS.; AND
RIVERSIDE DR. AND AUDUBON AVE., WASHINGTON HEIGHTS

ANTHONY RADZIWILL WAS JOHN'S COUSIN and lifelong best friend. Anthony had a five-year struggle with cancer before succumbing on August 10, 1999, just three weeks after John Jr.'s crash. The thought of losing Anthony weighed heavily on John in the final months of his life. John and Carolyn were both vigilant in caring for Anthony and his wife, Carole, during the long ordeal of Anthony's illness. In her book *What Remains*, Carole recounts an incredibly touching scene of John (still in a tuxedo) visiting Anthony late one night in the ICU here. The two had a unique way of communicating, as brothers often do. John took Anthony's hand and comforted him by the children's song "The Teddy Bears Picnic" to him until Anthony slowly began to sing along.

ETHEL AND JEAN WERE STUDENTS at Manhattanville beginning in September 1945. It was via their friendship that Bobby first met Ethel on a ski trip to Mont Tremblant, Quebec, in December 1945. Strangely enough, Bobby was initially more taken with Ethel's more studious older sister Pat, whom he had been seeing casually and even escorted to a dance here in early 1946. Still, after a few years — during which time Bobby was in a serious relationship with British actress Joan Winmill in 1948, and Ethel flirted with becoming a nun — the exuberant cut-up soon won him over, her personality a seemingly ideal counterbalance to Bobby's shyness. They began going steady during Ethel's junior year. Bobby came to Manhattanville from Harvard most weekends to take Ethel out. They were married on June 17, 1950, at St. Mary Church in Greenwich, Connecticut. JFK served as best man, and Jean was one of Ethel's attendants.

Manhattanville is a Catholic school for women run by the Society of the Sacred Heart, which encouraged its charges to do good works in the world. Eunice was a student here from 1939 to 1941. Manhattanville college president Mother Grace Dammann's decision to admit a black student in 1938 was both courageous and unusual for the time. Her 1938 "Principles versus Prejudices" speech helped shine a light on the racism present in the Catholic church. It would soon shame other institutions to follow Manhattanville's lead. One journal described the speech as "The Magna Carta of Desegregation."

After selling the campus land to the city in 1950, Manhattanville College relocated to Purchase in Westchester County, where it operates today. Each year, the college presents the Ethel Kennedy Human Rights Award to a recipient working to foster equity and social justice. CUNY buildings, including Aaron Davis Hall, and the Y-Building, are presently located on the South Campus. Joan Bennett graduated from Manhattanville in 1958 and married Ted that November.

## SHELTON PLAZA HOTEL
### 300 W. 116TH ST.; CLOSED

ON SEPTEMBER 5, 1979, BOBBY and Ethel's troubled twenty-four-year-old son David claimed he'd been robbed here, at the time a "known narcotics location," according to police. David claimed he'd been driving by (in a tan BMW) when he was flagged down by two pedestrians who robbed him inside the hotel. A few days following the incident, the *New York Times* quoted a hotel resident as saying that David had been seen here previously. The real story was that he'd been there scoring drugs. David had been shooting up heroin on and off for several years, but this incident made his private struggle public for the first time. He was soon hospitalized at Massachusetts General Hospital in "very serious condition" with a recurrence of endocarditis, a bacterial infection of the heart sometimes associated with the use of intravenous drugs.

By all accounts a kind, soft-spoken, and sensitive soul, David was about to turn thirteen when his father was murdered. Bobby had rescued David from drowning in the Malibu surf on June 4, 1968, the day of the California primary. David was found dead from an overdose of cocaine and Demerol at his Palm Beach, Florida, hotel room on April 25, 1984. A statement from Ted said: "We all pray that David has finally found the peace he did not find in life." He was twenty-eight.

# COLUMBIA UNIVERSITY'S FERRIS BOOTH HALL

## 2920 BROADWAY @ 116TH ST.; DEMOLISHED

IN A TIGHT RACE TO unseat incumbent Republican Kenneth Keating and with carpetbagging charges appearing to stick, Bobby held a Q&A here before an audience of 1,000 students on October 5, 1964. He took on the issue as follows:

> *"If it's going to be judged on who has lived here in the state of New York longer, then my opponent has. But then maybe you should elect the oldest man in the state of New York. ... I have had really two choices over the period of the last ten months. ... I could have retired ... my father has done very well and I could have lived off of him. Or I could have continued to work for the government. ... That's my major interest, and it's been the major interest of my family."*

While a retirement at the age of thirty-eight was probably never in the cards, with JFK's death and his election to the Senate, Bobby's life took on a certain inevitable trajectory that he could have scarcely imagined only a few years earlier. The Columbia event was later cited as turning the momentum of the campaign in Bobby's favor. When it was over, he spoke to and took questions from a raucous crowd of 2,000 students who had amassed on 114th St. between Broadway and Amsterdam Ave.

Ferris Booth Hall served as the Columbia Student Union from 1960 until it was torn down in 1996 and replaced by Alfred Lerner Hall. In the spring of 1968, it served as the headquarters when the students occupied campus buildings in protest of the Vietnam War and the policies of Columbia president Grayson Kirk.

# JOHN F. KENNEDY JR. RESIDENCE

## 56 W. 91ST ST. BETWEEN CENTRAL PARK WEST AND COLUMBUS AVE.

JOHN JR. MOVED INTO THE top floor of this four-story renovated townhouse in the fall of 1986. This coincided with his enrollment at New York University Law School downtown, but this move placed him five blocks farther *uptown* from where he'd been living on W. 86th St. Go figure. This building has a distinctive red door and is across the street from the P.S. 84 schoolyard. Columbus Avenue is just around the corner, and John's beloved Central Park is a short walk down the street, which had to be a major selling point for him.

The years prior to *People* magazine's "Sexiest Man Alive" cover story on John in September 1988 were a time in which John lived a relatively low-key life in New York. With the *People* cover, public fascination in his life increased and continued to gain intensity for the rest of his life.

# JOHN F. KENNEDY JR. RESIDENCE
## 309 W. 86TH ST. BETWEEN WEST END AVE. AND RIVERSIDE DR.

JOHN LIVED HERE FROM SOMETIME around late 1984 until the fall of 1986 when he moved to 56 W. 91st St. He sublet a two-bedroom apartment with his Brown roommate and friend Rob Littell. Littell later wrote[91] that John insisted on finding a place close to Central Park, although this place is closer to the Hudson River than it is to the park. Because one bedroom was much larger than the other, John and Rob agreed to switch rooms every six months so they could split the rent evenly. This renovated pre-war building has a doorman on a two-way street. After they moved out, the landlord here was reportedly less than thrilled with the condition in which Messrs. Kennedy and Littell had left the apartment. Something about a fist having gone through a wall. He initiated legal action, and the case was quietly settled out of court. Littell later admitted that he and John were not "model tenants."

It's worth noting that while Manhattan's Upper West Side is geographically just half a mile across Central Park from the wealthy Upper East Side environs in which John grew up, it is a world away both culturally and sociologically.

---

91   Robert T. Littell. *The Men We Became: My Friendship with John F. Kennedy Jr.*, New York: St. Martin's Press, 2004.

## ZABAR'S
### 2245 BROADWAY @ 80<sup>TH</sup> ST.

THIS NEW YORK INSTITUTION HAS been around since 1934 and offers bagels, smoked fish, and other traditional Jewish favorites. Publicist Ken Sunshine recalled the day he came here with John Jr. in the autumn of 1993 as he was campaigning with Mayor David Dinkins, who was seeking re-election:

> *"...As soon as we got there, John was absolutely*
> *attacked by a crowd of mostly over-70-year-old*
> *women. Now, I represent Leonardo DiCaprio,*
> *and I've never seen anything like this. They were*
> *climbing over the lox counter to get to him. Dinkins*
> *got separated from him. ... It was like the Beatles.*
> *... John never traveled with security, and Dinkins*
> *was the only one with a phalanx of security.*
> *So, it was just John and this screaming army of*
> *septuagenarians. ... We had to get him out of there."* [92]

www.Zabars.com

---

92    Maer, Roshan. "Prince of the City," *New York Magazine*, August 2, 1999.

# COLLEGIATE SCHOOL
## 241 W. 77TH ST. BETWEEN BROADWAY AND
## WEST END AVE.; RELOCATED

CHARTERED IN 1638, THIS IS the oldest independent school in the U.S. and one of the most prestigious. John Jr. was enrolled here in the fall of 1968. Jackie was photographed while escorting him to his first day of classes here that September. Despite the rigorous curriculum, John apparently thrived here and made a lot of friends. Actor David Duchovny was among his classmates. According to his fellow students, John wasn't averse to an occasional puff on a joint,[93] or to skipping class to play frisbee in Central Park. Hey, it was the '70s! In 1976, he left here after finishing the tenth grade, bound for Phillips Academy in Andover MA.

Although it was not widely publicized at the time – or since – John was forced to repeat a grade while at Andover. If he'd completed the tenth grade at Collegiate, he should have graduated from Andover in 1978 rather than when he did in 1979.[94] It's been alleged

---

93  According to Rolling Stone publisher Jann S. Wenner's book *Like a Rolling Stone: A Memoir* (New York: Little, Brown and Company, 2022), John was still an enthusiastic pot smoker in the summer of 1994, when he brought his foot-long bong to a Rolling Stones show at New Jersey's Giants Stadium.

94  Perhaps this wasn't noticed because a typical American student born in November 1960, like John, would have begun first grade in 1967 and graduated high school (as John did) in 1979. John was apparently "fast-tracked" while at St. David's.

that John suffered from a mild form of dyslexia.

John's first two apartments after graduating from Brown were located on the Upper West Side, so perhaps he became fond of the area while at Collegiate. Collegiate is now located at 301 Freedom Place South.

www.collegiateschool.org

## CAROLYN BESSETTE KENNEDY'S DOCTOR'S OFFICE

### 300 W. 72ND ST. BETWEEN WEST END AVE. AND RIVERSIDE DR.

CAROLYN WAS PHOTOGRAPHED LEAVING HERE on June 11, 1997, following a visit with her doctor. This illustrates the invasive nature of the paparazzi, which beset Carolyn daily, and the fact that, no, she didn't "know what she was getting into" when she married John. Once she became John's wife, she enjoyed precious little privacy, a situation that left her increasingly despondent, according to several people who knew her.

# THE DORILTON

## 171 WEST 71ST ST., NORTHEAST CORNER OF
## W. 71ST AND BROADWAY

ACTRESS DARYL HANNAH OWNED AN eighth-floor apartment at this elegantly distinctive, century-old, French Second Empire-style building when she dated John Jr. in the early 1990s. On the list of John's serious girlfriends — and allowing for some overlap — Hannah falls after Christina Haag (reportedly the only one Jackie had any use for) and model Julie Baker and before Carolyn Bessette. Jackie never met Carolyn, even though John was photographed with her at the New York City Marathon in September 1993, eight months before Jackie's death. John had known Carolyn since at least as far back as the summer of 1992, so it apparently took a while for things to heat up.

John lived here in 1993 and maybe a bit before and after, too. He'd had a casual relationship with Hannah for some time, but things got serious when John went to L.A. in October 1992 and returned to New York with her following a reported altercation between her and her boyfriend, singer Jackson Browne. In its August 16, 1993, cover story, *People* magazine featured photos of John and Daryl and proclaimed, "It's Love!" The pair was also photographed attending the wedding of John's cousin Ted Kennedy Jr. at Cape Cod that summer.

Knowing Hannah's reputation as a neat freak, friends were

amused to find John's clothes strewn all over the place here. They broke up shortly after Jackie's death, but their relationship left one lasting legacy in John's life: Hannah's brother-in-law, famed record (The Mamas and the Papas, Carole King) and film producer (*Up in Smoke*) Lou Adler suggested the name *George* — as in Washington — for John's new political magazine. His suggestion earned him a place on *George*'s masthead.

Built just after the subway opened in 1904, the Dorilton was one of the first large apartment buildings on the Upper West Side. Designed by famed architects Janes & Leo, the Dorilton is a building that must be seen to be believed. It was named a landmark in 1974 when the Landmarks Preservation Commission described it as "exceptionally handsome." Hannah sold her place here in 1994. Her unit was later converted into a duplex that carried an asking price of $5.49 million when it was listed in September 2022.

## CAFE LUXEMBOURG

### 200 W. 70TH ST. NEAR AMSTERDAM AVE.

CAROLE RADZIWILL RECALLED THAT THIS French restaurant was one of John Jr.'s favorite places. It was opened by Odeon (where John and Carolyn ate often) owners Keith McNally and Lynn Wagenknecht in 1983. Wagenknecht is now the sole owner.

www.cafeluxembourg.com

# ABC TELEVISION STUDIOS
## 77 W. 66TH ST. BETWEEN
## CENTRAL PARK WEST AND COLUMBUS AVE.

ALTHOUGH THE FIRST KENNEDY-NIXON DEBATE in Chicago on September 26 is the one enshrined in our collective memory, the candidates actually had four debates that autumn, two of which were broadcast from here. JFK was here while Vice President Richard Nixon was in L.A. for the October 13 debate, which was primarily taken up by the question of whether the U.S. should use force to defend the islands of Quemoy and Matsu — both of which are located in the Taiwan Strait close to the Chinese mainland — from Chinese Communist aggression. The format specified no opening or closing statements, just answers to the reporters' questions. Jackie accompanied JFK on this occasion.

Both candidates were here on October 21 for their final debate, which was devoted to foreign policy and permitted them to make an eight-minute opening and three- to five-minute closing statements. Although Nixon — a sharp and experienced debater — comported himself well in these two debates, Kennedy came across as cool and confident under pressure, and there is little doubt that the debates, taken in their entirety, boosted JFK toward victory that November.

# TAVERN ON THE GREEN

## WARNER LEROY PLACE, CENTRAL PARK BETWEEN W. 66TH AND 67TH STS.

JOHN JR. AND JACKIE ATTENDED a party for the movie *Bobby Deerfield* starring Al Pacino here on September 18, 1977. John attended the Robin Hood Foundation's Heroes Awards event here on December 11, 1991.

John, Carolyn, and her sister Lauren attended the Ninth Annual Robin Hood Foundation Awards breakfast here on December 2, 1998. (John and Carolyn reportedly left the event walking hand in hand down Central Park West.) John was a board member of the foundation, which works to fight poverty in New York. He presented a check for $25,000 to his friend Hans Hageman, who, along with his brother Ivan, started the East Harlem School on the site of Exodus House, a drug rehabilitation facility their parents founded in 1963. John met the brothers while attending Collegiate, where the brothers commuted from their Spanish Harlem home, which was then at Exodus House and is now the site of East Harlem School. They designed the school to be "A powerful response to a deeply segregated school system." One of the innovative school's credos is that "Creative flight can only be sustained by grounded discipline." Today, Ivan serves as head of the school.

www.Robinhood.org
www.eastharlemschool.org
www.tavernonthegreen.com

# LA PALESTRA

## 11 W. 67TH ST. BETWEEN CENTRAL PARK WEST AND COLUMBUS AVE.

JOHN JR. REPORTEDLY WORKED OUT at this upscale gym on the afternoon of July 15, 1999. Palestra is owned by Pat Manocchia, a Brown University friend of John's, and he and Carolyn were regulars here. This was the site of an unofficial memorial to John held following his memorial service on Friday, July 23. Attendees included John's cousins Tim Shriver and (his best friend) Anthony Radziwill, his old Brown roommate — and by now a famed international correspondent for CNN — Christiane Amanpour, plus John's erstwhile girlfriend Christina Haag. Haag later wrote that Anthony — who only had weeks to live — told her "I'm all cried out ... there's nothing left."[95]

---

95   Christina Haag, *Come to the Edge: A Love Story*. New York: Random House, 2012.

# DAVID GEFFEN HALL;
## FORMERLY PHILHARMONIC HALL (1962-73)
## AND AVERY FISHER HALL (1973-2015)
## LINCOLN CENTER FOR THE PERFORMING ARTS
### 10 LINCOLN CENTER PLAZA

ON SEPTEMBER 23, 1962, JACKIE attended the gala opening of Philharmonic Hall. Opening night seats ranged from $100 to $250, a lot of scratch in 1962. Jackie, accompanied by Mr. and Mrs. John D. Rockefeller, received a standing ovation as she entered the Hall. Unfortunately, she had to leave mid-concert to return to Newport, where she was scheduled to help JFK welcome the President of Pakistan, Ayub Khan, the following day. Conductor Leonard Bernstein led the New York Philharmonic in a program that consisted of Gloria from the *Missa Solemnis* by Beethoven; the premier of *Connotations for Orchestra* by Aaron Copland; Ralph Vaughan Willams' *Serenade to Music*, and *Symphony No. 8*, first movement by Mahler, a composer Bernstein consistently championed. Before leaving, Jackie met briefly with Bernstein, Copland, and the architect of the new Hall, Max Abramovitz.

Acoustical issues plagued the Hall from the outset, with *New York Times* critic Harold Schonberg describing the sound as "inconsistent" in his opening night review. A third renovation completed in 2022 was widely praised for (finally) resolving these issues. Still, the Philharmonic Hall and the performance spaces that were added in the ensuing years made Lincoln Center a cultural hub for New York and the nation.

Elevating the cultural life of the United States and its citizens was an essential part of what JFK and Jackie sought to accomplish during their time in the White House, and the new Lincoln Center undoubtedly contributed to that effort. Jackie was involved with Lincoln Center until the end of her life. While undergoing treatment in early 1994, it was announced that she'd agreed to serve as chairwoman for the American Ballet Theater's Spring Gala and that she planned to attend the event to be held here at Damrosch Park on May 9. Of course, Jackie was too ill to attend and passed away two weeks later.

John Jr. introduced the fourth episode of his *Heart of the City* program in the winter of 1994 while strolling outside what was then Avery Fisher Hall.

On May 1, 1995, John escorted Carole Radziwill to the American Ballet Theater's Spring Gala, held in honor of Jackie. On February 12, 1996, John attended the Council of Fashion Designers of America's (CFDA) Awards show here. He was photographed at the event with Mick Jagger and the singer's then-wife Jerry Hall.

# METROPOLITAN OPERA HOUSE
## 30 LINCOLN CENTER PLAZA

BOBBY AND ETHEL, ALONG WITH Ted and Joan, attended the opening night performance of Samuel Barber's *Antony and Cleopatra* at the Met's new Lincoln Center home on September 16, 1966. Although it starred renowned soprano Leontyne Price and was directed and designed by Franco Zeffirelli and choreographed by Alvin Ailey, the critics roasted this over-the-top production.[96] *New York Times* critic Charlotte Curtis wrote: "Almost everything about the evening, artistically speaking, failed in total impact. ... Good intentions cannot compensate for questionable taste and bad judgment." As we've seen, Bobby and Pat attended the premiere of Zeffirelli's movie *The Taming of the Shrew* in March of 1967.

Barber — well known even today for his *Adagio for Strings*[97] — never quite recovered from this artistic flop. Jackie was photographed with Barber here on December 7, 1967, for the 125th anniversary of the Met's first performance. Zeffirelli went on to direct the

---

96  "The Opera House," a 2018 episode of PBS's Great Performances, contains extensive footage of *Antony and Cleopatra* and includes Leontyne Price's memories of the production.

97  Paul McCartney plays a bit of *Adagio* on piano in the Beatles' *Get Back* documentary.

highly successful film *Romeo and Juliet* in 1969. He also directed many other operas at the Met, notably his much-loved 1981 production of *La boheme*, which was revived in 2018.

Jackie took John Jr. (who, at age eight, must have been bored to tears) and Caroline to a Royal Ballet performance here on May 6, 1970. Jackie attended a performance of the Royal Ballet here on May 7, 1974. She was photographed dining here at a gala with Mikhail Baryshnikov on May 18, 1977.

Peter Gelb has been the company's general manager since 2006. He has sought to expand the company's audience with *Live in HD* transmissions of performances to movie theaters around the world.

www.metopera.org

# MIDTOWN WEST

## WEST OF FIFTH AVE. BETWEEN
## W. 59TH ST AND W. 14TH ST

# KENNEDY FAMILY APARTMENT

## 24 CENTRAL PARK SOUTH BETWEEN FIFTH AND SIXTH AVES.

THIS BUILDING ADJACENT TO THE Plaza Hotel was the site[98] of a contentious meeting between Bobby and a group of prominent African-Americans concerning civil rights held on May 24, 1963. Writer James Baldwin (who'd roasted white liberals for their cowardice on civil rights), Harry Belafonte, *A Raisin in the Sun* playwright Lorraine Hansberry attended along with Clarence B. Jones, a New Yorker who as Martin Luther King's lawyer and adviser would soon help him draft the "I Have a Dream" speech. The Black participants were understandably angry and frustrated with the Kennedy administration's foot-dragging on civil rights. For more than two years, JFK had tried not to offend powerful Southern Democrats whose support he needed to enact his legislative agenda.

Jerome Smith, a young Freedom Rider who'd been beaten for his trouble, threatened that he was now "Ready to pick up a gun." Bobby, who envisioned himself a champion of civil rights, was taken aback by the vitriol directed at him during the meeting. Although Belafonte later told Dr. King that the meeting had been a "disaster,"

---

98  At least one prominent Kennedy family biography misstates this meeting as having taken place at Bobby's UN Plaza apartment, which had yet to be built at the time.

within weeks, Bobby strongly urged JFK to give a televised speech on civil rights in the wake of the Birmingham protests. In that speech, JFK proposed what would become the landmark Civil Rights Act of 1964, which — along with the Voting Rights of 1965 — finally prohibited discrimination based on race. While Belafonte became closer to Bobby after this meeting, Baldwin was so skeptical that he supported incumbent Republican Sen. Kenneth Keating when Bobby ran against him in 1964.

A sad postscript to the meeting came on January 12, 1965, when Hansberry succumbed to pancreatic cancer at the age of 34. Baldwin later wrote:

> *"It's not at all farfetched to believe that what she saw contributed to the strain which killed her, for the effort for which Lorraine was dedicated is more than enough to kill a man."*[99]

99    Baldwin introduction to Lorraine Hansberry, *To Be Young, Gifted and Black: An Informal Autobiography*, New York: Signet, 1970.

# THE INTERCONTINENTAL;
# FORMERLY THE NAVARRO

## 110 CENTRAL PARK SOUTH BETWEEN SIXTH AND SEVENTH AVES.

AN ELEGANT PRE-WAR BUILDING ORIGINALLY designed by famed architect James Carpenter, the Navarro later became the Ritz-Carlton and then the International Hotel. The building, which features breathtaking views of Central Park, was converted to condos around 2006. Judith Exner wrote in her book 1977 book *My Story*[100] that she and JFK hooked up here on August 4, 11, and 16, 1960, while she was staying at a friend's apartment (17E). JFK had accepted the Democratic Presidential nomination in Los Angeles on July 15 and spent part of August in Hyannis Port. Apparently, JFK had decided that the increased scrutiny inherent with becoming a major party Presidential candidate was not going to curtail his extramarital fun. Although their relationship continued until at least the spring of 1962, these would be the last of the couple's New York assignations. Although many Kennedy associates initially expressed skepticism regarding the claims in her book, Exner's relationship with JFK has been verified via White House phone logs and visitor records.

---

100  Exner, *My Story*, New York: Grove Press, 1977.

## THE NEW YORK ATHLETIC CLUB
180 CENTRAL PARK SOUTH BETWEEN SIXTH AND SEVENTH AVES.

JOHN JR. WAS A MEMBER of this private social and athletic club. Think moneyed, (very) old-school New York. He came here regularly to work out — lifting weights and playing racquetball. His friend Rob Littell wrote that John lived here for a few weeks between moving out of Daryl Hannah's apartment in 1994 and moving into his new place on Hudson Street downtown. The club was founded in 1868, and membership is by invitation only. Amenities include two restaurants, a cocktail lounge, and more than 187 guest rooms. John had planned to play racquetball here with Steve Gillon on July 19, 1999, but, of course, he never made it.

# THE PLAZA HOTEL

## 768 FIFTH AVE. @ CENTRAL PARK SOUTH

THE PLAZA HAD EIGHT HUNDRED rooms when it opened in 1907 and added three hundred more when it was remodeled in 1921. It is one of the world's most famous hotels and a favorite destination for New York's elite. The Kennedys were here on many occasions.

Joe Sr. stayed here often, and it was in his suite here that he met with John "Sea Wolf" Bulkeley, a Medal of Honor winner for his daring rescue of Gen. Douglas MacArthur — the Commander of the U.S. Army forces in the Far East — from Corregidor Island in March 1942. Bulkeley was now in charge of the Navy's P.T. (Patrol Torpedo) Boat program and was about to send two hundred new boats to the Pacific. At this meeting, Joe implored him to remove JFK from his Naval desk job and appoint him skipper of one of the boats. Joe must have been persuasive because — even though Bulkeley was aware that Joe might have had the ulterior motive of enhancing his son's record in preparation for a potential post-war career in politics — by April 1943, Lt. John F. Kennedy was dispatched to the Pacific Theater as commander of PT-109. It's impossible to overstate the importance of this meeting knowing that JFK's close aide and friend, Dave Powers, once claimed that "Without PT-109 you have no President John F. Kennedy."

Rose often stayed here during her trips to the city, including extended stays after Labor Day.

Jackie, Lee, and their mother, Janet, regularly met for tea here. Jackie and Ari often dined at the now-closed Oak Room here.

In her 1977 memoir *My Story*, Judith (nee Campbell) Exner wrote that she hooked up with JFK here on the night of March 7, 1960. This was the night before the New Hampshire Presidential primary (which JFK won with 85% of the vote) and a month after the pair had met at the Sands Hotel in Las Vegas. Exner claimed that the pair were intimate for the first time here (in room 1651, since you asked) and that following the main event, they shared some Jack Daniels. No doubt knowing that he had the next day's election in the bag, JFK didn't bring up New Hampshire once during the evening. His first real test against his opponent, Sen. Hubert Humphrey, wouldn't come until the Wisconsin primary scheduled for April 5.

The JFK/Exner relationship was revealed in 1975 after an investigation by the U.S. Senate Committee on Intelligence Operations, aka the Church Committee, chaired by Idaho Sen. Frank Church. Her simultaneous friendships with organized crime figure Sam Giancana, head of the highly profitable Chicago "Outfit" (with whom she was actually more than friends), and Johnny Roselli of Los Angeles made JFK's relationship with her risky in the extreme. The disclosure marked the first public confirmation of one of JFK's extramarital affairs.

Bobby, Jackie, and Franklin Roosevelt Jr. enjoyed cocktails here with new friend actor Richard Burton in October 1964.

Rose, Pat, Lee, and her husband, Stas, were among the notables at Truman Capote's legendary "Black and White Ball" held in the Grand Ballroom here on November 28, 1966. Jackie, along with Bobby and Ethel, were invited but declined to attend. Dubbed "The

Party of the Century," masked guests included Frank Sinatra and his new bride Mia Farrow, Katherine Graham, Gloria Vanderbilt, first daughter Lynda Bird Johnson, Harry Belafonte, and New York society folks like CBS founder William S. Paley and his wife Babe. Capote explained, "I wanted it at the Plaza because I think it's the only really beautiful ballroom left in the United States."

Bobby, Ethel, and Jackie attended a "Salute to New York State" Democratic Party fundraiser here on December 10, 1967. It was Jackie's first participation in a public political event since JFK's death. Bobby took the mic after dinner had been served and said, "Welcome to the Kennedy family Christmas party. ... And now, may I introduce this evening's guest of honor, Mrs. John F. Kennedy." Jackie then stood to a standing ovation from the crowd. She was escorted by former New York Gov. Averell Harriman, who would soon head the U.S. delegation at the Paris Peace Talks with North Vietnam.[101]

Attendees — who had shelled out $500 a plate — were then entertained by singer Tony Bennett and comedian Alan King. Also present was Sen. Eugene McCarthy of Minnesota, who had just announced his anti-war candidacy for the Presidency on December 1, putting Bobby in the uncomfortable position of not endorsing him despite their agreement on the Vietnam issue. Bobby and McCarthy were all smiles when they were photographed together that night. Outside, fifty women marched in support of McCarthy's candidacy in front

---

101  As Under Secretary of State, Harriman was involved with the ill-considered August 1963 weekend cable to Henry Cabot Lodge, the U.S. Ambassador in Saigon, indicating support for a potential military coup against South Vietnam President Ngo Dinh Diem. This set off a disastrous chain of events leading to Diem's overthrow and murder in November 1963, events which — since they were perceived to have been sanctioned by the Americans — cemented the U.S. commitment to South Vietnam and the series of military leaders that would succeed Diem.

of the Plaza. Bobby and many political pundits saw McCarthy as a one-issue candidate and doubted his ability to get elected. Even so, McCarthy became a hero to anti-war Democrats, and his near defeat of LBJ in the March 12 New Hampshire Democratic primary resulted in the President withdrawing from the race and leaving Bobby to contend against McCarthy during the spring primaries.

Bobby and Ethel attended the afterparty held in the Grand Ballroom here following the premiere of the Elizabeth Taylor—Richard Burton film Doctor Faustus on February 6, 1968. Bobby was photographed lighting Liz's cigarette. This was the same week Bobby traveled to West Virginia to shine a light on poverty in the Appalachian region, a testament to his ease with people from all rungs of society.

## MAREA RESTAURANT; FORMERLY SAN DOMENICO
### 240 CENTRAL PARK SOUTH,
### JUST EAST OF COLUMBUS CIRCLE

THIS HIGH-END ITALIAN EATERY WAS one of JFK Jr.'s favorite lunch spots. Jackie and Maurice Tempelsman regularly dined here, and Ted was said to have proposed to his wife, Victoria, here. San Domenico was the preferred power lunch spot for the media elite during the 1990s, so John Jr. was here often, especially after launching *George* in 1995. He reportedly had lunch here on July 15th, 1999, the day before he died, dining on spaghetti with tomato and basil and grilled sea bass. While here, he spotted Diane Sawyer — then married to Mike Nichols — and went over to give her a hug. Before leaving, he thanked owner Marisa May for always protecting his privacy. Since its opening in the summer of 1988, San Domenico was credited with gaining New York's Italian cuisine the same respect previously reserved for French fare. San Domenico closed in 2008 due to (what else?) rent issues.

## MOUNT SINAI WEST;
## FORMERLY ROOSEVELT HOSPITAL
### BETWEEN NINTH AND TENTH AVES. AND BETWEEN
### 59TH AND 60TH STS.

BOBBY AND ETHEL CAME HERE on January 10, 1965, to await the birth of their ninth child, Maxwell Taylor Kennedy, who was born in the early hours of January 11. Many of the original Roosevelt Hospital buildings from the 1960s were torn down to make way for two 49-story residential buildings at One Columbus Place. A new main hospital building opened in 1990.

## DEUTSCHE BANK CENTER; FORMER LOCATION OF THE NEW YORK COLISEUM

10 COLUMBUS CIRCLE, W. 58TH TO W. 60TH STS. BETWEEN EIGHTH AND NINTH AVES.; DEMOLISHED

ALONG WITH LBJ, JFK HELD a nationally televised speech here on November 5, 1960, the Saturday before Tuesday's Election Day. He spoke before an enthusiastic crowd of 9,000 supporters. "If we sleep too long in the 60s, Mr. Khrushchev will indeed 'bury' us," he warned. This was a reference to the Soviet leader's "We will bury you" statement to Western ambassadors in Moscow in 1956, which was widely interpreted as a threat to use nuclear weapons. The Coliseum was still new at the time, having opened in 1956. It served as New York's main convention center for the next three decades. It was hardly beloved by architectural critics, with *AIA's Guide to New York* remembering it as a "dreary white brick white elephant," and one writer describing it as "a low point for New York's public buildings." The Coliseum eventually lost national convention business to the far larger McCormick Place in Chicago. With the opening of the more spacious and modern Javits Center in 1986, it was evident that time had passed the Coliseum by, and it was shuttered that year. It then took more than a decade to sell the property. The Coliseum was razed in 2000, and the Time Warner (now Deutsche Bank) Center was constructed where it once stood.

# RAFFLES

## 171 W. 57TH ST. @ SEVENTH AVE. CLOSED

THIS WAS A PRIVATE CLUB founded by Earl Blackwell, located in a penthouse apartment here. George Plimpton's former wife, Freddy, later recalled[102] that following a dinner at the Smith's apartment, which she believed occurred in "early October" of 1963, JFK — "happy because he had eluded the Secret Service" — came here with her and Plimpton. "It was just about escaping, going to a fun place," Freddy remembered. According to her account, JFK didn't dance due to his bad back, and the trio later returned via taxi to the Smith's apartment, leaving JFK at the back entrance. (One wonders what the facial expression of the cabbie must have been as he beheld the leader of the free world hopping on board.) That a U.S. President would ride in cabs to go nightclubbing late at night in Manhattan without (or even with) Secret Service protection is mind-boggling. Still, October 1963 was a more innocent time in an era that was about to end forever.

In October 1969, photographer Ron Galella snapped a photo of Ari and Jackie leaving here in their limo.

---

102  Nelson W. Aldrich Jr., Editor, *George Being George: George Plimpton's Life as Told, Admired, Deplored and Envied by 200 Friends, Relatives, Lovers, Acquaintances, Rivals – and a Few Unappreciative Observers*, New York: Random House, 2009.

# THE DIRECTOR'S GUILD OF AMERICA THEATER; FORMERLY CINEMA RENDEZVOUS

## 110 W. 57TH ST. BETWEEN SIXTH AND SEVENTH AVES.

BOBBY AND ETHEL WERE AMONG the guests at the gala premiere of *Doctor Faustus* here on February 6, 1968. The film starred Elizabeth Taylor and Richard Burton. The crowd was so large and boisterous that it reportedly took Liz and Dick ten minutes to make their way from their limo to the theater entrance. Guests later went to dinner at the Plaza Hotel. The movie was a bomb.

Jackie and Ari attended the showing of the controversial X-rated Swedish movie *I Am Curious (Yellow)* here on October 6, 1969. When she went out into the lobby mid-film and saw photographers, Jackie — who was wearing a kerchief in a fruitless attempt to go unrecognized — immediately left the theater, leaving Ari to finish watching by himself. Once outside, *Daily News* photographer Mel Finkelstein claimed that an irate Jackie knocked him to the ground using a "judo trick," and another paparazzo took a photo of Finkelstein on the pavement with Jackie striding past him. This account was disputed by two other witnesses, one of whom was the theater doorman, who claimed that Finkelstein slipped and fell, and that Jackie hadn't touched him. Today, the theater is a pre-eminent state-of-the-art screening facility ... with a pretty cool history!

Despite – or perhaps because of – attempts to ban it as pornographic, *I Am Curious Yellow* was a box-office success in the U.S., grossing over $20 million and ushering in a new era where nudity became commonplace in mainstream movies.

https://www.dga.org/The-Guild/Theaters/New-York/MainTheater.aspx

# NICHOLAS KOUNOVSKY GYM
## 1940: 39 W. 54TH ST. /9 W. 57TH ST./ 25 W. 56TH ST.
## FROM MID-1969: 24 W. 57TH ST.

THE RUSSIAN-BORN KOUNOVSKY WAS A fitness guru credited with introducing European exercise and gymnastics techniques
to New York's high society during the 1960s and 70s. He opened his
first gym at the W. 54th St. location in 1940. Jackie was a regular
here, usually coming in on Tuesday and Thursday mornings but
rarely speaking much. Kounovsky had some unusual motivational
techniques, one of which was rewarding his charges with drinks
of champagne when they performed as requested. Workouts were
often followed by lunch at La Caravelle, making one wonder if the
clients should have just stayed home. Kounovsky died in 1993, but
his methods are still taught today.

# THE RUSSIAN TEA ROOM

## 150 W. 57TH BETWEEN SIXTH AND SEVENTH AVES.

THIS SMALL BUILDING WITH THE red awning next to Carnegie Hall was said to be Jackie's favorite lunch spot. Founded in 1927 by members of the Russian Imperial Ballet, this was a premier gathering place for New York's artists and dancers for many years. Given her love of Russian culture and history, it's not surprising that Jackie was very fond of this place, often bringing the writers she was editing here for lunch. Before escorting Jackie here, director Mike Nichols would call ahead to reserve two bowls of pelmeni (Russian dumplings) for their 3 p.m. lunch. In early 1992, John Jr. was spotted here with his recent ex, Christina Haag. Also in 1992, Jackie was here for the launch party of Edward Radzinsky's book *The Last Tsar*, which she edited. Pronounced "The Worst Restaurant in New York" in a 2023 *New York Post* article, the Tea Room would appear to have seen better days.

# CARNEGIE HALL
## 881 SEVENTH AVE. BETWEEN W. 56TH AND 57TH STS.

JOHN AND CAROLYN ATTENDED A benefit at this famed concert hall on December 1, 1997, to raise funds for the La Fenice Opera House in Venice, which was burned down by arsonists in January 1996. Guests included Barbara Walters, Anna Wintour, and John and Carolyn's friend, Donatella Versace. They heard music by Rossini, Verdi, and Donizetti, all of whom had their works premiere at La Fenice. Elton John then took the stage, saying he was there at the request of the recently assassinated Gianni Versace. "In his memory, and for all the beautiful things he has showed me in Venice, I'm going to sing this song." He then sang "Live Like Horses," a song extolling personal freedom from his album *The Big Picture*, which had been released that September. For Carolyn, Elton's performance must have brought back memories of when he sang at Versace's Milan memorial service in July.

Elton's Princess Diana tribute "Candle in the Wind 97" (the original 1973 version was about Marilyn Monroe) was the No. 1 song on the U.S. *Billboard* "Hot 100" chart on this night, amid an astonishing 14-week run at the top of the chart. An inescapable presence on U.S. radio that autumn and beyond, the song must have caused Carolyn anxiety given her empathy for Diana as a fellow target of the paparazzi.

The rebuilding of the La Fenice began in 2001, and it reopened in November 2004 with a performance of *La Traviata*.

# ORSINI'S

## 41 W. 56TH ST. BETWEEN FIFTH AND SIXTH AVES.; CLOSED

THIS PLACE WAS RENOWNED AS a celebrity hangout, and that attracted more diners than its simple Italian comfort food did. *New York Magazine* restaurant critic Gael Greene described it this way in 1970: "No one goes to Orsini's for the food. ... Orsini's is theater. ... One goes for the people, the mood." Jackie came here often and was photographed in the doorway after dining here in 1979. Bobby and Ethel ate here on January 10, 1968, along with Arthur Schlesinger, former astronaut John Glenn, actor Sidney Poitier, and director George Stevens Jr. and his wife. Bobby was wrestling with the question of whether to run for President, and he questioned the motives of California politicians such as Jesse Unruh, who were encouraging him to run and assuring him he could win the primary there in June.

# SHOREHAM HOTEL;
## FORMER HOME OF LA CARAVELLE
### 33 W. 55ᵀᴴ ST. BETWEEN FIFTH AND SIXTH AVES.

LOCATED IN THE SHOREHAM, LA Caravelle was owned by Fred Decré and Robert Meyzen, with Roger Fessaguet as head chef. Decré and Meyzen, had been maîtres d' at Le Pavillon, a Kennedy family favorite just down the street. At the urging of Joe Sr. — who'd had a falling out with Henri Soulé of Le Pavillon after he sought to have a photographer kicked out of the restaurant — they left there to open La Caravelle in September 1960. They hired Fessaquet, another veteran of Le Pavillon, as executive chef. Since he was very familiar with the Kennedys' culinary preferences, Fessaquet helped train René Verdon — the chef at the Essex House — before the latter went to Washington to serve as JFK's White House chef. Joe was present the night La Caravelle opened, September 21, 1960.

Although the owners were initially concerned that East Side denizens would not cross Fifth Avenue to visit the restaurant, their fears were soon averted. *New York Times* critic Craig Claiborne described La Caravelle as "the finest restaurant in New York on almost every count."

JFK was reportedly especially fond of the vichyssoise and chicken with champagne sauce served at La Caravelle, sometimes requesting these for takeout orders when he visited New York. Steve

Smith was at a business lunch here on November 22, 1963, when he learned that his brother-in-law had been assassinated. The following May, columnist Drew Pearson reported that the Kennedys had held a "family reunion" — Joe included — at La Caravelle to discuss the prospects of Bobby being named as LBJ's Vice Presidential running mate.

While undergoing rehab in 1962 at NYU Medical Center following his stroke, Joe got takeout meals from La Caravelle delivered.

A February 1966 *Times* article noted that the restaurant maintained a "royal station" described as "tables just inside the entrance that are more or less reserved for patrons such as Mrs. John F. Kennedy." The elegant atmosphere was enhanced with murals of Parisian Park scenes painted by Jean Pagès. A *New York Times* article on Bobby's relationship with New York published in the days following his death noted this as one of his favorite restaurants in the city.

Jackie was photographed outside La Caravelle in 1970, accompanied by her friend Nicole Alphand. Late in 1974, Jackie met with *New Yorker* editor William Shawn here to convince him to let her write an anonymous piece for the magazine's *Talk of the Town* section. Shawn agreed, and Jackie's article was published with the title "Being Present." She touted the opening of the International Center for Photography (ICP) museum, which Jackie, a former professional photographer herself, helped to get started.

La Caravelle
RESTAURANT
33 WEST 55th STREET
NEW YORK CITY

## STUDIO 54

THIS IS THE LEGENDARY CLUB that pretty much sums up the 70s, both in its best (disco music, sexual liberation, racial diversity, and tolerance) and worst (elitism, cocaine, and greed) aspects. John Jr. was photographed dancing here in 1977 when he was still just 16 or 17. On November 14, 1977, Jackie was photographed getting a hug from Leonard Bernstein at a party here celebrating the release of the ballet-themed movie *The Turning Point*. The following year, Caroline was spotted here several times. Jackie was photographed here with club denizen Raymond St. Jacques in 1979. The Roundabout Theatre Company now operates the space and includes the 54 Below cabaret in the basement.

# MUSEUM OF MODERN ART (MOMA)

## 11 W. 53RD ST. BETWEEN FIFTH AND SIXTH AVES.

GIVEN THE LIMITED NUMBER OF documented appearances she made here, it would seem that Jackie preferred the Met and the Whitney to MOMA. Or perhaps it was just a matter of proximity since MOMA wasn't as close to her home. Famed architect Philip Johnson recalled a somewhat puzzling meeting with Jackie in the sculpture garden here in 1964. Johnson assumed he was there to discuss the plans to build the JFK Library in Boston. He had just finished working on some improvements to the garden, but Jackie seemed unaware of his involvement. He later said:

> *"...It wasn't clear why we were meeting at all. She didn't speak very directly about the JFK Library, more generally about city planning, that sort of thing."* [103]

Johnson suspected that Jackie had already decided to give the library commission to I.M. Pei and that she was just going through the motions in their meeting. Pei's design was widely lauded when

---

103  C. David Heyman, *A Woman Named Jackie*, New York: Lyle Stuart, 1989.

the library finally opened in 1979, but not by Johnson, who stated that he had a "not very positive" impression of the building from the photos of it he'd seen.

# NEW YORK HILTON MIDTOWN
## 1335 SIXTH AVE. @ 53ᴿᴰ ST.

ON NOVEMBER 15, 1963, JFK gave a speech to the Catholic Youth Organization (CYO) meeting in the Grand Ballroom here. Although his speech lasted just five minutes, it was very enthusiastically received. The Hilton was brand new at the time, having opened on June 26, 1963. It had 2,153 rooms, making it the largest hotel in Manhattan. JFK had been in the same room a week earlier to accept the "Family of Man Award" from the Protestant Council of the City of New York. He spoke then about poverty in rural and urban areas and the importance of foreign aid in combating world poverty.

Bobby addressed the good government group Citizens Union in the Mercury Ballroom here on December 14, 1967, a speech in which he decried indifference to the poverty present in inner cities.

A much-reproduced photo of Carolyn and John Jr. laughing while she sits on his lap was taken at a dinner here in June 1996.

## SHERATON NEW YORK TIMES SQUARE HOTEL; FORMERLY THE AMERICANA HOTEL

### 811 SEVENTH AVE. BETWEEN W. 52ND AND W. 53RD STS.

RISING 51 STORIES AND BOASTING more than 1,000 rooms, the Americana opened on September 25, 1962. Like the nearby Hilton, it was built to accommodate the expected flood of tourists who would be attending the 1964-65 World's Fair. JFK spoke to a crowd of 5,500 at the AFL-CIO convention here on November 15, 1963. He decried the fact that there were four million still unemployed, calling it "...An intolerable waste in this rich country of ours." He advocated for his tax-cut plan as a way to reduce the high unemployment rate. While emphasizing the importance of passing his civil rights proposal, he said that reducing unemployment was equally important. Both of these proposals were currently bogged down in House committees and were deemed unlikely to pass in what was left of 1963. From here, JFK proceeded to the Hilton Hotel a block away, addressing attendees at a Catholic Youth Organization convention.

On November 1, 1966, Bobby was photographed at a Democratic fundraising dinner here with his future 1968 opponent, Vice President Hubert Humphrey and soon-to-be failed[104] New York

---

104  In an indication of his popularity, incumbent Governor Nelson Rockefeller carried Manhattan in his defeat of O'Connor. To date, he is the last Republican to do so in a statewide election.

gubernatorial candidate Frank O'Connor, with whom Bobby campaigned extensively that fall. After being sold in 1979, the hotel became the Sheraton Centre Hotel before it was renamed.

## 21 CLUB

21 W. 52ND ST. BETWEEN FIFTH AND SIXTH AVES. CLOSED

THE 21 WAS A STORIED Manhattan institution for more than ninety years. Known for its wrought-iron gates, gas lanterns, and the red-capped lawn jockeys on the stairs and balcony outside, the 21 Club was started as a speakeasy in 1930 during Prohibition. JFK was a regular here during his bachelor days and also ate here in January 1961 when he was President-elect.

Gore Vidal later claimed[105] that at a 1961 White House dinner party, caviar from 21 was served.

Sometime in 1966, Bobby had a secret meeting in one of the private rooms here with newly elected New York Mayor John Lindsay. The media had set up Bobby and the young Republican as rivals, but over drinks at their meeting, the pair agreed to work together on Bobby's Bedford-Stuyvesant anti-poverty project. Their doing so helped to make the project a success.

Bobby was here on the night of Tuesday, March 12, 1968, when Minnesota Sen. Eugene McCarthy shocked the political world by nearly defeating President Lyndon Johnson in the New Hampshire Democratic primary. Within hours, Bobby—who had vacillated for

---

105  Gore Vidal, *Palimpsest*, New York: Vintage Books, 1995.

months over whether to enter the race—said he was "reassessing" his possible candidacy in light of the New Hampshire results. Four days later, on March 16, he announced he was running.

Bobby had expected McCarthy to do well enough in New Hampshire to make clear how disenchanted many Democrats were with the Vietnam War, thus paving the way for RFK to enter the race. But not *this* well. By coming within seven points of LBJ with 42% to LBJ's 49%, it seemed McCarthy might be able to take out LBJ by himself, thereby removing the raison d'être of a Kennedy candidacy. Bobby's entry brought accusations that he was an opportunist capitalizing on McCarthy's success. Kennedy partisans countered that Bobby could defeat Richard Nixon in November, while McCarthy was unlikely to do so. Bobby wound up competing head-to-head with McCarthy for the anti-war vote in the primaries that spring instead of focusing on his expected opponent, LBJ, or later after LBJ withdrew, Hubert Humphrey.

Jackie and Ari were spotted here before their marriage. 21 has been described as Ari's favorite New York restaurant. A man of simple culinary tastes, Ari was happy ordering beer and knockwurst here.

In the spring of 1970, photographer Ron Galella snapped a photo of Jackie and Lee here for drinks before going on to the Alvin Theatre to see the opening night performance of the new Stephen Sondheim musical *Company*.

Jackie and Frank Sinatra were famously photographed together here on September 17, 1975. John Jr. and Carolyn were spotted having dinner here in February 1996. The 21 Club closed on December 11, 2020, ostensibly a victim of the COVID-19 pandemic, although many agreed that the restaurant had been in decline for years.

# THE NEIL SIMON THEATRE;
# FORMERLY THE ALVIN THEATRE

## 250 W. 52ND ST. BETWEEN BROADWAY AND EIGHTH AVE.

JACKIE, LEE AND HER HUSBAND Stas saw Stephen Sondheim's musical *A Funny Thing Happened on the Way to the Forum* here on February 5, 1963. Starring Zero Mostel and directed by George Abbott, this was the first hit show for which Sondheim composed both the music and lyrics. *A Funny Thing* ran for more than two years and won the Tony Award for Best Musical. Bobby reportedly also saw the show here during its initial run.

Jackie and Lee attended the opening night performance of Sondheim's groundbreaking musical *Company* here on April 26, 1970. *Company* was notable for its nonlinear storyline and for using the musical form to take a clear-eyed view of modern-day marriage and relationships. In a 1967 column by Liz Smith, Sondheim was listed as among the younger "groovier crowd" with whom Jackie preferred to socialize, a group that also included Sondheim's *West Side Story* collaborator Leonard Bernstein and his wife Felicia.

Sondheim later wrote the song "Bobby and Jackie and Jack" for his 1981 musical *Merrily We Roll Along*. The song is set when JFK was President and name-checks numerous Kennedys in addition to the ones mentioned in the title. Lee Harvey Oswald is among the rogue's gallery of Presidential assailants depicted in Sondheim's dark 1990 musical *Assassins*.

# ROSIE O'GRADY'S
## 800 SEVENTH AVE @ 52ND ST.; CLOSED

THIS VENERABLE IRISH PUB WAS located here in the Theater District from 1981 until exorbitant rent costs forced it to close in July 2023. John Jr. was a regular here while working at *George*, whose offices are just a couple of blocks away. On one occasion, he ordered the shepherd's pie and a Heineken.

"He was in Rosie O'Grady's two days before he died," remembered server Kathleen Carty. On his first visit, he asked Carty her name. When she told him it was Kathleen, he joked, "Oh, that's a strange name for an Irish girl."[106]

Second-generation owner Michael Carty said, "Celebrities knew they could come in here and be left alone." This atmosphere was undoubtedly appealing to John.

---

106 *The New York Post*, "Rosie O'Grady's Saloon Honors Celeb Customers from JFK Jr. to Bono in Final Toast" by Angela Barbuti, June 24, 2023.

# ARO TOWER; FORMER SITE OF ROSELAND BALLROOM

## 239 W. 52ND ST. BETWEEN BROADWAY AND EIGHTH AVE.; DEMOLISHED

THE ROSELAND RELOCATED TO THIS space — built in 1922 as the Iceland ice skating rink — in 1956. John Jr. was here on the evening of Valentine's Day 1995 for a benefit for Naked Angels, the theater repertory group of which he was a board member. Madeleine Kahn (who died a few months after John in December 1999) and Fisher Stevens (later to co-star in *Succession*) performed. An unaccompanied (on *Valentine's Day?*) John told the crowd, "I hope everybody is with the one they love." Roseland hosted many concerts through the years, including Nirvana in 1993, Oasis in 1995, and Madonna in 2000. Lady Gaga closed the venue with a series of seven shows in March and April of 2014.

# TOOTS SHOR'S RESTAURANT

33 W. 52^{ND} ST. BETWEEN FIFTH AND SIXTH AVES.; CLOSED

ORIGINALLY LOCATED AT 51 W. 51^{st} St. (there's a plaque commemorating it there), this was a classic New York saloon and celebrity hangout operated by Bernard "Toots" Shor. It was a particular favorite of athletes such as Joe DiMaggio and sports writers. Other clientele included everyone from mobster Frank Costello to Chief Justice Earl Warren. This was the site of the famed "drinking contest, " where Shor bested his good pal, Jackie Gleason. In the early hours of October 31, 1964, following his radio debate with Sen. Kenneth Keating hosted by Barry Gray on WMCA, Bobby, Ethel, and a group of friends that included Gray, former New York governor Averell Harriman, and Arthur Schlesinger gathered here. Seemingly acknowledging that the tide had turned in his favor, Shor greeted Bobby with, "How are you, Senator?" Toots' place was long past its glory days by 1964, and it closed for good in 1971.

# JUDSON GRILL

152 W. 52ND ST. BETWEEN 6TH AND 7TH AVES.; CLOSED

THIS WAS A LARGE, STYLISH restaurant serving American cuisine that was located in the Equitable Center here from 1994 to 2004. A February 1998 *New York Times* lunchtime review noted: "The energy in that big, handsome room is so electric that you feel you are in the very heart of Manhattan." This location is a short walk from where the *George* offices were located at Broadway and 51st St., and John Jr. would sometimes have lunch here. Writer and RFK biographer Jack Newfield later told of his experience going to lunch here with John:

> *"Walking next to him up Broadway to the Judson Grill one day, and having lunch in a room full of buzz, I got a glimpse of what it must be like to be so famous, how uncomfortably distorting it must be. Heads turned. People did double-takes. Pretty women smiled. Waiters stammered. People pointed at him. This level of Princess Di-Muhammad Ali celebrity robs you of all privacy. But John was never*

*harsh, never bitter.... He had a natural grace."* [107]

Of course, John had never known a time in his life when he *wasn't* famous.

Sarah Jessica Parker — still a few years away from starring in *Sex and the City* — dated John briefly in the summer of 1991. She later recalled:

> *"I never had any idea what real fame was until I met John.... We would go places where there wasn't a soul around, and the next day, I'd see pictures of us there in the tabloids."* [108]

Lest we paint too bleak a picture, John's fame had obvious advantages. Many people he met were in awe of him because of who his parents were and were eager to do whatever they could to please him. As for women, John had access to beautiful models, singers, and actresses that mere mortals could only fantasize about. And he was very wealthy. So yes, life had its challenges, but he understood that he was fortunate in many ways.

When his friend, CNN correspondent Jill Brooke, once said to him, "It must be hard being you," John smiled and replied, "Actually, I highly recommend it." [109]

---

107  Newfield, Jack, "Goodnight, Sweet Prince of a Noble Family", *The New York Post*, July 19, 1999.

108  https://www.closerweekly.com/posts/john-f-kennedy-jr-s-lovers-recall-memories-after-his-death/

109  Maer, Roshan, "Prince of the City," *New York* Magazine, August 2, 1999.

# RADIO CITY MUSIC HALL

## 1260 SIXTH AVE. BETWEEN W. 50TH AND W. 51ST STS.

JEAN LATER WROTE THAT THE whole family would see movies here during their Sunday trips to the city in the 1940s. On one such visit, they watched *The Little Colonel,* starring Shirley Temple and Lionel Barrymore.

John Jr. attended the MTV Music Video Awards here on September 8, 1994. The show was hosted by comedienne Roseanne Barr. The event is best remembered for its opening, in which Michael Jackson and his new bride, Lisa Marie Presley, strode out on the stage. Jackson concluded a short speech by stating, "And just think, nobody thought this would last," before the couple shared a kiss. Aerosmith won Video of the Year for "Cryin'" while R.E.M. took home several technical awards for "Everybody Hurts."

John and his cousin Rory attended *Time* magazine's 75th Anniversary Gala here on March 3, 1998. John offered a toast in honor of JFK's and LBJ's defense secretary Robert McNamara. McNamara was one of the architects of the escalation of the Vietnam War under LBJ and has long been blamed for the failure of American policy in Vietnam. McNamara had recently published his book *In Retrospect: The Tragedy and Lessons of Vietnam,* in which he accepted blame for policy failures in Vietnam ("we were wrong, terribly wrong") while trying to urge future American leaders to learn from the mistakes he and his colleagues made. Many met the book with anger and scorn, partly because McNamara had once seemed so sure of himself in his proclamations about the war, but also because many felt he should have spoken out against the war earlier. Bobby had repeatedly urged him to do so in the months before McNamara resigned as Secretary of Defense in late 1967. Would his doing so have changed the course of the war and kept it from dragging on for several more years? John was, of course, mindful of all of this and the anguish McNamara had lived with for decades when he gave his toast:

> *"...He took full responsibility for his decisions. Judging from the reception he got, I doubt many public servants will be brave enough to follow his example. So tonight, I would like to toast someone I've known my whole life, not as a symbol of pain we can't forget,*[110] *but as a man. And I would like to thank him for teaching me something about bearing great responsibility with great dignity. An adversity endured only by those who accept great responsibility."*[111]

Whatever one's views of McNamara, *In Retrospect* should be required reading at all U.S. military academies, not to mention for potential U.S. Presidents and Secretaries of Defense.

---

110  This is an allusion to the quote from the poet Aeschylus that Bobby had used in his speech in Indianapolis the night of Martin Luther King Jr.'s death: "In our sleep, pain which cannot forget falls drop by drop upon the heart, until in our own despair, against our will, comes wisdom through the awful grace of God."

111  https://time.com/6052980/vietnam-robert-mcnamara-memoir/

## *GEORGE* MAGAZINE OFFICES
### 1633 BROADWAY @ 51ST ST.;
### PARAMOUNT PLAZA, 41ST FLOOR

ALTHOUGH *GEORGE* WAS IN TROUBLE financially by the summer of 1999 and folded two years later in John's absence, the past twenty-plus years have seen politics mesh with pop culture as never before, proving that John's instincts in founding *George* were correct. Unfortunately, magazine advertising revenues plummeted in the ensuing decades with the rise of the internet, so it's unlikely *George* could have sustained itself under such circumstances, even if John's star power had still been propelling interest. During the final weeks of his life, John toyed with the idea of making *George* a web-only publication in an effort to save it.

## THE GERSHWIN THEATRE; FORMERLY THE URIS
### 222 W. 51ST ST. BETWEEN BROADWAY AND EIGHTH AVE.

JACKIE ATTENDED FRANK SINATRA'S SHOW here on September 17, 1975. A photo shows Sinatra pal Jilly Rizzo escorting Jackie that night. The Chairman appeared with Ella Fitzgerald and the Count Basie Orchestra. They were in the middle of a two-week run of shows that began on September 8. It marked the first time Sinatra had appeared at a theater in the city since his legendary Paramount shows in the 1940s.

While at Doubleday, Jackie was said to have repeatedly implored Sinatra to pen a memoir, but she couldn't persuade him. The singer was reportedly so distraught when Jackie died that he could not perform two scheduled concerts in the days following her death. The Uris was renamed in honor of George and Ira in 1983. The Gershwin is steps away from what is now Azalea Ristorante, where John Jr. ate lunch on the afternoon of his plane crash.

## AZALEA RISTORANTE;
## FORMERLY TRIONFO RISTORANTE
### 224 W. 51ST ST. BETWEEN BROADWAY AND EIGHTH AVE.

JOHN JR. ATE LUNCH AT Trionfo on July 16, 1999, a meal that proved to be his last. The location is at the base of the same Paramount Plaza building that housed *George*. John — hobbled and still on crutches despite having had the cast removed from his left foot the previous day — chose this convenient location because it was too painful to walk anywhere farther. Richard Blow — now serving as *George*'s executive editor — accompanied John and later wrote[112] that John removed his shoe from his left foot and propped up his injured left leg on a chair as he settled in. You don't have to be a doctor to conclude that maybe it wasn't such a good idea for a man in such a condition to take the controls of a small plane.[113] Blow remembered that John ordered a salad and chicken in white wine sauce and that he expressed optimism about *George*'s future during the final hours of his life.

---

112  Blow, *American Son.*

113  In the NTSB (National Transportation Safety Board) report on John's crash, a flight instructor who flew with John to Martha's Vineyard at night on July 1 said that the cast on John's left ankle meant the instructor had to "taxi the airplane and assist the pilot with the landing."

# WINTER GARDEN THEATRE
## 1634 BROADWAY BETWEEN W. 50TH AND 51ST STS.

JACKIE WAS REPORTEDLY IN ATTENDANCE at the opening night performance of *West Side Story* here on September 26, 1957. JFK and Jackie saw the 1961 film version while in the White House. Composer Leonard Bernstein had become friendly with the future First Couple earlier in the 1950s. He conducted the 70-piece orchestra assembled for JFK's pre-inaugural gala in Washington DC — composing *Fanfare* for the occasion — and was a White House guest while JFK was President. In a long and diverse career in music, Bernstein's score for *West Side Story* is arguably his greatest artistic achievement and the work he is likely to be best remembered for.

The Winter Garden is directly across the street from Paramount Plaza, which housed John Jr.'s *George* offices. John would have encountered the marquee for the Andrew Lloyd Webber musical *Cats* every day as he went to work at *George*. He saw *Cats* at least once during its long run. *Cats* opened in October 1982 and finally closed on September 10, 2000, making it, at the time, the longest-running show in Broadway history. Like John Jr.'s death the previous year, the closing symbolized the end of one era and the beginning of a new one.

## THE TIMES SQUARE CHURCH; FORMERLY THE MARK HELLINGER THEATRE

### 237 W. 51ST ST. BETWEEN BROADWAY AND EIGHTH AVE.

ALTHOUGH THERE IS SCANT DOCUMENTATION to verify it, it is very likely that JFK and Jackie saw the hit Lerner & Loewe musical *My Fair Lady* here after it opened on March 15, 1956. The original production starred Rex Harrison as Henry Higgins and Julie Andrews as Eliza Doolittle.

Jackie saw the Alan Jay Lerner-Burton Lane (Loewe had retired to Palm Springs) musical *On a Clear Day You Can See Forever* here on December 7, 1965. She was escorted by Lerner and photographed visiting the cast backstage after the performance. The show starred John Cullum and Barabara Harris. Lerner — whose father founded the Lerner Department Store chain — went to Choate and Harvard with JFK and the two were lifelong friends. Lerner provided the lyrics to Frederick Loewe's music for *Camelot*, which is now, thanks to Jackie, forever associated with the Kennedy administration. Like JFK and Jackie, Lerner was a patient of the notorious Dr. Max Jacobson. JFK and Jackie hosted Lerner and Loewe at the White House, and Lerner organized JFK's 1963 birthday bash at the Waldorf.

*On a Clear Day* opened in October 1965 and closed in June 1966, a disappointing run compared to Lerner's earlier successes with *My*

*Fair Lady* and *Camelot*. Critics pointed out problems with the show's book, but the musical score — including the excellent title song — was and is highly regarded by critics and fans. The Nederlander Organization sold the Mark Hellinger to the Times Square Church, which was already renting it, in December 1991.

# IRISH ARTS CENTER

### 553 W. 51ST ST. @ 11TH AVE., HELL'S KITCHEN

SINCE 1972, THE IRISH ARTS Center has aspired to be the premier multi-disciplinary home for Irish arts in the U.S. John Jr. acted in several plays while at Brown, and on August 4, 1985, he made his New York debut here in *Winners,* a four-character play by renowned Irish playwright Brian Friel. *Winners* premiered in Dublin in 1967 before moving to Broadway. John's co-star was his long-time acquaintance, now girlfriend, Christina Haag, and they played Joe and Meg, a young Irish couple dealing with first love. They are to be married because Meg is pregnant. Eerily, at the end of the play, John and Haag's characters drown while trying to reach an island in a boat. Two other eerie coincidences redolent of the 1999 tragedy: As searches for Joe and Meg are conducted, clothes wash up on shore, and a search for the missing bodies is conducted over three days.

Attendance at the performances was by invitation only, and after six shows, *Winners* closed on August 9. As for a future as an actor in the theater, John told a reporter: "This is not a professional acting debut by any means ... it's just a hobby." Nye Heron, the Arts Center's executive director at the time, told a reporter: "He's one of the best young actors I've seen in years." John's romance with Haag lasted until 1991. Haag later stated that John had the makings of becoming an excellent actor. His mother apparently dissuaded him from pursuing acting as a career, although some of his friends dispute this. If he had done so, "He would have had a lot of opportunities," Haag recalled. Friel's *Dancing at Lughnasa* won the Tony Award for Best Play in 1992.

The Irish Arts Center is still a great institution, and it recently relocated to a new home around the corner at 726 11ᵗʰ Ave.

https://irishartscenter.org/

## RICE N BEANS
### 744 NINTH AVE. BETWEEN W. 50TH AND W. 51ST STS., HELL'S KITCHEN

JOHN JR. LIKED THIS PLACE and often ordered takeout from here while working late at night at *George* two blocks away. Described as a "hole in the wall" by the *Zagat Guide*, Rice n Beans is known for its excellent Latin American food. It is still thriving today.

# THE TIME-LIFE BUILDING

## 1271 SIXTH AVE., WEST SIDE BETWEEN 50<sup>TH</sup> AND 51<sup>ST</sup> STS.

A PARTNERSHIP BETWEEN ROCKEFELLER CENTER and Time. Inc., this 48-story sleek and stylish building costing $70 million was designed by architect Wallace Harrison of Harrison, Abramovitz & Harris. In need of more office space, *Time* moved from 1 Rockefeller Center nearby. Marilyn Monroe was on hand to cut the ribbon when construction began in 1957. Tenants began moving in late 1959. Writing in the *New York Times,* architecture critic Ada Louise Huxtable lauded the building for having a "still rare etheistic excellence."

JFK had a private meeting with publisher Henry Luce here on August 5, 1960, after accepting the Democratic nomination in L.A. on July 15. The *New York Times* reported that one thousand people, "mostly women," gathered at the building entrance to greet him and that police had difficulty escorting him through the crowd. Luce was quoted in the next day's *New York Times* as claiming he had yet to decide to support Republican Richard Nixon. With its regular articles and countless photos of the Kennedy family, Luce's *Life* magazine did more than any publication to promote a positive image of the Kennedys during the 1960s. *Time* was a different story, and JFK wanted Luce to know that he expected better treatment in the future. One wonders if the rumor that Joe had a thing with Luce's wife Claire while serving as U.S. Ambassador in London complicated matters.

Time Inc. was once the largest publishing enterprise in the world. As magazines continue to go the way of the buggy whip, it is worth remembering that the *Time* empire once included its namesake magazine with a circulation of 4 million, *Life* (read by one in ten Americans), *Sports Illustrated*, and later, *People*. Leaf through an old edition of *Time* or *Life* with its in-depth articles and be astonished about how well-versed a typical American was about current events sixty years ago compared to today.

*Time* abandoned its offices here in 2015. In designating the lobby as an NYC landmark, the Preservation Commission described the building as "A rare intact example of mid-century modernism." Thus, it was appropriate the building served as the fictional headquarters of Sterling Cooper Draper Pryce in the *Mad Men* television series, which was set beginning in the optimistic years of the New Frontier era.

# NBC STUDIOS

## RCA BUILDING, 30 ROCKEFELLER CENTER

JFK WAS INTERVIEWED BY *Tonight Show* host Jack Paar in Studio 6B on June 16, 1960. Bobby was a guest on the show just five days before the election in 1960. Paar ceded the *Tonight Show* job to Johnny Carson in the autumn of 1962 and by 1964 was hosting *The Jack Paar Program* in primetime. Bobby was interviewed by Paar here on March 13, 1964, his first TV interview since the assassination. He had first appeared with Paar while promoting his book on his investigations into labor rackets, *The Enemy Within,* in June 1959. At that time, Paar described Bobby as "the bravest, finest young man I know."

Asked about Jackie, a fragile-looking Bobby said, "She's fine, really. She's making an adjustment and doing it well. She spends almost all of her time with the children now. I think she's making a good deal of progress." He went on to discuss the JFK Library and showed various mementos, including a draft of his inaugural address.

On February 5, 1968, Bobby appeared on the *Tonight Show* here during the extraordinary week that Harry Belafonte guest-hosted the show. (Belafonte also welcomed Dr. Martin Luther King Jr., among others, that week.) Bobby joked that Harry didn't look like

Johnny Carson, his fellow UN Plaza resident. Bobby refused to let Belafonte pin him down on whether he would run for President in 1968, probably because he had still yet to make up his mind. He also questioned why marijuana was illegal while cigarettes — "which kill far more people every year than marijuana" — weren't. Jimmy Fallon now hosts the *Tonight Show* from Studio 6B.

# ROCKEFELLER CENTER SKATING RINK
## ROCKERFELLER CENTER

BOBBY AND ETHEL HELD A party for 200 "associates" from the New York area here on January 24, 1968. Bobby was casually attired in a turtleneck shirt, a check jacket, and a navy beret. Partygoers later repaired to the adjacent Promenade Cafe for an elaborate buffet. At the time, the cafe consisted of the English Grille on the north side of the rink and the Cafe Francais on the southern side. JFK dined at the Cafe Francais in 1960. In addition to Arthur Schlesinger, guests included Bobby's young aide Carter Burden and his wife Amanda, who remains a prominent figure on New York's social scene to this day.

The next day's *New York Times* carried the headline "The Robert Kennedys Dress Up to Go Skating on Thin Ice," which claimed that Bobby had been "skating on thin ice politically in recent weeks" and noted that the ice at the famed rink is only two inches thick. Bobby was, of course, publicly vacillating over a presidential run at this time. Photographer Ethan Russell (soon to be renowned for his photos of the Beatles and the Rolling Stones, among other rock luminaries) took pictures at the event. He later wrote that Bobby was nonplussed when told that police were beating anti-war demonstrators not far away in Midtown.

Jackie and John Jr. were photographed at the tree lighting festivities here in December 1969.

## WORLDWIDE PLAZA COMPLEX; FORMER SITE OF THE OLD MADISON SQUARE GARDEN RAZED

### WEST SIDE OF EIGHTH AVE. BETWEEN 49TH AND 50TH STS.

THIS WAS THE SITE OF the most iconic Kennedy-related happenings in New York, or anywhere else: Marilyn Monroe's "Happy Birthday, Mr. President" serenade for JFK on May 19, 1962. Some things you might not know:

- It was "a hot, rainy night," according to the *Village Voice*.
- The event had not sold out, and tickets were given away on the street to fill the seats.
- For the book *Popography,* the author interviewed photographer Bill Ray, who took the iconic photo from behind Marilyn as she sang. Lee said there was a collective gasp from the crowd when a spotlight shined on Marilyn in the otherwise darkened arena as she came out on stage in her skin-tight dress.

Understandably overshadowed by Marilyn that night were Miriam Makeba, who sang "Wimoweh," aka "The Lion Sleeps Tonight," Harry Belafonte, who sang "Michael," and Peggy Lee, who sang a song that (according to Mimi Alford) was a favorite of JFK's, "I Believe in You," from *How to Succeed in Business Without Really Trying.*

If you want to see what MSG looked like then, check out the 1962 movie *The Manchurian Candidate*.

The next day, JFK returned here for a senior citizen rally to build support for a national health program for seniors, a goal achieved by the establishment of Medicare in 1965.

Bobby spoke here before a crowd of more than 18,000 at the United Jewish Appeal's "Stars for Israel" rally on June 11, 1967. Held in the wake of the Six-Day War in the Middle East, performers included Peter, Paul & Mary, Alan King, and Leslie Uggams. Bobby spoke in favor of Sen. Jacob Javits' proposal for direct negotiations between Israel and the Arab states backed by the major powers, stating, "Israel has earned the right to a final peace settlement" as opposed to an armistice. A year later, Bobby's accused assassin would cite Bobby's support for Israel as a reason for shooting him. Bobby's assassination occurred exactly a year to the day after the start of the Six-Day War. A new Madison Square Garden was built after the old Penn Station was torn down. This inspired an effort to save Grand Central, including the creation of the NYC Landmarks Preservation Commission.

# THE BARKING DOG;
## FORMERLY THE NEW WORLD GRILL
### 329 W. 49TH ON WORLDWIDE PLAZA BETWEEN
### EIGHTH AND NINTH AVES.

JOHN JR. OFTEN ATE LUNCH at the casual American New World Grill restaurant while working at *George*. Chef Katy Keck was a partner and consulting chef at the New World. "A cheerful spot, tucked away in the Worldwide Plaza complex ... (with a) spirited mix of styles — Asian, Southwestern and Italian," noted a *New York Times* review in 1997. John was said to enjoy dining al fresco here so he could catch some rays and work on his tan. Richard Blow later wrote[114] that John rejected his suggestion that they have lunch here on July 16, 1999, because it was too far for him to walk from their *George* office while on crutches and still in pain with his injured ankle. The Barking Dog is not visible from 49th St. It lies in the back of the building, facing the plaza.

www.barkingdognyc.com

---

114  Blow, *American Son*.

## CINERAMA THEATRE
### 1579 BROADWAY BETWEEN W 47<sup>TH</sup> AND W. 48<sup>TH</sup> STS.; DEMOLISHED

ALTHOUGH LITTLE REMEMBERED TODAY, THE last big social event of JFK's administration took place not in Washington but here on Sunday evening, November 17, 1963. JFK was in Florida and Jackie was in Washington, but just about all the other Kennedys, including Bobby, Ethel, Ted, Joan, Jean, and Pat attended the benefit premiere of director Stanley Kramer's all-star comedy *It's a Mad, Mad, Mad, Mad World*. The film was shown on a giant screen measuring 81 feet wide by 30 feet tall to showcase the wide-screen Cinerama process. By the end of the week, the film's title wouldn't seem very funny anymore. The Cinerama was torn down in 1987, but the Cinerama Dome in L.A. — which premiered *Mad World* on its opening night on November 2, 1963 — is still open.

## CHARLEY O'S BAR
### 33 WEST 48TH ST. BETWEEN FIFTH AND SIXTH AVES.; CLOSED

CHARLEY O'S WAS ONCE DESCRIBED by the *New York Times* as "the ultimate modern Irish bar." Bobby stopped in here on his way to march in the 1968 St. Patrick's Day Parade and might have returned after marching. Given the raucous and seat-of-your-pants nature of Bobby's campaign, one reporter later stated that it was appropriate that it kicked off in a bar. SEE ALSO: La Grenouille.

## THE JAMES EARL JONES THEATRE; FORMERLY THE CORT THEATRE

138 W. 48ᵀᴴ ST. BETWEEN SIXTH AND SEVENTH AVES.

JOHN JR. AND CAROLYN ATTENDED a performance of David Hare's play *The Blue Room* here on January 27, 1999. The play — directed by Sam Mendes — generated considerable publicity because it starred Hollywood actress Nicole Kidman, who appeared in the nude for a few dimly lit moments during the show. Not coincidently, *The Blue Room's* 14-week run was 95% sold out by the time it opened on December 13, 1998, and scalpers were said to be asking $500 a ticket. The production played to capacity houses throughout its run.

"Pure theatrical Viagra!" was how one London critic notoriously described the production. The New York critics were a bit less enthusiastic. *The Blue Room* remains Kidman's only Broadway turn to date. Hare's play is an adaptation of Arthur Schnitzler's play *Der Reigen*, which was popularized by the 1950 movie *La Ronde* by director Max Ophüls. The story concerns a chain of sexual encounters, with Kidman and co-star Iain Glen each playing five characters.

Kidman and her then-husband Tom Cruise had recently completed work on director Stanley Kubrick's film *Eyes Wide Shut*, an adaption of another Schnitzler novella, *Traumnovelle (Dream Story)*, which was published in 1926. Kidman and Cruise play an upscale married couple tempted by sexual situations in a somewhat hallucinatory story. Like Hare, Kubrick had taken a Schnitzler story set in Vienna and set it in the modern day, in this case, New York City. Kubrick died on March 7, 1999, after completing a final edit of the film. As fate would have it, *Eyes Wide Shut* opened in theaters in the U.S. on July 16, 1999, the day John's plane went down. Although *Eyes Wide Shut* took in almost $22 million and outperformed all other movies that weekend, Kidman later cited John's crash as having kept moviegoers home that weekend, thus tamping down *Eyes Wide Shut's* U.S. box office numbers:

> *"There was a lot of interest in Eyes Wide Shut before it was released. But the weekend it came out, July 16, 1999, was the death of JFK Jr. ... a black, black weekend. And for Stanley to have died before the film opened. ... Well, it all felt so dark and strange."*[115]

Middling reviews didn't help, but this mysterious film's reputation has surely grown in the decades since 1999. Director Martin Scorsese is among the film's champions, calling *Eyes Wide Shut* "misunderstood" at the time of its release, and, like other Kubrick films, "unlike anything else before or since."

In 2022, the Cort was renamed for actor James Earl Jones following an extensive $47 million renovation that began when the theater shut down at the outset of the COVID-19 epidemic in 2020.

---

115  https://www.hollywoodreporter.com/movies/movie-news/nicole-kidman-stanley-kubricks-lens-382186/

# LAUREN BESSETTE OFFICE, MORGAN STANLEY DEAN WITTER

## 1585 BROADWAY BETWEEN W 47TH AND W. 48TH STS.

THIS BUILDING — NOTABLE FOR its stock market ticker displays — is just four blocks down Broadway from where John's *George* offices were located. Lauren was a vice president at Morgan Stanley, working in the corporate finance division. She started with the company in 1987, left for two years to earn her MBA at the Wharton School of Business at the University of Pennsylvania, then returned in 1991. In 1994, she began a four-year stint working out of Morgan's Hong Kong office. Soon after returning to New York in February 1998, she was promoted to principal, one step below becoming a managing director.

According to John's assistant, RoseMarie Terenzio,[116] the plan on July 16 1999, was for Lauren to meet John in the downstairs lobby of his Paramount Plaza office at 6:30 p.m. when John would drive them to the Essex County Airport in Caldwell, New Jersey. *Time* magazine later reported that a meeting here that ran late that afternoon kept Lauren from meeting with John at his office until 6:45. If so, it joins a series of individual incidents that, had they not occurred, might have prevented the tragedy. But perhaps it wouldn't have mattered

---

116  *Fairy Tale Interrupted*, p. 200.

because Carolyn reportedly had yet to show up at the airport when John and Lauren arrived at around 8 p.m. Undoubtedly, the Friday night Manhattan traffic delayed all three parties.

According to some reports, Lauren was dating Kennedy's cousin Bobby Shriver at this time and requested to be dropped off at Martha's Vineyard, where she planned to meet him that night. John and Carolyn were going to Hyannis Port, so this necessitated John's fatal detour away from the lights of the coastline toward the dark and foggy open sea on their way to the island. In hindsight, a better choice would have been for John to hug the coast up to around New Bedford and then turn south toward the Vineyard. This way, he would have had to fly over the ocean for no more than eight miles. Of course, if accounts describing the meeting between John, Carolyn, and Lauren at the Stanhope were accurate, Carolyn may not have made the trip at all had Lauren not agreed to go along with them.

# ETHEL BARRYMORE THEATER

241 W. 47<sup>TH</sup> ST. BETWEEN BROADWAY AND EIGHTH AVE.

DURING AN UNANNOUNCED VISIT TO the city as President-elect on January 7, 1961, JFK came here to see Henry Fonda starring in the comedy *Critic's Choice* by Ira Levin. Yes, the guy who later scared the hell out of readers and moviegoers with *Rosemary's Baby*, *The Stepford Wives*, and *The Boys from Brazil* thought he'd try his hand at comedy! Otto Preminger was the director. JFK's one-time girlfriend Gene Tierney had starred in Preminger's 1944 movie *Laura*. Here, Fonda plays a drama critic who is forced to review his wife's really awful play. In his *New York Times* review, Howard Taubman[117] opined that *Critic's Choice* "is not much of a play" and that Preminger's "ideas for comedy run thin, like the playwright's."

JFK's friendship with Fonda was probably the reason he came to see *Critic's* Choice. The actor had been very active in the campaign, starring in television ads and even interviewing JFK and Jackie in a paid program that aired on November 2, 1960, less than a week before the election. *Critic's Choice* opened on December 14, 1960, and ran until May 1961. Bob Hope and Lucille Ball starred in a 1963 movie adaptation.

---

117  Howard Taubman "Theater: Integrity Comes First in 'Critic's Choice," *The New York Times*, December 15, 1960.

# THE SAMUEL J. FRIEDMAN THEATRE; FORMERLY THE BILTMORE THEATRE

## 261 W. 47TH ST. BETWEEN SEVENTH AND EIGHTH AVES.

ON DECEMBER 17, 1970, JACKIE attended a performance of the rock musical *Hair* here accompanied by her friend (and possibly more?) and advisor, financier André Meyer. Photographer Ron Galella snapped a picture of her wearing a black cape as she entered the theater. Although tame by today's standards, *Hair* was very controversial in its day; an anti-Vietnam War show that brought rock music to Broadway and whose characters did drugs and got naked on stage. Strangely enough, Michael Butler, the producer who brought *Hair* to Broadway after seeing it at the Public Theater, was a friend and advisor to Sen. John F. Kennedy during the 1950s. Small world! Whatever else can be said about Jackie, the woman was no prude. She had no problem seeing nude performers in a Broadway musical, viewing X-rated films, or sunbathing in the nude.

# GOTHAM BOOK MART
## 41 W. 47TH ST. BETWEEN FIFTH AND SIXTH AVENUES; CLOSED

FOUNDED IN 1920 BY A feisty book lover with avant-garde tastes named Frances Steloff, the Gotham became a haven for New York writers and artists over the decades. Customers included George Gershwin, Eugene O'Neill, Charlie Chaplin, Saul Bellow, James Joyce, J.D. Salinger, and Woody Allen. They were often in search of rare titles unavailable elsewhere. Steloff defiantly continued to sell D.H. Lawrence's *Lady Chatterley's Lover* and Henry Miller's *Tropic of Cancer* after they were declared obscene. Andreas Brown was a customer who purchased the Gotham from Steloff in 1967 and went on to run it for forty years. Steloff never left, staying on as a consultant and living in an alcove apartment above the store before dying at 101 years old in 1989. Brown later recalled that Jackie was an avid shopper at his store, buying books "Almost every day ... hundreds a year. Her taste is eclectic — fiction, non-fiction, history, art — and she's fascinated with current social issues."[118] Brown introduced Jackie to the drawing of Russian illustrator Boris Zvorykine, which resulted in her editing and writing the introduction for the book *The Firebird and Other Russian Fairy Tales*, which Viking published in

118  Quoted in Lawrence, *Jackie as Editor.*

1978, becoming one of only two books to carry Jackie's name during her years in publishing. The Gotham closed in 2007, and Brown passed away in 2020.

## JOSEPH P. KENNEDY OFFICE
### 1560 BROADWAY BETWEEN W. 46TH AND 47TH STS.

THIS 17-STORY TIMES SQUARE BUILDING was built in 1925 and recently underwent a design overhaul and upgrade. Joe had an office here in the 1920s and early 1930s when he ran Film Box Offices Corp. from this location. His friend Eddie Moore assisted him here and would soon lend his name to Joe's last child, born in 1932. All the major Hollywood studios had offices nearby at the time because it was in New York that studios made their financial decisions. By 1928, Joe had merged FBO into other companies controlled by associates to form RKO (Radio Keith Orpheum), the first studio devoted exclusively to "talkies." He also managed the career of (and bedded) actress Gloria Swanson at this time. The building is now home to the Actor's Equity Association. It's interesting to note that some sixty years later, Joe's grandson John worked in his *George* offices just four blocks north of here.

## K. WRAGGE

48 W. 46<sup>TH</sup> ST., SECOND FLOOR, BETWEEN
FIFTH AND SIXTH AVES.; CLOSED

IN BOBBY'S AUTOPSY REPORT, LOS Angeles County coroner Thomas Noguchi noted that the shirt Bobby wore on the day of his assassination came from this high-end shirtmaker. K. Wragge started in 1872 and was known for their made-to-order custom shirts.

# THE RICHARD RODGERS THEATRE; FORMERLY THE 46TH ST. THEATER

## 226 W. 46TH ST. BETWEEN EIGHTH AVE. AND BROADWAY

FOLLOWING A MEETING WITH NEW U.N. Secretary-General U Thant earlier in the day, JFK attended a performance of the hit musical *How to Succeed in Business Without Really Trying* here on the evening of January 19, 1962. The front page of the next day's *New York Daily News* carried a photo of JFK exiting his limo outside the theater along with the headline "JFK learns how to succeed." The show starred Robert Morse (who appeared decades later in *Mad Men*, a show set in the JFK era) and singer Rudy Vallée. JFK owned the show's original cast album, and White House intern Mimi Alford — with whom he had an affair — later wrote:

> *"Something about Robert Morse crooning the lyrics — 'You have the cool, clear eyes of a seeker of wisdom and truth' — seemed to light up some pleasure center deep inside his brain. He liked the song so much."* [119]

---

119 Mimi Alford, *Once Upon a Secret: My Affair with President John F. Kennedy and Its Aftermath*, New York, Random House, 2012.

The next day, the *New York Times* reported that upon his entrance to the theater, the "audience rose and applauded enthusiastically."

Actress and writer Patricia Bosworth claimed that JFK attended a showing of *How to Succeed* here on November 15, 1963. She was appearing in the play *Mary, Mary* at the old Helen Hayes Theatre (since demolished) next door. She later wrote that when she saw Morse on the street that afternoon, he excitedly told her that JFK was going to attend his show that night. Since *Mary, Mary* ended before *How to Succeed* did, she arrived in time to witness Morse singing the rousing final number "Brotherhood of Man" "directly to the President. Once the house lights went up, she noticed JFK had jumped to his feet as he applauded Morse and the cast. Bosworth remembered:

> *"(JFK) looked tanned and incredibly handsome. ...*
> *He seemed enveloped in an absolute wave of love*
> *and yearning as the entire audience stood up and*
> *applauded him. The emotional intensity contained*
> *in that theater was palpable."*[120]

Although JFK's visit to *How to Succeed* that night is virtually absent from biographies of his life, Bosworth's account is supported by the fact that JFK *was* in New York that night, and the two shows in question were playing in the adjacent theaters to which she assigns them. Also, it is logical to assume the event was vividly imprinted on her memory due to the fact that the assassination took place one week later to the day.

The theater was renamed for composer Richard Rodgers in 1990. It has been home to *Hamilton* since 2015.

---

120  Patricia Bosworth, "JFK on Broadway," April 10, 2005,
      https://mrbellersneighborhood.com/2005/04/jfk-on-broadway

## MINSKOFF THEATER

### 1515 BROADWAY AT W. 45TH ST. NEAR TIMES SQUARE

THE MINSKOFF HAS BEEN HOME to *The Lion King* since it moved here in 2006. John and Carolyn were here on April 6, 1998, for the Municipal Art Society's Chairman Event, at which John and Caroline presented the Jackie Kennedy Medal to Stephen Swid, recognizing his preservation efforts as long-time chairman of the organization. Jackie had served on the Municipal Art Society's Board of Trustees. Swid was a significant player in the music business — the "S" in SBK Entertainment — credited with turning the performing rights organization SESAC into a major player against rivals BMI and ASCAP. Swid headed SESAC for 20 years, signing such notables as Bob Dylan and Neil Diamond.

www.mas.org

## BARBETTA
### 321 W. 46TH ST. BETWEEN EIGHTH AND NINTH AVES.

A NEW YORK INSTITUTION SINCE 1906 specializing in the cuisine of Northern Italy's Piedmont region, this restaurant was a favorite of Jackie's. Upon the publication of Martha Graham's autobiography *Blood Memory* — which had been rushed due to the author's death in April 1991 — Jackie took her colleagues here for a celebratory lunch in the garden.

www.barbettarestaurant.com

## DOUBLEDAY OFFICES
### 1540 BROADWAY BETWEEN W. 45TH AND W. 46TH STS.

JACKIE HAD AN OFFICE HERE after Doubleday relocated its offices in 1992.

## BERNARD B. JACOBS THEATRE;
## FORMERLY THE ROYALE THEATRE
### 242 W. 45ST ST. BETWEEN SEVENTH AND EIGHTH AVES.

WHILE FIRST LADY, JACKIE SAW the S.N. Behrman comedy *Lord Pengo* here on December 4, 1962. The show starred Charles Boyer as an art dealer in the title role and Agnes Moorehead. The show got so-so reviews and closed the following April.

Bobby and Ethel were photographed with their friend Lauren Bacall backstage here on January 17, 1966. Bacall was then starring in the comedy *Cactus Flower*. John Jr. saw the Cold War spy drama *Pack of Lies* here on February 13, 1985. When Madonna was starring in David Mamet's Hollywood satire *Speed-the-Plow* here in 1988, John was spotted entering the theater by himself to catch a performance. He was seen chatting with Madonna while biking

The Jacobs Theatre as photographed in 2023.

300

in Central Park shortly after that. *Speed-the-Plow* was a hit, running for 297 performances from May until the end of 1988. Actor Ron Silver won the TONY Award for Best Actor. To date, Madonna has not returned to act on a Broadway stage. The theater was renamed for Jacobs in 2005.

# NEW YORK MARRIOTT MARQUIS;
## FORMER SITE OF THE MOROSCO THEATER
### 217 W. 45TH ST. AND BROADWAY BETWEEN
### W. 45TH AND 46TH STS.; DEMOLISHED

AS PRESIDENT-ELECT, JFK ATTENDED A performance of Gore Vidal's political drama *The Best Man* here on December 6, 1960. He sat in the third row with his friend Charles Spalding. A Secret Service agent occupied the seat behind him. At the end of the performance, Vidal[121] —who was related to Jackie by marriage — and the rest of the cast applauded JFK, who then walked up to the stage to greet them. The play captured the inside political machinations that take place at a national party convention, with main characters loosely resembling Adlai Stevenson (whom JFK was about to disappoint by not choosing him to be his Secretary of State, but instead relegating him to the post of U.N. Ambassador), President Harry S. Truman, and the late Wisconsin senator, Joe McCarthy. JFK and the rest of the audience laughed uproariously when one of the characters stated, "I suppose that we had better try for a Catholic. That seems to be the thing this year."

---

121  Following a White House altercation with Bobby, Vidal had a falling out with the Kennedys and was a member of the "Democrats for Keating" organization when Bobby ran for the Senate in 1964.

Jackie and Rose saw the play *Forty Carats* here on May 21, 1969. The Jay Preston Allen comedy centers on a May-December romance between a 40-year-old American woman and a 22-year-old man whom she meets when her car breaks down in Greece. The show starred Julie Harris. Allen had a long and successful Hollywood career as a screenwriter (Hitchcock's *Marnie*, for one) and script doctor, one of the few women doing those jobs at the time. She later created the ABC Television drama *Family* (1976-80), for which Mike Nichols was among the executive producers.

Built in 1917, the Morosco was one of the theaters controversially torn down to make way for the construction of the Marriot Marquis — which includes the Marquis Theatre — in 1982.

# GERALD SCHOENFELD THEATRE;
## FORMERLY THE PLYMOUTH THEATRE
### 236 W. 45ᵀᴴ ST. BETWEEN TIMES SQUARE AND EIGHTH AVE.

*DANCING AT LUGHNASA* OPENED HERE on October 24, 1991, and ran for just more than a year. Jackie attended a performance of the Brian Friel play here during its run. Jackie was part of a foursome that included singer Carly Simon, her husband Jim Hart, and actor Alec Baldwin, who was 33 at the time. Baldwin later told Howard Stern that he "freaked out" that night when he realized Jackie would be joining him. Simon later wrote that the following day, Jackie described the outing as a "magical night." [122]

John Jr. — who had acted in Friel's play *Winners* in 1985 — also saw *Dancing at Lughnasa* during its run here. Set in County Donegal, Ireland, in 1936, *Dancing at Lughnasa* examines a changing Irish society (and life in general) via the lives of the five unmarried Mundy sisters. The sisters were based on a real family that Friel knew as a child growing up in Ireland. *Dancing* won the 1992 TONY Award for Best New Play.

---

122  Simon, *Touched by the Sun.*

# THE JOHN GOLDEN THEATRE

252 W. 45ᵀᴴ ST. BETWEEN SEVENTH AND EIGHTH AVES.

JFK AND JACKIE SAW THE cutting-edge British comedy review *Beyond the Fringe* here on February 9, 1963. A crowd of 2,000 gathered outside the theater to watch them enter. Once inside, the prolonged ovation they received delayed the start of the show for several minutes. JFK was seen laughing as the performers poked fun at him and other world leaders. *Beyond the Fringe* starred four of England's funniest and most creative young performers: Peter Cook, Dudley Moore, Alan Bennett, and Jonathan Miller. *Monty Python*'s Michael Palin later reflected:

> *"Beyond the Fringe, like rock and roll, was perceived as something fresh and new and dangerous. It was shocking and thrilling but was done with such skill and intelligence that it could not easily be shot down, dismissed, or shrugged off."* [123]

---

123  William Cook, Ed., *Tragically I Was an Only Twin: The Complete Peter Cook*, New York: St. Martin's Press, 2003.

With its willingness to poke fun at people and institutions normally previously off-limits to mockery, *Beyond the Fringe* was hugely influential on *Monty Python* and younger comedians. If you've never seen Moore and Cook's 1967 flick *Bedazzled*, do so immediately, if not sooner. Bennett later claimed that Cook had a flirtatious relationship with Jackie.

# THE BROADHURST THEATER

## 235 W. 44ᵀᴴ ST. BETWEEN SEVENTH AND EIGHTH AVES.

JACKIE SAW THE HIT KANDER & Ebb musical *Cabaret* here on December 11, 1966. She was escorted by Joseph Kingsbury-Smith, a Pulitzer Prize-winning journalist who later served as the national editor of Hearst Newspapers. Bobby very likely also saw *Cabaret* around this time. Set in Weimar, Berlin, *Cabaret* has had numerous Broadway revivals in the years since and is considered one of the greatest Broadway musicals of all time.

On April 8, 1976, Jackie was back to see Katherine Hepburn in Enid Bagnold's play *A Matter of Gravity*. The play centers on an eccentric dowager who lives in one room of her mansion. One can't help but think that play must have reminded Jackie of her eccentric aunts — "Big Edie" and "Little Edie" Beale, the subjects of the Albert and David Maysles' documentary *Grey Gardens*,[124] then in theaters. Bagnold was the author of *National Velvet*, but *A Matter of Gravity* received so-so reviews and closed after 79 performances.

On January 2, 1981, Mike Nichols escorted Jackie to the premiere of *Amadeus* here. The play concerns a fictional rivalry between

---

124  Decades later *Grey Gardens* would be adapted into its own Broadway show (a musical, strangely enough) and an HBO film.

Mozart and an Italian composer named Salieri. Director Milos Forman's film adaptation won the Oscar for Best Picture in 1985.

The Broadhurst dates back to 1917 and is operated by the Schubert Organization.

# THE SAINT JAMES THEATER

## 246 W. 44ᵀᴴ ST. BETWEEN SEVENTH AND EIGHTH AVES.

WHEN HE WAS PRESIDENT-ELECT, JFK saw the musical *Do Re Mi* here on January 9, 1961. The show starred comedian Phil Silvers of *Sgt. Bilko* fame, and Nancy Walker, who became both famous and infamous in later years: famous as Rosie on the Bounty paper towels commercials and infamous as the director of the 1980 Village People movie *Can't Stop the Music*, a train wreck often cited as one of the worst movies of all time. *Do Re Mi* had a book by Garson Kanin — who also directed the show — and featured songs by Jule Styne, Betty Comden, and Adolph Green, the most remembered of which is "Make Someone Happy." Silvers and Walker play a husband and wife whose get-rich-quick schemes get them mixed up with mobsters. JFK was surrounded by a crowd of well-wishers at intermission and had to leave before the final curtain. As a result, the Secret Service realized that any future visits to the theater would need to be carefully planned.

Bobby visited with Carol Channing backstage here on April 17, 1964, to congratulate her on her performance in the Jerry Herman musical *Hello, Dolly!* Channing later campaigned with Bobby that fall.

# THE HARVARD CLUB

## 35 W. 44TH ST. BETWEEN FIFTH AND SIXTH AVES.

IF YOU DIDN'T GRADUATE FROM Harvard or have a spouse who did so, you can forget about becoming a member here. The original façade dates back to 1895 and was designed by Charles Follen McKim of McKim, Mead, and White. The architecture was intended to emulate the buildings on the Harvard campus in Cambridge, Massachusetts.

A 1927 *Photoplay* article notes that Joe was here on a snowy February day the previous year as he was completing the purchase of R-C Pictures Corp. and the Film Booking Office Inc., a move he'd plotted for six years. The story quotes Joe as saying, "I seem to have bought a movie studio," as he explains that he will not be able to travel to Palm Beach as planned. Joe's tenure in Hollywood proved remarkable and has been the subject of several books. Had he not been the founder of America's most prominent political family, he still would have been recognized as a uniquely important figure in the history of the movie industry in Hollywood.

Movies were one of America's fastest-growing businesses during the 1920s and Joe wanted in, musing that if "pants pressers" — as he derisively called the other studio heads — could get rich there, imagine what he could accomplish with his sharp banking skills. While there, he ran three studios simultaneously, Pathé being the other one. He also helped usher in the talkie era while finding time to bed the most prominent female star of the day, Gloria Swanson. "Kennedy was the first and only outsider to fleece Hollywood," recalled Betty Lasky, the daughter of Paramount founder Jesse Lasky.[125]

Bobby's JFK-organized bachelor party was held here on June 15, 1950, and his rowdy new Skakel brothers-in-law, along with his Harvard football pals, turned the event into a booze-fest that ended with someone spraying the elegant wood-paneled Slocum Room with a fire extinguisher. "A couple of young men got out of hand," JFK later explained. One wonders what condition they were in by 8 a.m. the following day when Cardinal Spellman was scheduled to celebrate a Mass for them at his residence on Madison Ave.

In a letter to the club's manager, Clifford Howes, dated July 19, 1950, JFK enclosed a check for $256.96, writing, "I believe this covers completely all expenses incurred." This was likely sent to settle the booze tab. In the runup to the party, JFK — a millionaire many times over — hit up each of the attendees for $10.87, their share of a $174 engraved cigarette case that Bobby — also a millionaire many times over — was to be gifted. For the dinner menu, the cost-conscious JFK selected the $4.50 roast beef and stuffed chicken option rather than the $7.00 lobster and filet mignon combo. Today, a portrait of JFK hangs in the dining room here.

Less than three months before his death, John Jr. gave a revealing, if unpublicized, talk here on April 28, 1999. Addressing the American Society of News Editors, John explained how his life experiences had affected what he had hoped to accomplish with *George*:

125  Cari Beauchamp, *Vanity Fair*, June 2015, "The Mogul in Mr. Kennedy."

"I wanted to tweak this whole aspect of family history. ... Some of this pressure needed to be let out. You had this generation before me which just kind of stopped. Everything was frozen, and this icicle was bigger and bigger and bigger and was just about to drop. I used the (George) covers to address some of those ... feelings I had about politics and celebrities ... in a way that I understood."[126]

---

126  Richard Blow *American Son*

# SARDI'S RESTAURANT
## 234 W. 44<sup>TH</sup> ST. BETWEEN BROADWAY AND EIGHTH AVE.

SARDI'S IS A NEW YORK institution that has been located here since 1927. Bobby attended the New York Film Critics Circle Awards reception here on January 28, 1968, during which he presented the Best Picture Award to director Norman Jewison for his film *In the Heat of the Night*. The film starred Sidney Poitier as a Philadelphia detective dealing with the racial prejudice he encounters in a small Southern town. Bobby had an accidental meeting with Jewison during the 1966 Christmas holidays at a Sun Valley, Idaho, hospital after both had a son injured on the ski slopes. After Jewison told Bobby about the plot of *In the Heat of the Night*, Bobby was immediately intrigued and told the director, "This is a very important film, Norman. Timing is everything in life, in art, in politics." Jewison later wrote that Bobby provided him with research on young people in the South and stayed in touch as the film was in production.

Jewison was surprised to find Bobby handing him his award at Sardi's later recalling, "As I went up to get the award (accompanied by the film's producer Walter Mirisch), he says, 'See, I told you timing was everything!'" Bobby was right about the importance of *In the Heat of the Night*. The film contains at least two iconic scenes of black empowerment that sear themselves in the viewer's memory:

Poitier's "They call me Mr. Tibbs!" line and the scene in which he slaps a wealthy and powerful white man who has just slapped him. Poitier was at Sardi's that night and presented the Best Director award to Mike Nichols for *The Graduate*. Nichols would soon be spotted escorting Jackie around town.

## STEPHEN SONDHEIM THEATRE;
## FORMER SITE OF XENON

124 W. 43ᴿᴰ ST. BETWEEN SIXTH AVE AND BROADWAY CLOSED

THIS WAS THE SITE OF Henry Miller's Theater (not the writer) which opened in 1918. By the 1970s, it was a porno theater. Xenon was a very popular disco that opened in 1978 and closed in 1984. It tended to attract the fashion crowd, while the Hollywood types preferred rival Studio 54. Unlike Studio 54, mere (non-famous) mortals at least had a fighting chance of being admitted here. John Jr. enjoyed hanging out at Xenon and was photographed here with his friend Christiane Amanpour and his then-girlfriend Sally Munro in February 1982. To see what Xenon was like back in the day, you can check out the 1978 movie *Eyes of Laura Mars* starring Faye Dunaway, which filmed party sequences there. After being completely redesigned — save for the façade which was landmarked in 1987 — the Miller was renamed for Sondheim in 2010.

## CHEZ JOSEPHINE

### 414 W. 42ND ST. BETWEEN NINTH AND 10TH AVES.

FOUNDER JEAN-CLAUDE BAKER OPENED CHEZ Josephine in 1986, naming it after his "adoptive mother," the legendary African-American singer and member of the French Resistance in World War II, Josephine Baker. With its velvet curtains and life-sized paintings of Baker, this Theater District French brasserie and piano bar evokes the era of the Folies Bergère in which she was a star. Jackie — who had a special place in her heart for Paris in the 1920s — was a regular here, as were John Jr. and Carolyn. John requested the pianist play Elton John's "Your Song" during a visit here in the spring of 1999. Jackie usually stopped in for lunch and conversed with Jean-Claude in fluent French. She once told him that to avoid causing a commotion, she had to enter Broadway theaters after the shows had begun, but she disliked doing so due to her fear that she was distracting the actors on stage. Jean-Claude passed away in 2015, but his restaurant is still thriving today.

www.chezjosephinenyc.com

# JOHN KENNEDY JR. WORKPLACE, MCGRAW-HILL BUILDING

## 330 W. 42ND ST. BETWEEN EIGHTH AND NINTH AVES.

DESIGNED IN THE INTERNATIONAL STYLE, this 33-story skyscraper dates from 1931 and includes Art Deco detailing. John Jr. worked for the 42nd Street Development Corporation as "Acting Deputy Executive Director" here beginning in early 1986 before he started law school at NYU that fall. His mother's friend and fellow building preservationist, legendary advertising man Fred Papert, headed the non-profit corporation, and Jackie sat on its board. The corporation was tasked with cleaning up and revitalizing the sleazy and crime-ridden blocks of 42nd St. east of the Port Authority Bus Terminal. John's duties included negotiating with developers and city agencies. Papert credited Jackie with inspiring the plans to save W. 42nd St., a feat he described as "my proudest accomplishment." Papert also later spoke highly of John:

> *"John was an intelligent bargain... He knew his way around the city. He's unpredictable in a good way. He was both orderly and passionate — a rare combination."*[127]

---

127 Michael Gross, "Favorite Son," *New York* Magazine, March 20, 1989.

# OVERSEAS PRESS CLUB
## 54 W. 40<sup>TH</sup> ST (1968); MOVED

BOBBY APPEARED HERE ON APRIL 1, 1968, to give his reaction to LBJ's announcement the previous evening that he wouldn't be a candidate in 1968. One reporter described him as looking "dazed." After lambasting LBJ on the campaign trail for the previous two weeks, Bobby now called the President's decision to withdraw "truly magnanimous." He requested a meeting with LBJ, which took place two days later at the White House with Ted Sorenson accompanying Bobby.

The club is currently located at 40 W. 45<sup>th</sup> St. SEE ALSO: East Side location.

www. opcofamerica.org

# THE OLD METROPOLITAN OPERA HOUSE

1411 BROADWAY @ W. 39TH ST. AND THE ENTIRE WEST SIDE
OF THE STREET BETWEEN 39TH AND 40TH STS.

IN 1966, JACKIE WAS INVOLVED in unsuccessful efforts to save this building from the wrecking ball after the Metropolitan Opera Company completed its move to Lincoln Center. The company had called this building home for 83 years. It took up the entire western side of the block on Broadway between W. 39th and 40th Sts. Although it had been among the buildings the newly created Landmarks Preservation Commission had initially designated for landmark status in 1965, they ultimately voted not to vote to preserve it. Ironically, the Metropolitan Opera Company opposed the granting of landmark status, fearing possible competition. Many notables sang here, including Enrico Caruso, who debuted here in 1903 and went on to perform here more than in all the world's opera houses combined. Renowned Russian dancer Vaslav Nijinsky made his U.S. debut here in 1916.

Jackie took ballet lessons here as a child, and it seems she had fond memories of her time here. Jackie made a surprise appearance here when she was First Lady when she attended the Royal Ballet's American premiere of *Marguerite and Armand*.

On March 19, 1965, Maria Callas performed at the Metropolitan for the first time in seven years. Jackie was on hand to watch the performance. The two women would soon be in a reported love triangle with Ari Onassis. Operatic! Jackie, Bobby, and Ethel were photographed with Leonard Bernstein in the dining hall here on April 28, 1965, after watching the Royal Ballet's performance of *Giselle*.

In a letter to the committee fighting the teardown, Jackie revealed the thinking that would guide her later preservation efforts:

> *"A city which tears down the fine things of its past sets a bad example. ... Is another office building as valuable as a historic building which can provide a setting for artists of the future?"*

Although the effort was unsuccessful, and the building was torn down in January 1967 with a 40-story office building – 1141 Broadway — erected in its place, Jackie's efforts to preserve old structures such as Grand Central Station would prove both successful and highly influential in the ensuing decades

# CALVIN KLEIN CORPORATE HEADQUARTERS

## 205 W. 39TH ST. BETWEEN SEVENTH AND EIGHTH AVES.

THIS IS A 17-STORY BUILDING in the heart of the Garment Center. Considering that John Jr. and Carolyn are one of the most legendary couples, it's startling to learn that there's no firm consensus about where — or when — they first met. This business is a likely candidate for the where, since some of their friends agreed that Carolyn, in her capacity of assisting celebrity shoppers, helped John pick out suits when he came here to shop one day. Carole Radziwill — who married John's cousin and best friend Anthony Radziwill in 1994 — recalls encountering Carolyn for the first time when the latter emerged from John's bedroom at his rented house in Sagaponack in the Hamptons two years before the couple got serious in 1994. Klein later (somewhat inaccurately) recalled how Carolyn came to work for him:

> *"I found Carolyn Bessette[128] in a store we had... in Boston. I took one look at her and said, "Come to*

---

128  The store was in Chestnut Hill, and Carolyn lived in an apartment on North Beacon St. at the time. Klein did not encounter Carolyn in Boston, but he personally interviewed her when she came to New York.

*New York." She was in the PR department."* [129]

Carolyn worked as a personal shopper for celebrities, including actress Annette Bening and Diane Sawyer. She soon became an essential assistant to Calvin Klein himself. She was reportedly crucial in his decision to use model Kate Moss in their advertising. Carolyn and Moss lived at the same address, 112 Waverly Place, in 1995. She became friends with Klein's wife, Kelly, and went on to become the director of show production, a crucial post in which she ran the company's high-profile Bryant Park fashion shows in 1994 and 1995. She worked long hours and was not shy about voicing her opinions or being demanding when she needed to be. Carolyn's decision to quit her job in the run-up to her wedding in early 1996 was later seen by some people close to her as unfortunate, depriving her of a day-to-day routine and a sense of purpose.

---

129  Marc Jacobs, August 28, 2013, *Interview* magazine, "The Visionary: Calvin Klein." https://www.interviewmagazine.com/fashion/calvin-klein.

# KENNETH JAY LANE JEWELRY SHOWROOM

20 W. 37TH ST. BETWEEN FIFTH AND SIXTH AVES.; MOVED

DUBBED "THE KING OF JUNQUE," Lane helped popularize costume jewelry in the U.S. and became quite wealthy doing so. His expertise at creating "fakes" that were nearly indistinguishable from the real thing made his creations very popular with Manhattan society ladies. When Jackie's possessions hit the auction block at Sotheby's in April 1996, Lane was quoted in the catalog:

> *"Jackie had been wearing my jewelry since the
> middle sixties, often visiting my showroom, where
> she was like a kid in the candy shop."*

Jackie once tasked Lane with creating a replica of a Van Cleef & Arpels necklace that Ari had given her. After producing twenty-five of the necklaces to keep the cost down, Lane received a call from Jackie informing him, "I saw our necklace again on *Dynasty*." She was referring to the popular prime-time drama that ran on ABC television from 1981 to 1989, which was name-checked in Prince's[130] song "Kiss."

https://kennethjaylane.com/

---

130  At their wedding, John Jr. and Carolyn danced to Prince's "Forever in My Life"— a track from his *Sign O' the Times* album.

# JACOB K. JAVITS CONVENTION CENTER

655 W. 34TH ST. @ ELEVENTH AVE. BETWEEN 34TH AND 38TH STS.

DESIGNED BY I.M. PEI, THIS huge black building stretches over a four-square block along the Hudson River. After failing his New York State bar exam twice, John took the test for a third time here on July 24, 1990, and passed. After facing public humiliation ("The Hunk Flunks") after the first two attempts, he was undoubtedly thrilled to finally succeed. The pressure was on because John stood to lose his job as an Assistant District Attorney had he failed. D.A. Robert Morgenthau's office had a strict policy that assistants were only permitted three attempts to pass the bar. Several sources claim that John was given a private room here to take the exam, away from the distraction of fellow test takers gawking at him. There are also claims that he took the exam offsite.

## STATLER HILTON HOTEL AKA HOTEL PENNSYLVANIA

401 SEVENTH AVE. BETWEEN W. 32ND AND 33RD STS., DEMOLISHED

BOBBY HELD HIS ELECTION NIGHT victory rally here on November 3, 1964, when he won election to the Senate, defeating incumbent Republican Kenneth Keating. Bobby addressed what the *New York Times* described as a "screaming, youthful crowd" of more than a thousand people in the ballroom at 1:22 a.m. The Pennsylvania closed permanently on April 1, 2020. Demolition began in December 2021, and the hotel is to be replaced by a new high-rise, 15 Penn Plaza.

# MADISON SQUARE GARDEN
## BETWEEN SEVENTH AND EIGHTH AVES. AND 31ST AND 33RD STS.

BOBBY WAS PRESENT FOR THE opening night gala performance hosted by Bob Hope on February 11, 1968. This old-school show (viewable on YouTube) also featured Bing Crosby and Barbara Eden and seems anachronistic considering the times.

John Jr. attended the second Muhammad Ali-Joe Frazier fight here on January 28, 1974. This was the second of the pair's three fights and the least celebrated of the trio. Ali won the 12-round bout by a unanimous decision. John later told his friend Steven Gillon that he met Ali in the dressing room after the fight and that Ali gave him the silk robe that he wore when he entered the ring. Ali and John became friends, with the ex-champ once visiting John at his *George* office and attending his memorial service in 1999.

Jackie attended a Paul McCartney and Wings concert here on May 24, 1976. She was photographed with Paul and his wife Linda after the show. A few months later, she attended the Democratic convention here. She was present when the Democrats held their convention here in 1992 when Bill Clinton was nominated.

On August 12, 1980, at the Democratic National Convention here, Ted delivered his famous "The dream shall never die," speech in which, while conceding defeat to President Jimmy Carter in his campaign for the party's Presidential nomination, offered a robust defense of American liberalism:

> *"For me, a few hours ago, this campaign came to an end. For all those whose cares have been our concern, the work goes on, the cause endures, the hope still lives, and the dream shall never die."*

The speech had a valedictory quality to it, marking as it did the end of any reasonable hope of a Kennedy brother again reaching the White House. Along with his 1968 eulogy for Bobby, it is the speech for which Ted is best remembered today.

John was backstage at least one of the two concerts Madonna held here on June 10-11, 1985, as a part of her "Virgin" tour. (He was photographed backstage with artist Keith Haring and hip-hop legend Fab Five Freddy.) John and Madonna reportedly had a brief fling a few years later. They remained friends, however, and Madonna authored an "If I Were President" column in the first issue of *George* in 1995. John and Daryl Hannah were spotted at the Aerosmith concert here on February 17, 1994 (first song: "Eat the Rich").

Jackie, Caroline, and Maurice Tempelsman were here on May 19, 1989, to see John receive his degree upon his graduation from NYU Law School. Afterward, John told reporters, "I'm very glad it's over."

John was a Knicks season-ticket holder, and he was often spotted at courtside here during the 1990s when he attended countless games. Mike Lupica recalled John once saying of the Garden, "I love this place. ... They just let you be part of the crowd here." This was when center Patrick Ewing led the team and Pat Riley was the coach. Lupica wrote of John:

*"...He sat at the Eighth Ave. end of the Garden. First row under the basket, maybe ten seats away from the end of the Knicks bench, over to his left. ... There was never a big entrance. He was there to see the game."*[131]

131   Mike Lupica, "Kennedy Genuine Article," *New York Daily News*, July 19, 1999.

# PENN SOUTH HOUSES AKA MUTUAL REDEVELOPMENT HOUSES, AKA PENN SOUTH

### BETWEEN W. 23RD AND W. 29TH STS. AND BETWEEN 8TH & 9TH AVES. NEAR PENN STATION

THIS IS A HOUSING COOPERATIVE development started by the International Ladies' Garment Workers' Union (ILGWU). Now, everybody over 60 sings, "Look for the union label..." Yes, this is the union we're talking about. JFK spoke here at the opening ceremonies on May 19, 1962. It was a hot afternoon, and JFK opened by humorously complaining of the "sweatshop conditions." He emphasized the importance of unions in improving workers' welfare and moving the country forward. Eleanor Roosevelt, Gov. Nelson Rockefeller, and labor leaders George Meany and Alex Rose were among the many dignitaries on the dais with him. Today, there are 2,820 apartments in the complex, which is now home to many retirees.

JFK addresses the crowd at the dedication of the Penn South Houses, May 18, 1962. *Cecil Stoughton. White House Photographs. John F. Kennedy Presidential Library and Museum, Boston.*

JFK greeting the crowd at the Penn South Houses, May 19, 1962. *Stoughton, JFK Library.*

# DOWNTOWN BELOW 23RD ST.

## TRAMPS
## 51 W. 21ST BETWEEN FIFTH AND SIXTH AVES., CLOSED

THE CLUB STARTED LIFE ON 15th St. as a venue for blues and roots music before moving to this location in 1989. It then became one of the city's best venues to hear live music. The club's booking agent, Steve Weitzman, recalled that John Jr. regularly came to see a favorite band of his, Trouble Funk, whenever they played at the club. Weitzman said of John:

> "(He) insisted on paying for his ticket even though I spotted him in line outside the club and walked him to the front of a long line. That's the only favor he allowed me to do for him; he wouldn't accept a free ticket."

John's friend John Perry Barlow later said that John first told him about Carolyn while here in early 1994. John was still dating Daryl Hannah at the time.

Trouble Funk is a Washington DC funk and R&B outfit that is still active today. Their 1982 song "Pump Me Up" was sampled on Public Enemy's "Fight the Power" and MARRS' "Pump Up the Volume."

The list of notables who played Tramps in the 90s includes Bob Dylan, Bruce Springsteen (an E Street Band reunion performance from February 1995 was immortalized in the documentary *Blood Brothers*), Ray Charles, and Prince. Son Volt had appeared at Tramps often, and they played the final shows here in September 1999.

# THE GRAMERCY PARK HOTEL
## 2 LEXINGTON AVE. @ E. 21ST ST.

BEFORE MOVING INTO THEIR NEW home in the Riverdale section of the Bronx, the Kennedys lived on the second floor here during the summer of 1927. They had the entire floor to themselves. JFK and his siblings were said to have played in the park across the street. While there, they would have seen the statue of Edwin Booth, a famous 19th Century actor and Gramercy resident now remembered — if at all – as the brother of Abraham Lincoln's assassin, John Wilkes Booth. Gramercy Park had long had a Bohemian vibe, attracting writers such as Hart Crane, Edith Wharton, and Herman Melville. Theodore Roosevelt was born on nearby E. 20th St.

Gramercy Park is the only private park in Manhattan, with access limited by locked gates, the keys distributed among the residents of the surrounding buildings.

Opened in 1925, the hotel was built on the site of architect Sanford White's former home. The Gramercy has a rich history during which it welcomed guests including Babe Ruth, who hung out in the bar; actor Humprey Bogart, who married his first wife Helen Menken here in 1926; and rock bands, including the Rolling Stones, David Bowie, U2 and the Clash. The Gramercy's bar is seen in the 2000 movie *Almost Famous*. The Gramercy has been closed since the onset of the COVID-19 pandemic in 2020, but new leaseholder MCR Hotels is renovating, and a reopening is planned for 2025.

# MAX'S KANSAS CITY
## 213 PARK AVE. SOUTH BETWEEN
## 17<sup>TH</sup> AND 18<sup>TH</sup> STS. CLOSED

THIS WAS THE FIRST ITERATION of the legendary rock club. According to the late Bob Neuwirth, Bobby once came here hoping to meet the ill-fated Warhol "It Girl" Edie Sedgwick. "(Bobby) was having a good time. He was ready to boogie," Neuwirth recalled.[132] However, when his bodyguard, Bill Barry, smelled marijuana in the air, he urged Bobby to leave immediately. "But I've just ordered a drink," Bobby protested. The ex-FBI agent Barry insisted, saying "Senator, we must get out of here at once." And out they went.

Max's was home base for the Warhol and the Velvet Underground. Later, Patti Smith would launch her career from here. Just about anyone associated with New York rock music played here, including the New York Dolls and Bruce Springsteen. After the original club closed in December 1974, the reopened club became the epicenter of punk rock and new wave music in the United States.

---

132 Jean Stein, Edie: *American Girl*, New York: Grove Press, 1994.

# PETE'S TAVERN

## 129 E. 18TH ST. @ IRVING PLACE

ESTABLISHED BACK IN 1864 (WHEN Abe Lincoln was President), Pete's is the oldest continually operating bar and restaurant in New York. Legend has it that O. Henry wrote "The Gift of the Magi" in a booth here in 1905, when the place was named Healy's. The owners cleverly pretended to be florists during Prohibition, but the bar was still active for those in the know.

Robert Mitchum drank here in the 1962 movie *Two for the Seesaw*. Miranda proposed to her boyfriend Steve here in a *Sex and the City* episode.

JFK and Jackie were said to have dined here. John Jr. was said to have become a regular after spying a photo of his parents on the wall. Pete's is still beloved for its burgers and charming atmosphere.

www.petestavern.com

# FORMER OFFICE OF DR. JANET TRAVELL

## 9 W. 16TH ST. BETWEEN FIFTH AND SIXTH AVES.; CLOSED

FOLLOWING HIS SURGERIES AT THE Hospital for Special Surgery in October 1954 and February 1955, JFK returned to the Senate on crutches on May 24, 1955. Two days later, he flew to New York and came here accompanied by Dr. Ephraim Shorr, an expert on adrenal insufficiency who had been consulting on JFK's case with the doctors at HSS. Travell was a renowned expert in pain management, having served as an associate professor of clinical pharmacology at Cornell University. Travell later recalled that JFK's condition was such that he had great difficulty navigating the two steps down to her office from street level.

> *"He was thin, he was ill, his condition was poor, he was on crutches. ... He couldn't step up or down a step with his right foot. We could hardly get him into the office."*[133]

JFK had problems with his right knee due to an old football

---

133   Janet Travell, JFK Library Oral History Interview, https://www.jfklibrary.org/asset-viewer/archives/JFKOH/Travell%2C%20Janet%20G/JFKOH-JGT-01/JFKOH-JGT-01.

injury, and Travell applied a coolant spray that, in a mere 15 to 20 minutes, increased the range of motion when he bent his knee. JFK was impressed that Travell had quickly succeeded where others had failed. Upon his request, Travell immediately had JFK admitted to New York Hospital, where he spent the long Memorial Day weekend. JFK found that his discomfort eased a bit while sitting in a wicker rocking chair in the office here and said, "This is so comfortable; why can't I have one of these?" Travell later brought the rocker uptown to his hospital room. As President, JFK would be strongly associated with rocking chairs, and it appears his love of them started here on W. 16th St.

At the hospital, JFK received procaine injections for his back in addition to muscle stimulation and passive exercises (in which a therapist exercises the patient's muscles) before being released on June 1. Travell prescribed regular procaine injections to relieve his chronic back pain. When she discovered that JFK's left leg was shorter than his right, causing his spine to be misaligned, she prescribed lifts for his left shoes. JFK saw Dr. Travell again that July and August and again in October and November after a trip to Europe. He was a regular visitor here in the late 50s, sometimes seeing Travell every week. On occasion, she would see him at the Waldorf. She also oversaw his secret admissions to New York Hospital at this time. Her treatments allowed him to put his pain under control and permitted him to endure the grueling campaigns of 1958 and 1960. One could make a convincing argument that JFK would not have been elected President had he not become Dr. Travell's patient.

Upon becoming President, JFK appointed her White House physician, the first woman to hold that post. She remained in the job when LBJ became President. There, her two or three daily injections of nonvaccine administered to JFK began to alarm her colleagues, who feared that it might result in JFK seeking to use stronger and more addictive narcotics. Dr. Eugene Cohen had recommended Travell for the White House job but was soon blasting her in scathing terms, calling her, "A deceiving, incompetent, publicity-mad physician who had only one consideration in mind and that was herself."

Travell was eased out as JFK's chief doctor by Christmas 1961, although she maintained her title as White House physician until July 1963 when vice admiral George Burkley replaced her. Despite a series of surgeries and the ministrations of so many doctors, even in 1963, JFK was still using crutches when he was out of the public eye.

Travell left the White House in 1965 to focus on her writing, although she still saw patients. She died in 1997. This brownstone dates from 1840. Dr. J. Willard Travell, Janet's father, bought it in 1928 following the death of Florence Prentice, the original owner's daughter. Both Janet and her father had their practices here for a time. J. Willard was a pioneer in the field of relief of muscle pain, and his daughter followed in his footsteps.

## GLUCKSMAN IRELAND HOUSE
### 1 FIFTH AVE. WASHINGTON MEWS

THIS IS NYU'S CENTER FOR Irish Studies founded by Lewis and Loretta Brennan Glucksman. It is housed in a pair of two-story Greek Revival style buildings built in 1939. Lew was a philanthropist and former head of Lehman Brothers.

John Jr. – an alumnus of NYU's Law School - was an avid supporter of the project and was present when it was announced at NYU on May 20, 1991. He was photographed on that occasion with Loretta Brennan Glucksman and former Taoiseach Charles Haughey. John spoke at the opening of Ireland House on April 26, 1993 when he declared: "The creation of Ireland House will be a wonderful academic and cultural addition to NYU." He was right. In 2023 the *Irish Star* described Ireland House as "a home away from home for generations of Irish artists, writers, musicians, and historians in New York."

Loretta was honored for her work in promoting Irish culture by being named the Grand Marshall of the 2018 St. Patrick's Day Parade.

ireland.house@nyu.edu

# WASHINGTON SQUARE PARK
## FOOT OF FIFTH AVE., GREENWICH VILLAGE

JFK HELD A CAMPAIGN RALLY here on October 27, 1960. Long a home for beatniks and bohemians, the Village would soon be the epicenter of the 60s counterculture both musically and politically. John Jr. spent a lot of time in the area from 1986 to 1989 while attending law school at NYU, located just across the street at the southwest end of the park. In 1994, John was filmed in front of the park's Stanford White-designed marble arch for an episode of his *Heart of the City* television series. He described Greenwich Village as one of New York's "quintessential neighborhoods." The series allowed John to show his love and passion for his hometown by showcasing regular citizens trying to improve people's lives. The arch was dedicated in 1889 to commemorate the centenary of Washington's first Presidential inauguration.

# THE GREY ART GALLERY
## 100 WASHINGTON SQUARE EAST; CLOSED/RELOCATING

THIS IS NEW YORK UNIVERSITY'S fine art gallery, and its works include pieces from modern artists like Picasso and Joseph Cornell and specialized collections focusing on Iranian, Turkish, and Indian art. On April 15, 1999, Carolyn attended an event here celebrating the opening of an exhibition of the designs of the Italian ready-to-wear brand Krizia and its founder Mariuccia Mandelli. Per *The New York Times,* Krizia's designs went "from plain to fancy to sexually daring to architecturally astonishing." The gallery plans to reopen at 18 Copper Square in the spring of 2024. Mandelli died in 2015 at the age of 90.

greyartgallery.nyu.edu

# NEW YORK UNIVERSITY SCHOOL OF LAW, VANDERBILT HALL

## 40 WASHINGTON SQUARE SOUTH

ACCORDING TO HIS ROOMMATE, ROB Littell,[134] John had previously applied to Harvard Law School and was devasted when he was not accepted. (So much for legacy admissions!) John enrolled here in the fall of 1986 and graduated on May 20, 1989. John had a long commute from his W. 91st St. apartment, sometimes making the trip on his bike and other times taking the subway. After graduation, John went to work at the Manhattan DA's office. In the summer of 1989, he failed the New York State Bar exam for the first time.

---

134  Littell, *The Men We Became*

## CAROLYN BESSETTE RESIDENCE
### 112 WAVERLY PLACE BETWEEN
### MACDOUGAL ST. AND SIXTH AVE.

CAROLYN MOVED INTO A FIRST-FLOOR apartment at this restored 200-year-old carriage house after leaving her place on Second Ave. It's located just down the street from Washington Square Park. In his book, *The Other Man,*[135] Carolyn's ex, Michael Bergin, remembers an April 1996 incident that occurred after he'd spent the night here. (Recall that John and Carolyn had been dating for over half a year at this point. This was two months after the Battery Park fight during which she appeared to take off what press accounts described as her engagement ring.) He writes that he high-tailed it out of here half-dressed the following morning when they learned that John — concerned when he could not contact Carolyn because she'd taken the phone off the hook — was on his way here to make sure Carolyn was okay.

This property has a courtyard and an unusual restored "back house" cottage built around 1900 by the artist Everett Shinn, which was the subject of a *New York Post* article in 2019.[136] Eager to avoid

135  Bergin, Michael *The Other Man: A Love Story*; John F. Kennedy Jr., Carolyn Bessette, & Me. Harper Collins, 2004.

136  https://nypost.com/2019/01/09/back-houses-are-nycs-best-kept-secrets/

paparazzi, Kate Moss and Johnny Depp reportedly kept company in the rear house during the 1990s. Carolyn reportedly urged Klein to build his advertising campaigns around Moss. The campaigns would prove controversial, with critics claiming that they promoted "heroin chic."

# ANTA WASHINGTON SQUARE THEATRE

## 40 W. FOURTH ST. BETWEEN MERCER ST. AND LAGUARDIA PLACE; RAZED.

THE MUSICAL *MAN OF LA Mancha* opened here on November 22, 1965. Bobby's friend Richard Goodwin later wrote that Bobby saw the show here at least three times in the coming years. A loose retelling of the Miguel Cervantes story, *Man of La Macha* featured Richard Kiley in the role of the idealistic Don Quixote and won the Tony Award for Best Musical in 1966. Bobby clearly related to the show's theme of doing right no matter the cost. He was especially fond of the show's hit song "The Impossible Dream," and played it often in his New York apartment and at Hickory Hill. The song became the unofficial theme song of his 1968 presidential campaign.

Opening in January 1964 with a production of Arthur Miller's *After the Fall*, the ANTA was designed to be the temporary home of the Lincoln Center Reparatory Company while the Vivian Beaumont Theater at Lincoln Center was being built. Because it was meant to be a temporary structure, the ANTA cost only $630,000 to build. *Man of La Mancha* had its 974th and last performance here on March 17, 1968 (the day Bobby marched in the St. Patrick's Day Parade) before moving to the Martin Beck Theatre, where it ran for another three years. NYU's Tisch Hall occupies the site today.

# LE POISSON ROUGE; FORMER SITE OF VILLAGE GATE
## 160 BLEECKER ST. @ THOMPSON ST.

THE FAMED VILLAGE GATE NIGHTCLUB was opened by Art D'Lugoff in 1958. It played host to a host of jazz greats, including John Coltrane, Sonny Rollins, and Charles Mingus. Nina Simone, Herbie Mann, and Coltrane all recorded live albums here. D'Lugoff once turned down a young Bob Dylan's request to perform here.

Bobby and Ethel attended an event held by George Plimpton here on April 28, 1966, at which the Velvet Underground performed. The purpose of the gathering was to raise money for Plimpton's *Paris Review*. A crowd of 1,000 occupied the three floors of the club. The Velvets were in the midst of their famed monthlong run at "The Dom" on St. Mark's Place, so they either had the night off or squeezed both events into their schedule. The April residency at the Dom is seen as the height of Velvet Underground's career as a live band. Jackie saw the band at the Dom that April.

The Velvets were the final act to take the stage on this night and were possibly not even introduced. D'Lugoff turned down the volume several times during the band's performance, only to have Lou Reed and company turn it right back up again.

A then-little-known Yoko Ono was also at Plimpton's party doing a performance piece called "Painting to Shake Hands," in which curious attendances put their arm through a canvas in order to shake hands with whoever was on the other side.

Bobby and Ethel hosted a party at the Dom's location a year later on the opening night of the newly christened Electric Circus. The Velvet Underground's setlist at Plimpton's party would have likely consisted of songs from their as-yet-to-be-released first album (some — such as "Femme Fatale" and "I'll Be Your Mirror" were sung by their blonde chanteuse, Nico) plus at least one eardrum-piercing noise improvisation.

Under the sponsorship of Andy Warhol, the Velvets attracted an interesting mix of followers that included both the wealthy "beautiful people" in addition to the downtown freaks. Other guests on this night reportedly included director Mike Nichols and Frank Sinatra.[137] Describing the Velvets performances at this time, Warhol later said:

*"We all knew something revolutionary was happening. We just felt it. Things could not look this strange and new without some barrier being broken."*[138]

The Village Gate closed here in 1994 and was soon replaced on its ground floor by a CVS that still occupies the corner. Le Poisson Rouge is a multimedia arts cabaret founded by musicians that has become a favorite downtown venue for music fans. It occupies the basement space here that was once home to the Village Gate. Happily, the Village Gate sign still adorns the building, a reminder of its illustrious past.

---

137  Richie Unterberger, *White Light/White Heat: The Velvet Underground Day-By-Day, Revised and Expanded eBook Edition*, 2017.

138  Warhol quoted in Legs McNeil and Gillian McCain, *Please Kill Me: The Uncensored Oral History of Punk*, New York: Grove Press, 2016.

## MERCBAR
### 151 MERCER ST., BETWEEN
### W. HOUSTON AND PRINCE STS., SOHO; DEMOLISHED

NAMED FOR THE MERCER HOTEL next door, this bar and lounge opened in 1993 and quickly became a favorite hangout for downtown hipsters and professionals. The interior was designed to look like a lodge and featured a canoe suspended above the bar. John Jr. and Carolyn were here in 1998 and very likely at other times, too. MercBar was still going strong in 2013, but it had to close that year for a pretty good reason: The building was falling down.

# FLORENT

## 69 GANSEVOORT ST. BETWEEN WASHINGTON AND GREENWICH STS., MEATPACKING DISTRICT

JOHN JR. AND *GEORGE'S* CREATIVE director Matt Berman[139] hung out at the bar here one night in the summer of 1997, downing Coronas and recalling their favorite gags from the recently released *Austin Powers* movie. This discussion would result in *Austin Powers* co-star Elizabeth Hurley gracing *George's* October 1997 cover.

When he opened this French-American bistro/diner in 1985, charismatic host Florent Morellet was paying a monthly rent of $1,350. He was forced to close in 2008 when his landlord demanded $30,000 in monthly rent. Such was his reward for investing in the area when few others would. Florent opened when prostitutes and the denizens of raunchy BDSM clubs like the all-male Anvil and Mineshaft populated the cobblestone street outside. Sometime in the 90s, the Meatpacking District became a "hot" area, transformed by scores of new businesses and hotels like Soho House and Gansevoort Hotel, along with upscale restaurants like Spice Market, Pastis, and Vento. John would have been heartened to see his beloved Whitney Museum now housed in its new and much larger home in the neighborhood.

---

139  Matt Berman, *JFK Jr., George & Me: A Memoir*, New York: Gallery Books, 2014.

## VILLAGE EAST BY ANGELIKA CINEMA
### 189 SECOND AVE @ 12<sup>TH</sup> ST.

JOHN JR. WAS HERE ON the night of September 13, 1991, for the premiere of the comedy *A Matter of Degrees*. The film co-starred John's former girlfriend, Christina Haag, and included a brief cameo of John singing (badly) while accompanying himself on acoustic guitar and saying a line or two. The film is set in Providence (with parts filmed on the Brown campus) and was written and directed by W.T. Morgan. Morgan is best known for his 1986 documentary *X: The Unheard Music*, which focuses on the L.A. punk band X. John Doe of X co-stars in *A Matter of Degrees* along with Tom Sizemore. Future stars Wendel Pierce (*The Wire*) and Michael Imperioli (*The Sopranos*) also appear in the film.

The building here dates back to 1925. Both the interior and exterior have been designated as landmarks.

# CAROLYN BESSETTE RESIDENCE
## 166 SECOND AVE., 10<sup>TH</sup> FLOOR BETWEEN
## E. 10<sup>TH</sup> AND E. 11<sup>TH</sup> STS., EAST VILLAGE

CAROLYN WAS LIVING IN THIS 15-story pre-war building when she first met John Jr in the spring of 1992. She moved here in the summer of 1989 when she came to New York to work at Calvin Klein headquarters in midtown. This was a homecoming of sorts as she had spent her early years in White Plains, a city in Westchester County 18 miles north of Manhattan, where she was born in 1966.

This building is across the street from St. Mark's in the Bowery Episcopal Church and not far from Washington Square and Union Square Parks. Carolyn lived in a rent-controlled apartment here, which she shared with a roommate. This was at a time before the neighborhood became gentrified.

Carolyn later recalled living here:

> *"I used to step over drunks and crack dealers to get to my apartment. ... Everybody at Calvin thought I was crazy, but I couldn't imagine coming to New York and living anywhere else. Even with all the weirdness, I felt comfortable, and I had fun."*[140]

---

140  "Paradise Lost," by Mark Ganem, Women's Wear Daily, July 19, 1999.

It's worth noting that although Carolyn had a doorman here, she didn't have one at the Waverly Place apartment or John's place on North Moore St. The lack of a doorman, or any other security at North Moore St., undoubtedly increased Carolyn's anxiety level especially after she'd married John and became one of the most famous women in the world.

---

Https://wwd.com/fashion-news/fashion-features/article-1089543/.

# THE ELECTRIC CIRCUS

19-25 ST. MARKS PL, BETWEEN SECOND AND THIRD AVES; CLOSED

JACKIE TURNED UP HERE IN 1966 to see the Andy Warhol-sponsored Velvet Underground when they played here during the month of April. At the time, this venue was known as "The Dom," so named because this was once the Polish National Home, later becoming the Dom Restaurant, dom being the Polish word for home. In later 1966, the venue was briefly called The Balloon Farm.

Bobby and Ethel hosted an opening night party for 2,000 guests at the Electric Circus on June 27, 1967. The event benefited the Children's Recreation Fund, which Bobby helped found in 1966. The Electric Circus was a legendary three-level New York rock music venue launched at the start of the "Summer of Love" by Jerry Brandt, featuring kaleidoscopic light shows, male and female go-go dancers, and circus performers. Writing in the *Village Voice* about the club's opening night, Bobby's friend Jack Newfield noted the huge crowd and the contrasting mix of hippies and "beautiful people" that The Electric Circus attracted. According to an account of the evening that appeared in *Billboard* magazine, the Kennedy party featured all of these elements plus the ejection of a man who'd discarded his clothes.

The Electric Circus was the first East Coast club to emulate the psychedelic San Francisco clubs that featured the music of bands like the Grateful Dead and the Jefferson Airplane.[141] The innovative use of lighting at the Electric Circus would later prove influential on the discos of the 1970s. It was not exactly a place you would expect a sitting U.S. senator to be hosting a party, but it was downtown New York in the summer of 1967, and Bobby wasn't running for anything at the time. The Beatles had released the era's touchstone album, *Sgt. Pepper's Lonely Hearts Club Band* at the beginning of June, and Bobby was photographed sporting "love beads" at a party at Hickory Hill around this time. The Paupers, a Canadian band fresh from the landmark Monterrey Pop Festival, played at the party.

If you want to see for yourself what it was all about, the Clint Eastwood movie *Coogan's Bluff* (1968) contains scenes shot in the club in late 1967. Brandt went on to greater success in the 1980s when he operated the Ritz club at Webster Hall.

---

141  The Airplane's *Surrealistic Pillow* album was spotted at Hickory Hill around this time. In my book *Popology*, I recount the story of how Bobby and Ethel hosted the band at their home the day after the group played at their Junior Village Telethon in Washington on February 16, 1968.

## WEBSTER HALL; FORMERLY THE RITZ
### 119 E. 11TH ST. BETWEEN THIRD AND FOURTH AVES.

JOHN SAW GEORGE CLINTON AND the P-Funk All-Stars here on September 20, 1992, when it was known at The Ritz. His friend John Mosley later recalled that John declined an offer to jump the line, which stretched around the block. "We're going to wait in line like everyone else," he said. And they did, for an hour and a half.

# IL CANTINORI RESTAURANT
## 32 E. 10ᵀᴴ ST. BETWEEN BROADWAY AND UNIVERSITY PLACE

WHEN IT OPENED IN 1983, Il Cantinori was just the second New York restaurant to serve rustic Tuscan fare, following in the footsteps of Da Silvano. As the 1980s progressed, both restaurants became known for their celebrity clientele.

This was one of John and Carolyn's favorite places to eat in Greenwich Village. In the spring of 1999, John and Carolyn reportedly dined at an outdoor table here with his cousin Maria Shriver and Arnold Schwarzenegger. In a 2021 tweet in response to a bonkers fringe conspiracy theory that John was still alive, Maria wrote, "You never get over these losses."

# SEN. JACOB JAVITS BIRTHPLACE
## 85 STANTON ST. BETWEEN ALLEN AND ORCHARD STS.

ONE OF THE MOST FAMOUS and poignant photos of Bobby was taken here on May 8, 1967. Photographer Fred McDarrah snapped a photo of him under a picture of Christ, an image that took on greater resonance after his assassination. Bobby — who was described as a "good-doer" by his friend Sammy Davis Jr. — undoubtedly had a strong Catholic faith that compelled him to do right as he saw it. Bobby, Javits, and Senators Pell and Clark were holding hearings to examine the effectiveness of New York's anti-poverty programs, and their tour of the Lower East Side brought them to this building, where Javits was born in 1904. Deemed a "tenement" in 1967, in recent years, units in the building have sold in the $700,000-800,000 range. McDarrah's photo graces the cover of the paperback edition of one of the better books on Bobby, Jack Newfield's *RFK: A Memoir*.

# FINE FARE SUPERMARKET/PAUL TAYLOR DANCE COMPANY; FORMER SITE OF THE COOPERATIVE AUDITORIUM

## 551 GRAND ST. @ JACKSON ST., LOWER EAST SIDE

BOBBY ATTENDED THE SENATE SUBCOMMITTEE on Poverty hearing here on May 8-9, 1967. The hearings were to examine the effectiveness of New York's anti-poverty programs. Bobby was especially critical of the state's efforts, claiming that the programs "have broken up family life" and had wasted money because of poor administration. Under intense questioning from Bobby, an official of the state Labor Department conceded that the state's job-training efforts had been minuscule. The senators — chairman Joseph Clark of Pennsylvania, Jacob Javits of New York, and Claiborne Pell of Rhode Island — had a gefilte fish lunch on the afternoon of the eighth at Ratner's Restaurant on Delancy St.

# DOWNTOWN BOATHOUSE AT PIER 26

## HUDSON RIVER WALK

THIS BUILDING IS LOCATED JUST north of North Moore St. John Jr. stored his two kayaks here, close to his home. He was fond of kayaking on the Hudson River or sometimes heading over to Brooklyn. The Boathouse is still there today, operating from May to October.

https://www.downtownboathouse.org/

## AREA NIGHTCLUB
### 157 HUDSON ST. BETWEEN HUBERT AND LAIGHT STS.
### CLOSED

ALTHOUGH IT HAD A BRIEF shelf life, lasting only from September 1983 until early 1987, Area made a lasting impression. The club occupied 13,000 square feet of space in this building, which was built in 1866.

Area attracted downtown VIPs like Andy Warhol, Keith Haring (who was once photographed with John), and Jean-Michel Basquiat, all of whom helped decorate the club. Area was designed to be a work of art itself, offering newly themed décor every six weeks, such as "Suburbia," "Sex," and "Gnarly," all featuring appropriate props such as 100 cereal boxes and Velveeta slices for "Suburbia." The bathrooms were unisex and home to a variety of nefarious activities. John Jr. was a regular here during his bachelor days in the 1980s. He lived down the street at 71 Hudson beginning in the spring of 1990 before moving a couple of blocks north to his North Moore St. apartment just three blocks south of where Area was located.

Area co-owner Eric Goode would go on to direct the *Tiger King* crime documentary television series.

# JOHN KENNEDY JR. AND CAROLYN BESSETTE RESIDENCE

## 20 NORTH MOORE ST. BETWEEN VARICK AND HOUSTON STS., TRIBECA

NOT LONG AFTER JACKIE DIED in 1994, John Jr. bought his ninth-floor two-bedroom loft here for a reported $700,000. Visiting shortly after Carolyn had moved in, Carole Radziwill later described the place as:

> *"...the ultimate bachelor pad, with bad furniture, bad lighting, ill-placed bathrooms, and small closets. ... We gave it nicknames: Home Depot, the Warehouse."*[142]

What might have seemed okay as a bachelor pad would prove a less-than-ideal refuge as the media's focus on John ramped up with Jackie's death, especially after he married Carolyn in September 1996. The building was a refurbished warehouse, and the apartment still looked it even after John renovated his floor. Carolyn moved in with John a year before their wedding. With no doorman, no security, only one door in and out, and a linoleum-lined space instead of

---

142 Carole Radziwill, *What Remains: A Memoir of Fate, Friendship & Love*, New York: Scribner, 2005.

a lobby, you can sympathize with Carolyn's increased anxiety as she began her marriage to one of the most famous men in the world set upon each day by 10-20 paparazzi waiting on her doorstep. It was not an ideal state of affairs, to say the least. By most accounts, she was increasingly upset about the situation as time went on, yet there was no apparent solution to the problem of her lack of privacy since John was reluctant to move out of the city.

An unnamed "friend" later told author Edward Klein:

> "(Carolyn) didn't feel at home in the North Moore Street apartment. She hated it. She didn't like where it was located. And John had decorated it — badly. It was very cold, like a young man's first loft."[143]

Carolyn thus became increasingly reclusive, putting further stress on the marriage.

Their apartment occupied the top floor and had access to the roof deck, on which John and his friends would sometimes toss a football. In the days after their deaths, the building became a shrine to the couple and Lauren Bessette, with flowers, candles, and photos placed outside the building.

Following their deaths, John and Carolyn's loft was put up for sale with a minimum bid price of $2.5 million. Actor and filmmaker (*The Brothers McMullen*, *She's the One*) Ed Burns purchased the unit in 2000, reportedly paying just below the asking price. The interior of John's former loft can be viewed extensively in Burns' 2011 flick *The Newlyweds*, an ultra-low-budget (but still pretty good) affair in which the director used his home as a set to keep expenses to a minimum.

---

143 "Secrets and Lies" by Edward Klein, *Vanity Fair*, August 2003.

## BUBBY'S

### 120 HUDSON ST. @ NORTH MOORE ST., TRIBECA

THIS WAS AND IS A friendly neighborhood joint just down the
street from John Jr.'s North Moore St. home. If you had to name one
place as John's "go-to" restaurant, this would be it. John often ate
breakfast here (he was said to be especially fond of the blueberry
pancakes) and often hung out at the bar. Bubby's has been in business since 1990, thus preceding John in the neighborhood by four
years. John and Carolyn were often captured in paparazzi photos
outside Bubby's. The couple was photographed on the street outside
Bubby's after lunch with Lauren Bessette on November 15, 1997.
Carolyn was said to often order the matzo ball soup here. Owner
Seth Price later recalled sometimes letting Carolyn leave through
the back door to protect her privacy.

www.bubbys.com

## TAMARIND TRIBECA;
## FORMER SITE OF THE SOCRATES DINER
### SOUTHWEST CORNER OF HUDSON AND FRANKLIN STS.

THE SOCRATES OPENED IN 1983 and was more than just a diner with outstanding pancakes; it was a home away from home for many of its customers. Located just down the street from their apartment on North Moore St., John Jr. and Carolyn were regulars here, with John often enjoying a hearty breakfast while sitting at the counter and reading the *New York Post*. Owner George Dourountoudakis would later recall that John would sometimes speak in rusty Greek to him. After his landlord converted the apartments on the upper floors of the building to office space, forcing many of his best customers to relocate, Dourountoudakis was forced to close in May 2007. On the diner's sad closing day, one of the last things he did was remove John's framed photo from behind the register.

With its striking interior and excellent food, Tamarind Tribeca is considered by many to be the best Indian restaurant in the city.

www.tamrindtribeca.com

## WALKER'S

16 N. MOORE ST. BETWEEN HUDSON AND VARICK STS., TRIBECA

WALKER'S IS A FRIENDLY BAR and restaurant next door to John's Jr.'s building on North Moore St. This place opened in 1987, so it was well established by the time John moved to North Moore in 1994. John and Carolyn were reportedly fond of the screwdrivers here. John was said to be drowning his sorrows here following a fight with Carolyn in March 1999.

www.walkersbarnyc.com

# LAUREN BESSETTE RESIDENCE
## 17 WHITE ST. @ SIXTH AVE.

LAUREN PURCHASED A LOFT IN this five-story 19<sup>th</sup>-century cast-iron building in 1998, paying $925,000. She had recently returned to New York after working in Morgan Stanley's Hong Kong office, where her fluency in Mandarin was an asset. Not coincidentally, the address is just a couple of blocks east of John and Carolyn's place on North Moore St., and Carolyn often took refuge from the omnipresent paparazzi here, often staying until late at night and sometimes even sleeping over.

Following Lauren's death, neighbors had fond memories of her, with one woman recalling, "She was just a lovely person. She was sweet and smart." [144] Lauren's loft was sold for a reported $1.7 million in early 2000. Today, units in the building sell for $5-6 million.

---

144 https://nypost.com/1999/07/22/lauren-lived-quietly-two-blocks-from-fame/

## TRIBECA GRILL

375 GREENWICH ST. BETWEEN NORTH MOORE
AND FRANKIN STS.

AS YOU WILL SURMISE BY the address, this was and is just a few streets west of John and Carolyn's place on North Moore St. Robert De Niro and Drew Nieporent opened this upscale bar and grill in April 1990. It is decorated with the abstract expressionist paintings of De Niro's artist father, Robert Sr.

This was the site of a somewhat bizarre luncheon date that John Jr. had with the 28-year-old blonde Brazilian singer and host of a TV show for kids[145] Xuxa (Maria da Graça Meneghel) on February 14, 1992. John had seen a video of Xuxa that apparently met with his approval. John refused Xuxa's offer of a limo to pick him up at his assistant DA job, preferring to walk to the restaurant instead. The lunch went well, but John was said to be upset when film footage of their encounter turned up on the tabloid television show *A Current Affair* the following week. He felt he'd been unwittingly duped into a PR stunt and wasn't happy about it. Interviewed around the time of John's 1996 wedding to Carolyn, Xuxa vehemently denied that she had set John up in 1992:

---

145  Think *Wonderama* but with a hot hostess wearing revealing outfits.

*"It was too bad.... He is very handsome. He is a really good guy. I tried to talk to him after that to tell him I didn't do it, but I couldn't. He wouldn't talk to me."*[146]

John and Carolyn celebrated his 35th birthday here on November 25, 1995.

John and Carolyn reportedly ate brunch here on Sunday, February 25, 1996, before their infamous brawl in Battery Park. Perhaps the bloody marys (and/or mimosas) were to blame!

www.tribecagrill.com

---

146 https://www.orlandosentinel.com/1996/10/02/tv-star-not-celebrating-jfk-jrs-wedding/

# EL TEDDY'S RESTAURANT
## 219 W. BROADWAY BETWEEN WHITE AND FRANKLIN STS.
## RAZED

JOHN JR. AND CAROLYN WERE regulars at this noisy Mexican restaurant, a favorite of Tribeca locals. The original building dates back to the 1920s and was home to various restaurants through the years.

John and Carolyn began seeing each other in the summer of 1992, but a strange incident at El Teddy's caused them to separate for the next two years. As they sat down to dinner, John confronted Carolyn with a letter he'd received from one of his friends. The writer accused Carolyn of being a golddigger, among other nasty claims. John apparently accepted the letter at face value and left El Teddy's without giving Carolyn an opportunity to respond.[147] John reportedly celebrated at least one — and possibly several — of his birthdays here in the mid-90s. These were small affairs with just a few close friends. The décor here was funky, with a lot of found objects, and the cuisine was inventive. Artist Antoni Miralda's 2,500-pound replica of the Statue of Liberty crown adorning the building (left when El Internacional went out of business) was seen during *Saturday Night Live's* opening montage for

---

147  Beller, *Once Upon a Time.*

many years. El Teddy's closed in January 2004 due to a business downturn following the 9/11 terror attacks. A six-story condo now stands on the site of the late, lamented El Teddy's.

# JOHN F. KENNEDY JR. RESIDENCE
## 71 HUDSON ST. BETWEEN JAY AND HARRISON STS.

JOHN JR. MOVED HERE IN the spring of 1990 (or possibly earlier), and occupied an entire floor. Dating from 1880, 71 Hudson was designed to be a duplicate of 73 Hudson, which stands next to it. At the time, Tribeca was undergoing a transformation from old warehouses to trendy bars and restaurants. John Jr. obviously enjoyed his new neighborhood because he purchased an apartment two-and-a-half blocks up Hudson St. at 20 North Moore St. a few years later. It's interesting to note that John never lived near his mother's Upper East Side home — or anywhere else on the Upper East Side other than temporarily — once he was on his own as an adult.

## ECCO RESTAURANT

### 124 CHAMBERS ST. BETWEEN WEST BROADWAY AND CHURCH ST., TRIBECA; CLOSED

THIS CLASSY AND MUCH-LOVED OLD-SCHOOL Italian restaurant — dubbed "The Italian Saloon" — was a favorite of John Jr.'s. Episodes of *Law and Order* and *The Sopranos* were filmed here, showcasing the old-school décor consisting of mahogany booths and mirrored panels. It closed in late 2019 after more than 35 years at this location.

## MUDVILLE 9

JOHN JR. WAS A FAN of this saloon, a Tribeca institution since 1977. John celebrated at least two of his birthdays here: in 1995 with Carolyn—where the celebration morphed into an all-night dance party—and in 1992 with Daryl Hannah.

https://www.mudville9.com/

# THE ODEON

## 145 W. BROADWAY @ THOMAS ST., TRIBECA

BY THE EARLY SUMMER OF 1994, John Jr. had been seeking to reunite with Carolyn for some time. It finally happened one evening when Carolyn was working a private event for Calvin Klein here, to which John showed up. Carolyn intervened before he could be turned away at the door, and the pair then spent the rest of the night talking.[148] But by the end of the summer, they were going steady.

This was one of the few restaurants in the area when Keith McNally, his brother Brian, and Lynn Wagenknecht opened it in October 1980. Famed for its neon sign, it's been a local favorite, especially with artists (Andy Warhol and Jean-Michel Basquiat) and writers. The iconic Odeon sign graced the cover of Jay McInerney's era-defining novel *Bright Lights, Big City*, and the characters in the book do drugs in the bathroom here. John Jr. and Carolyn lived just four blocks away on North Moore St. and were regulars here. Its sister restaurant, Café Luxembourg, was another of John's favorites. An October 1994 *New York Times* article noted the presence of Madonna, Robert De Niro, and John Jr. as proof that the restaurant was hip again after experiencing a lull following its 1980s heyday.

---

148  Beller, *Once Upon a Time.*

## EDWARD'S RESTAURANT;
## FORMER SITE OF BODEGA

### 136 WEST BROADWAY @ THOMAS ST.

LOCATED NOT FAR FROM THEIR apartment, John Jr. and Carolyn were said to have often eaten breakfast here. "The bright airy dining room feels like a luncheonette with high ceilings," per a *New York Times* review of Bodega.[149] The food might be described as Mexican comfort food, but it was also renowned for its frozen margarita machine.

John and Carolyn were dining here on January 28, 1997, when John became infuriated when he spotted paparazzi petting his dog, Friday, who was tied outside. John rushed out and screamed at them: "If you guys are going to be inhumane to my wife, you shouldn't pet my dog!" [150]

---

149 "Running the Gamut in Tribeca" *The New York Times*, January 17, 1999.

150 Beller, *Once Upon a Time*.

# FRANKLIN STREET SUBWAY STATION
## BETWEEN WEST BROADWAY AND VARICK ST., TRIBECA

LOCATED JUST A BLOCK SOUTH of John Jr.'s home on North Moore St., this stop could hardly have been more convenient for him. Writer and family friend (and Bobby biographer) Jack Newfield recalled seeing John riding the 1 Train regularly. Commentator Jeff Greenfield was once surprised to see John on the subway returning home from a Knicks game at Madison Square Garden. John often got on the 1 Train to go uptown to go to work at *George*, getting off at the Broadway and 50th St. stop just outside his Paramount Plaza office at 1633 Broadway.

# THE PUBLIC THEATER

## 425 LAFAYETTE ST. @ ASTOR PLACE

BUILT IN 1853 WITH A $400,000 bequest from John Jacob Astor, this was originally the site of New York's first free public library. The groundbreaking musical *Hair* opened here on October 17, 1967. Two weeks later, on October 30 — an off night for the show — Bobby and Ethel hosted a benefit for his Community Services Benefit Committee, which aided underprivileged kids. Ella Fitzgerald was the headline performer, and the next day's *New York Times* carried a photo of Bobby gazing up at Ella with a smile on his face as he sat on the edge of the stage. Ella sang "Goin' Out of My Head," among other tunes. Performers that night included Young-Holt Unlimited, who would have a big hit in 1968 with "Soulful Strut," and a rock band from Long Island called The Hassles, which featured a young Billy Joel.

## 310 BOWERY BAR

310 BOWERY BETWEEN BLEECKER AND E. HOUSTON STS.

JOHN JR. AND CAROLYN DINED here on October 15, 1995. In his book *American Son,* Richard Blow — who accompanied John that night along with John Perry Barlow and others — described how uncomfortable it felt for an ordinary person to be in the eye of the hurricane that surrounded John. It seemed other patrons were eavesdropping on all of John's conversations, making it difficult to speak candidly in his presence. A phalanx of aggressive paparazzi besieged John's group as it left around 1 a.m. and John unlocked his bike. "Again!" John shouted at paparazzo JD Ligier, who had been following him in recent days. After walking a block or two, Blow encountered John in the darkness. John noted that Blow "looked a little freaked back there" and asked if he was okay. A regular night for John was a surreal night for anyone else.

www.310Bowery.nyc

## PRAVDA

281 LAFAYETTE ST. BETWEEN PRINCE AND JERSEY STS.,
SOHO CLOSED

THIS RUSSIAN-THEMED VODKA BAR WAS the brainchild of
Keith McNally. The windowless Pravda was a hotspot in the late 90s
and early aughts. Carolyn and John celebrated RoseMarie Terenzio's
birthday with her here in January 1999. Pravda closed in 2016.

## SZECHUAN TASTE RESTAURANT
### 23 CHATHAM SQUARE, CHINATOWN; CLOSED

JACKIE ENJOYED THIS PLACE, THE first of 23 restaurants owned by David Keh. In its 1979 guide, *Fodors* described it as having "Probably the city's best Szechuan menu and food." Keh said his goal in starting Szechuan Taste was to create a "Chinese Lutèce." They eventually had branches on the Upper East and Upper West Sides. Keh was credited with introducing authentic Szechuan cuisine to New York and changing the image of Chinese restaurants to something beyond the typical takeout items. On February 19, 1969, Jackie and Ari dined here with architect I.M. Pei (who would soon design the JFK Library in Boston) and (Black Jack Bouvier's old flame) heiress Doris Duke.

## MANHATTAN DISTRICT ATTORNEY'S OFFICE
1 HOGAN PL. BETWEEN BAXTER AND CENTRE STS.

JOHN JR. WORKED HERE AS an assistant DA from August 21, 1989, to July 9, 1993. There were said to be 100 photographers outside the office on John's first day at work. Michael Cherkasky was the chief of investigations and, as such, John's boss. He later recalled:

> *"Citizens would come in with a complaint, and John's job was to interview them. It was funny to see the way they'd react. Having this legend sit down and scribble your complaint has got to be a little strange."*

Jackie apparently concurred. While John was working here, she asked a friend to speak to John about finding more suitable employment, befitting his family legacy.

# CITY HALL

CITY HALL PARK BETWEEN BROADWAY, PARK ROW,
AND CHAMBERS ST.

JFK SPOKE FROM THE FRONT steps at a rally held here on October 19, 1960. The rally followed a ticker-tape parade up Broadway that had, according to Mayor Robert Wagner's estimate, drawn a million people to see JFK and Jackie as they rode in a Chevy convertible. At times, the crowd brought the motorcade to a standstill. Police estimated that the crowd assembled in City Hall Plaza to hear JFK's speech numbered 50,000.

# NEW YORK CITY OFFICE OF BUSINESS DEVELOPMENT

## 17 JOHN ST. BETWEEN BROADWAY AND NASSAU ST.

BEFORE GOING TO LAW SCHOOL, John worked here for about a year, beginning in October 1984. He was an assistant to the Commissioner of Business Development, Lawrence Kieves, and earned a reported annual salary of $20,000. Deputy Mayor Kenneth Lipper oversaw the agency at the time during the administration of Mayor Ed Koch.

Interviewed by Daily News reporters after his second day on the job, John said that so far, it was "Going real good." He described himself as an "office associate." Asked exactly what his duties entailed, John replied, "I have to find out...I'll do whatever they throw on my desk." John told the reporters that he had interviewed with several private foundations and city agencies before deciding to take this job with the Office of Business Development, tasked with attracting and keeping businesses in New York City.[151]

Kieves later said of John:

> *"He worked in the same crummy cubbyhole as*

---

151   Peter McLaughlin and Alton Slagle, "Just Another Working Joe," *The New York Daily News*, October 18, 1984.

*everybody else. I heaped on the work and was*
*always pleased."*[152]

One of his colleagues, Shaaz Ali, later said of John:

*"He was like a really big kid.... When he was*
*walking through the stairs from one floor to*
*another, he would yell out just to hear his echo."*

This was said to be John's first paying job after graduating from Brown, but according to Ali, John absentmindedly lost his first paycheck, and another one had to be issued. While working here, John met Michael Berman. This would prove to be a fateful meeting, as the two men became fast friends. John asked Berman to begin assisting him with scheduling and preparing for his public appearances. A decade later they later partnered to create *George* magazine.

---

152  Michael Gross, "Favorite Son," *New York Magazine*, March 20, 1989.

## NOBU

### 105 HUDSON ST., BETWEEN FRANKLIN AND NORTH MOORE STS. RELOCATED

NOBU OPENED ITS FIRST LOCATION here in 1994. The name-sake restaurant of chef Nobu Matsuhisa, Nobu quickly became one of the most highly regarded and influential restaurants in the city. It's now expanded to three dozen locations around the globe. Nobu offers a Japanese-Peruvian fusion menu whose most renowned dish is the black cod with miso sauce.

John often went here for business dinners or with Carolyn. While they were still dating, they were photographed here on February 6, 1996. John often saw co-owner Robert De Niro, who lived close to John's place in Tribeca, on the neighborhood streets. Legendary music producer Quincy Jones met John here one night, and the pair discussed their respective magazines, Jones having recently launched *VIBE*. Jones was impressed by John's modesty. "I know people who've had a No. 13 record that had more attitude than he did."

On the weekend John and Carolyn died, co-owner Richie Notar brought food to John's apartment for a distraught RoseMarie Terenzio, John's *George* assistant to whom John had lent his place for the weekend after learning that the air conditioning in her apartment wasn't working.

After over 20 years on Hudson St., Nobu relocated to 195 Broadway in 2017. It has another NYC location at 40 W. 57$^{th}$ St.

www.noburestaurants.com

# FEDERAL HALL

## 26 WALL ST. @ NASSAU ST.

THIS WAS THE SITE OF John Jr.'s famous press conference on September 7, 1995, introducing *George* magazine to the world. Appropriately, it was held at the location — if not the same building — where the magazine's namesake, George Washington, first took the Presidential oath of office on April 30, 1789. The news conference was nearly upstaged by the news that John had become engaged to Carolyn, which the *New York Post* had broken days earlier. He stood next to a photo of the new magazine's first cover, which featured supermodel Cindy Crawford dressed up as George Washington (with a bare midriff).

John performed admirably, appearing confident while throwing in dashes of self-deprecating humor such as, "I haven't seen so many of you in one place since I failed my bar exam." The press conference and cover did the trick, and *George* sold out its initial run of half a million copies plus an additional 100,000 more, an astonishing success. Unfortunately, after the first two issues (which were sold in tandem to advertisers), newsstand sales and the number of ad pages declined and never quite recovered.

## FULTON FISH MARKET

SOUTH ST. BETWEEN BEEKMAN AND FULTON STS.

BOBBY KICKED OFF HIS SENATE campaign here at dawn on September 2, 1964. Asked what he thought of the place, he very astutely commented, "They have a lot of fish." Bobby promised to return here whether he won or lost the election. He made good on his word when he left an election night celebration at the Hotel Delmonico to return here at around 4 a.m. on November 4.

## DOWNTOWN ATHLETIC CLUB
### 20 WEST ST. NEAR MORRIS ST.

BEST KNOWN AS THE SPONSOR of the Heisman Trophy that annually honors the best college football player, this was also a private athletic and social club that counted John Jr. among its members. The place opened in 1926 but had seen much better days by the time John went there in the 1990s. Still, John enjoyed swimming, racquetball, steams, and massages here and appreciated the club's old-school charm.

John threw a bachelor party for his cousin Anthony Radziwill here in the summer of 1994. *Rolling Stone* publisher Jann Wenner recalled[153] that the event included typical amenities such as "booze (and) strippers" and a reminder from John to "please bring marital aids for Anthony from the porn shop."

Richard Blow later wrote[154] that John invited him and a few other *George* colleagues here on March 3, 1999, to watch Barbara Walters' much-hyped interview with Monica Lewinsky. For the past year, Lewinsky had been at the center of a scandal involving President Bill Clinton that had consumed the media (if not the public), and

---

153 Wenner, *Like a Rolling Stone.*

154 Richard Blow *American Son.*

now she was to give her side of the story. So, the interview was a big deal at the time. John believed in the quaint notion that even public servants were entitled to a private life. Blow noted John's discomfort as he watched the spectacle — including a groan when Walters asked the inevitable "blue dress" question.

The Athletic Club building is just four blocks from the World Trade Center site, and the club was forced to close after the area was inaccessible for months following the 9/11 attacks. The building is a landmark and today houses the Downtown Club condominiums.

# WHITEHALL TERMINAL STATEN ISLAND FERRY LANDING

## 4 SOUTH ST. @ WHITEHALL ST.

AFTER VISITING THE NEARBY FULTON Fish Market early in the morning of September 2, 1964, Bobby stopped here, making this the second stop of his 1964 senate campaign. He received an "uproarious reception" as he shook hands with commuters while standing on top of a car.

# BATTERY PARK EAST COAST MEMORIAL
## BATTERY PARK

ON MAY 23, 1963, JFK dedicated the East Coast Memorial to those missing at sea. The monument consists of eight massive 19-foot-tall granite pylons honoring the 4,601 American service members who lost their lives in combat in the Atlantic Ocean during World War II. The columns face the Statue of Liberty and list the names of those who were lost. The bronze statue of the eagle clutching a funeral wreath over a wave was designed by sculptor Albino Manca and symbolizes mourning for the dead. In tying the sacrifices of those memorialized to the present day, JFK stated during his remarks that "All Americans must always be prepared to play their proper part in a difficult and dangerous world."

Battery Park was the site of the infamous heated shouting match between John Jr. and his then-girlfriend Carolyn Bessette on February 25, 1996. The fight reportedly concerned Carolyn's concern that John was letting people take advantage of him via his willingness to attend weddings of casual acquaintances. However, the intensity of this exchange suggests it might have concerned more intimate matters. The fight involved pushing and shoving, and at one point, John appeared to be attempting to take the engagement ring off of Carolyn's finger. Unfortunately for both of them, a *National*

*Enquirer* photographer and someone taking video were on hand to document the scene.

"Carolyn, more than anyone who John had been with, would stand up to him, and confront him, and I think that John to an extent needed that," John's friend Steve Gillon later told *InStyle magazine*. Whether he needed it or not, by all accounts, he got it. By the mid-1990s, the wide availability of portable video cameras had brought scenes — such as the Rodney King beating — into people's living rooms that would not have been filmed or made known to the public in earlier times.

## NATIONAL MUSEUM OF THE AMERICAN INDIAN/
## ALEXANDER HAMILTON U.S. CUSTOM HOUSE[155]
### 1 BOWLING GREEN @ BRIDGE & STATE STS.

ON MAY 19, 1999, THIS Beaux-Arts turn-of-the-century building was the location of one of John Jr. and Carolyn's last public events in New York, the Newman's Own — George Awards ceremony honoring companies for their philanthropic work. For years, actor Paul Newman had successfully raised money for charity with his Newman's Own brands of tomato sauces, salad dressings, and the like. *George* contributor Tim Hotchner[156] grew up around Newman and later observed that John and the actor had a lot in common:

> "...John and Paul both shared very similar
> sensibilities. They were both superstars, "Sexiest
> Man Alive" in People magazine. But they were also
> the humblest guys I knew, didn't take themselves
> too seriously, and wanted to do good in the world." [157]

---

155  In the days before the federal income tax was imposed in 1913, customs were of great importance as an essential source of income for the government.

156  His father, writer A.N. Hotchner, co-founded Newman's Own in 1982.

157  *JFK Jr.: The Final Year*, A & E, 2019.

The National Museum of the American Indian/Alexander Hamilton U.S. Custom House as photographed in 2023.

Among the honorees at the event was fashion designer Kenneth Cole, who was one of the first in the fashion industry to advocate for AIDS awareness and funding. John joined Newman in presenting Cole with his award. Like John's cousin, Kerry Kennedy, Cole had married into the Cuomo family when he wed Maria Cuomo in 1987, thus making him (sort of) related to John.

Despite reports of troubles in their marriage at this time, John and Carolyn seemed happy and playful with each other as reporters interviewed them on their way into the building. This was one of the few times Carolyn's voice was recorded publicly

# THE OUTER BOROUGHS
# AND BEYOND

# BROOKLYN

## MCCARREN PARK

### NASSAU AVE., BAYARD, LEONARD, AND NORTH 12ᵀᴴ STS., WILLIAMSBURG

BOBBY'S VISIT HERE WAS IMMORTALIZED in a Jimmy Breslin column titled "Kennedy's Arithmetic"[158] that emphasized his appeal to young voters in a prospective future Presidential race. As darkness fell on a late autumn afternoon in 1966, Bobby had a bit of time to kill and came here when he noticed that the St. Francis Prep football team was holding practice in the park. Informed that they were one of the best teams in the city, Bobby said, "Good. I like to watch the good ones." He then inquired with the coach about various players and offered them encouragement ("Two hands!" he shouted when a receiver dropped a pass) as they ran through their plays. Bobby had hoped to catch their game that Sunday afternoon, but he couldn't make it. St. Francis was victorious that day and voted the game ball to Bobby. At the time, St. Francis was located on nearby N. 6th St. It relocated to its present location in Fresh Meadows, Queens, in 1974.

---

158  Breslin's article was published in the very short-lived (September 1966 to May 1967) *World Journal Telegram* and ended up in Bobby's FBI file.

# JFK MEMORIAL, GRAND ARMY PLAZA
## FLATBUSH AVE.

BOBBY AND ETHEL WERE PRESENT at the unveiling of a JFK memorial here on May 31, 1965, which was Memorial Day. He was greeted by a boisterous crowd of 20,000 people, some of whom were "nearly hysterical." At one point Bobby was knocked down, according to a report in the next day's *New York Times*.[159] The bust, designed by Neil Estern, was originally supposed to be accompanied by an eternal flame, but Jackie nixed the idea, preferring that the one in Arlington stand alone. The memorial's base was damaged by rain and vandalism, so the JFK bust was removed in October 2003, and the monument was upgraded and rededicated in 2010.

---

159   Eric Pace, "Admirers Mob Kennedy at Memorial to Brother," *The New York Times*, June 1, 1965.

## JFK MOTORCADE

FULTON ST. BETWEEN ADAMS AND DUFFIELD STS.

ON THE EVENING OF OCTOBER 20, 1960, JFK rode for 15 miles on the back of an open black convertible through the streets of Brooklyn. The next day's *New York Times* headline noted, "Candidate Almost Mobbed by Thousands of Women Shoppers." The story said that when he reached this five-block area of Fulton St., a crowd of 10,000 got so rowdy that JFK's convertible began to rock back and forth. The police quickly blared their sirens and got the 20-car caravan through.

## ACADEMY OF ARTS AND LETTERS; FORMERLY P.S. 305.

### 344 MONROE ST.

ON DECEMBER 9, 1966, BOBBY, Mayor John Lindsay, and Sen. Jacob Javits established the private non-profit Bedford-Stuyvesant Restoration Corporation (BSRC) here. Like many urban communities, by the mid-1960s, Bed-Stuy was experiencing widespread poverty due to white flight to the suburbs. The idea was to get businesses, foundations, and the government involved in underwriting the corporation to empower community members to address their problems by rehabbing old buildings, building new housing, and cleaning up the streets. Bobby was inspired to do something innovative after seeing the deplorable conditions in the area and hearing the anger and frustration in the voices of Bed-Stuy residents when he visited there on February 4, 1966.

The corporation's work reflected Bobby's current critique of the government's welfare bureaucracy as too top-heavy and ineffective in meeting the needs of those it was designed to help. At the P.S. 305 event, Bobby admitted that he "sounded like a Republican" by calling for private action to address poverty but claimed that governmental welfare and housing programs, "Don't have their origin in the community but are imposed from outside, and the community has no stake in their success."

An old milk plant purchased by the BSRC served as the corporation's first headquarters. By 1972, it had morphed into Restoration Plaza, which today is home to numerous stores and restaurants and includes the Billie Holiday Theatre, a supermarket, and two banks. It stands as a monument to the practical ways Bobby sought to help and empower the less fortunate. Ethel and many of the Kennedys have visited Bed-Stuy through the years to attend BSRC-associated events.

# BROOKLYN BRIDGE

JOHN JR. STOOD NEAR THE bridge on the Brooklyn side while introducing the sixth and final episode of his *Heart of the City* program for WNYC-TV in 1994.

# THE BRONX

## YANKEE STADIUM
### E. 161ST ST. @ RIVER RD., DEMOLISHED

ON SEPTEMBER 18, 1965, BOBBY was on the field here before a crowd of 50,000 fans for Mickey Mantle Day, which celebrated "The Mick's" 2000th game. Mantle was hobbled with injuries at the time, and there was speculation that he might not play another year, although he would play for an additional three seasons before retiring in 1968. Joe DiMaggio was also present that day. Did he make any small talk with Bobby? Probably not.

Bobby often attended New York Giants home football games here during the mid-60s.

With just 24 hours to live, John Jr. watched the Braves beat the Yankees, 6-2, on the night of July 15, 1999. Future Hall of Fame pitcher Tom Glavine got the win, and the Yankees' Roger Clemens was tagged with the loss. Then-Yankees owner George Steinbrenner later recalled that he told John he was welcome to sit in the owner's box seats, but John declined. "He wanted to sit downstairs. He liked being close to where the action was."[160] Steinbrenner had a long history with the Kennedys and even once hosted Bobby at his Ohio home.

---

160  Dale Russakoff and Lynne Duke, "JFK Jr.'s Joyful, Fateful Final Hours," *The Washington Post*, July 20, 1999.

The Yankees were having a good year in 1999 and were on their way to a World Series championship. This would be their third championship in the midst of four over the five seasons spanning 1996 to 2000. Yankee mainstays Derek Jeter, Bernie Williams, and Jorge Posada took the field that night facing a Braves team that included future Hall of Famer Chipper Jones and second baseman Bret Boone, the brother of future Yankees manager Aaron Boone. When the television camera showed John in the stands in the middle of the sixth inning, the Atlanta Braves announcer noted: "I hear his magazine is about to go down the old porcelain facility. That was the rumor in the New York papers today." On-screen, we see a smiling John sharing a laugh with his friend Gary Ginsberg as the familiar strains of Frank Sinatra's "New York, New York" plays over the stadium's PA system.

## ALBERT EINSTEIN COLLEGE, FORCHEIMER
## MEDICAL SCIENCES BUILDING, SOUTH CAMPUS
### 1300 MORRIS PARK AVE.

BOBBY, ROSE, AND PEACE CORPS director Sargent Shriver held a news conference here on March 18, 1965, to announce the Joseph P. Kennedy Jr. Foundation's $1 million grant to Yeshiva University to build a center to aid the developmentally disabled.

## ROSE KENNEDY CHILDREN'S EVALUATION AND REHABILITATION CENTER AT MONTEFIORE

### 1225 NORTH CAMPUS MORRIS PARK AVE. NEAR PELHAM PARKWAY SOUTH

BOBBY AND ROSE ATTENDED THE groundbreaking cere-mony for this building, which was part of Albert Einstein College and financed by the Joseph P. Kennedy Jr. Foundation, on May 1, 1966. Both had come to champion the cause of the developmen-tally disabled via the tragic life of Rosemary Kennedy, confined to a Wisconsin convent following a catastrophic lobotomy surgery in November 1941. Incredibly, none of her family members visited her in the twenty years following her surgery.[161] It was only after Joe's stroke in 1961 that her siblings were made aware of Rosemary's lobotomy and her present whereabouts — St. Coletta's Catholic home in Wisconsin. Although Rose described Rosemary as "retarded," in a 1963 interview, according to some doctor's accounts, she actually had a mental illness and suffered from depression before her lobot-omy. Rosemary lived a long life, dying at age 86 on January 7, 2005, surrounded by her surviving siblings, Ted, Jean, Eunice, and Pat. Tragic as her story was, Rosemary's plight no doubt spurred JFK's successful efforts on behalf of the mentally disabled as president and Eunice's life work with Special Olympics.

---

161    There is an unconfirmed rumor that JFK visited Rosemary in 1958.

In his remarks, Bobby spoke of the center's mission:

> *"Here, all will join in the commitment that every child can learn; that every child can be brought at least partway to full sharing in society."*

Bobby and Rose were accompanied at the groundbreaking by Samuel Belkin, the president of Yeshiva University, under which Albert Einstein College operated at the time. Mayor John Lindsay was also on hand. With a focus on intensive research, Albert Einstein is considered one of the top medical schools in the United States. The College became part of Montefiore in 2015, although it still maintains its association with Yeshiva.

# GAELIC PARK

BROADWAY AND 240TH ST. RIVERDALE, BRONX

THIS 2000-SEAT STADIUM IS LOCATED near the Westchester border and has been a part of Manhattan College since 1991. Prior to that, it was a social hub for the Irish immigrants of the area, hosting Gaelic football and hurling events. On October 25, 1964, Bobby stopped here during his senate campaign and tossed out the first ball at a match between County Dublin and a New York all-star team before a crowd of 10,000 fans. "We remember where we came from," the grandson of Irish immigrants told the crowd. Dublin won, 19-9, but the busy candidate left long before the game ended.

# KENNEDY FAMILY RESIDENCE
## 5040 INDEPENDENCE AVE. @ 252ND ST., BRONX

WITH JOE NOW ESTABLISHED AS a Hollywood film producer, the family moved here in September 1927 so he could be closer to his Manhattan office. Jean later recalled[162] that her father once told a reporter, "Boston was no place to bring up Irish Catholic children," and this belief undoubtedly also drove his decision to move his family to New York. Rose's stationery listed their home here as being in "Riverdale-On-Hudson," which sounds fancier than "The Bronx."

Then, as now, Riverdale is an upscale enclave in the northwest corner of the Bronx. The Kennedys lived in a rented home here that was surrounded by woods and featured views of the Hudson River. They relocated to Bronxville in Westchester County in 1929. It's interesting to note that although Rose was pregnant when the family moved here, she insisted on having her baby back in Boston at St. Margaret's Hospital in Dorchester, where Jean was born on February 20, 1928. Rose returned to St. Margaret's to give birth to Ted on February 22, 1932.

---

162  Jean Kennedy Smith, *The Nine of Us: Growing Up Kennedy,* New York: Harper, 2016.

Bobby was fighting charges of being a carpetbagger in his 1964 senate campaign, and so he returned here along with John Jr., reminding voters that he'd lived most of the first twenty years of his life in New York.

## RIVERDALE COUNTRY SCHOOL
### 5250 FIELDSTON RD., BRONX

CONTINUALLY RANKED AMONG THE BEST private schools in the country, JFK, Joe Jr., and their sisters Kathleen, Eunice, Pat, and Rosemary were all students here when the family lived on Independence Avenue in Riverdale starting in the fall of 1927. Joe Jr. left for Choate in 1929. JFK was a student here from grades five through seven, from 1927 until 1930. According to his *New York Times* obituary, his classmates here remembered him as "likable, moderately studious, polite, and hot-tempered."

# CONCOURSE PLAZA HOTEL

GRAND CONCOURSE @ E. 161ST ST., BRONX, CLOSED

OPENED IN 1923, IN ITS heyday, this imposing building was the most desirable place to hold social and political events in the Bronx. Visiting baseball teams playing at nearby Yankee Stadium — just three blocks to the west — often stayed here. The hotel's grand ball-room can be seen in two memorable movies: the 1955 Best Picture winner *Marty* and *The Catered Affair* from 1956, both of which starred Ernest Borgnine. Actor/director John Cassavetes filmed scenes for his 1980 movie *Gloria* here.

By 1960, the hotel had already seen better days. A February 1965 *New York Times* article lamented the decline of the "Once-Grand Concourse." Rising crime in the South Bronx made a stay at the hotel a less desirable prospect as the 1960s wore on, and it eventually became a welfare hotel. The city of New York purchased the hotel in 1974, converting it into a senior residence, which it still is today. Campaigning for the Presidency here on November 5, 1960, just days before the election, JFK reminded voters of his Bronx roots:

> *"I said up the street that I was a former resident*
> *of the Bronx. Nobody believes that, but it is true.*
> *I went to school in the Bronx. Now, Riverdale is*

*part of the Bronx, and I lived there for five or six years. No other candidate for the Presidency can make that statement. In fact, I do not know the last time that a candidate from the Bronx ran for the Presidency, but I am here to ask your help. I don't think we are going to run all right in Riverdale, but we will be here."*

# WILLIAM HODSON COMMUNITY CENTER

## 1320 WEBSTER AVE. NEAR E. 169TH ST., BRONX

BOBBY AND JACKIE ATTENDED A Christmas party for under-privileged kids here on December 15, 1965. The event featured a performance by the cast of the Broadway show *On a Clear Day You Can See Forever*, and the show's composer, Alan Jay Lerner, was on hand. This was the first of 26 such parties around the city paid for by Bobby's Community Trust Holiday Fund. Lerner's shows written with Frederick Loewe included *Brigadoon*, *Camelot* and *My Fair Lady* plus the 1958 film musical *Gigi*.

Due to Jackie's post-assassination interview with Theodore H. White, in which she recalled that JFK enjoyed listening to the original cast album of *Camelot* before turning in at night, the show became associated with memories of his Presidency, even though no one thought to make the connection while JFK was still alive. Lerner wrote *On a Clear Day* with composer Burton Lane. The show opened in October 1965 and ran for nine months; a respectable run but hardly up to the standards set by Lerner's previous triumphs. The Hodson Center, which is now focused on seniors, has been serving the Bronx for eighty years.

## THE BRONX ZOO
### 2300 SOUTHERN BLVD.

AT 265 ACRES, THIS IS the largest zoo located in a metropolitan area in the U.S. and one of the largest in the country. Bobby, Ethel, and seven of their eight kids visited here on election day, November 3, 1964. They were joined by JFK's lifelong best friend, Lem Billings. After a hard-fought campaign, internal polls told Bobby that he would win. However, he ended up running far behind LBJ, due in part to the fact that LBJ's opponent (Sen. Barry Goldwater) was way out of step with New York voters, whereas Bobby's (the more moderate Keating) wasn't. Jackie attended a fundraising ball here on June 28, 1978.

## SEDGWICK HOUSES; FORMER LOCATION OF CONVENT OF THE SACRED HEART, MAPLEHURST BETWEEN UNDERCLIFF AVE. AND MARTIN LUTHER KING BLVD.,[163] SOUTH OF W. 174TH ST. AND NORTH OF THE CROSS BRONX EXPRESSWAY; RELOCATED

ETHEL, JEAN, EUNICE, AND PAT all attended this Catholic prep five-day-a-week boarding school for girls not far from the Washington Bridge (not to be confused with the *George* Washington Bridge, a mile west on the other side of Manhattan). The campus was enclosed by an imposing high wall. Its main building was designed by Calvert Vaux, Frederick Law Olmsted's partner in designing Central and Prospect Parks.

Joe had put Rose in charge of selecting the schools their daughters attended. Rose chose for them to be educated by the Sisters of the Sacred Heart, who'd taught her as a child.  She thought it important the girls be taught a consistent curriculum whether here or at Noroton, Connecticut, Torresdale in Northeast Philadelphia, or Roehampton when they lived in London. Jean, Eunice, and Pat went here when the family lived in Bronxville. The Maplehurst estate was home to the school here from 1903 to 1945, the year Ethel graduated. Sacred Heart then moved to Greenwich, Connecticut, where it still operates today. The property was later taken over by the city of New

---

163   This section of the street was still named University Ave. during the time the school existed.

York in order to build the Cross Bronx Expressway.

Eunice, Pat, and Jean commuted here from their home eleven miles away in Bronxville. Ethel lived thirty miles away in Greenwich, Connecticut, so she boarded here five days a week. Constantly breaking the rules and rebelling against the school's spartan atmosphere, Ethel was quite the cut-up and a thorn in the sides of the nuns in charge. Jean went here from 1939 to 1941, so her time didn't overlap with Ethel's, who didn't start here until 1943. However, Ethel met some of Jean's friends here, who suggested they'd make good roommates for each other when they started at Manhattanville College of the Sacred Heart in September 1945. The two hit it off, and Jean soon introduced Ethel to Bobby. So, we can say that Ethel's time at Maplehurst changed her and Bobby's lives forever.

www.shgreenwich.org

## FORDHAM UNIVERSITY
### 441 E. FORDHAM RD., BRONX

BOBBY SPOKE TO A CROWD of 4,000 in the gymnasium here on November 2, 1964, one of his final stops before his election to the U.S. Senate the following day. The *New York Times* reported that he was "booed as well as cheered" at the rally.

Bobby gave the commencement address at this private Jesuit school here on June 10, 1967. Urging the graduates to get involved in trying to improve their communities, he quoted from his own "Ripple of Hope" speech that he'd given at the University of Cape Town in South Africa in June 1966:

> *"Each time a man stands up for an ideal, or acts to improve the lot of others, or strikes out against injustice, he sends forth a tiny ripple of hope, and crossing each other from a million different centers of energy and daring, those ripples build a current which can sweep down the mightiest walls of oppression and resistance."*

Today, those words adorn his spartan gravesite at Arlington National Cemetery.

He cautioned the grads that they were entering, "A world aflame with the desires and hatreds of multitudes." Just days after the Six-Day War in the Middle East, Bobby expressed strong support for Israel and lamented that Arab populations had been plagued by "irresponsible leaders" content to blame their nations' problems on outside forces.

Before long, Bobby would fall victim to some of the hatred he'd described, with a Jordanian immigrant who'd expressed his disdain for Bobby's support of Israel convicted of shooting him. The following year's Fordham graduation ceremony — which Bobby had indicated that he hoped to attend — was held almost a year to the day later, on June 8, 1968, the day of Bobby's funeral, and included a Requiem Mass for him. This marked the first time in 123 years that a mass was included as a part of the graduation ceremony.

# HUNTS POINT PRODUCE MARKET

BOBBY VISITED THIS HUGE WHOLESALE food market on January 25, 1968, during a tour of the Bronx. State Sen. Robert Garcia (later a congressman from the Bronx) told him about conflicts between Blacks and Hispanics regarding how anti-poverty funds were dispersed. A dinner honoring Garcia at Chateau Madrid Restaurant at 48th and Lexington Ave. was among the stops on Bobby's proposed schedule for June 9, 1968, when he planned to be campaigning in the New York primary election.

Other Bronx stops on this day included: The YMHA at 1130 Grand Concourse; the Lavelle School for the Blind at 221 Pauling Ave; and the Casita Maria Settlement House (now called the Casita Maria Center for Arts & Education) at 928 Simpson St.

# QUEENS

## SUNSET GARDEN ARENA
QUEENS BOULEVARD @ 45TH ST., SUNNYSIDE; DEMOLISHED

THIS WAS A POPULAR VENUE for wrestling and boxing starting in 1947 until the building was torn down in December 1977. The
façade was made of red brick and distinguished by a large clock in its
center. JFK campaigned here in 1960, as did Bobby in 1964. Bobby
appeared here on November 4, 1967, at a rally supporting a new
New York State constitution that voters defeated three days later.
The new constitution was the product of a constitutional convention that voters had approved in 1965. Among the provisions of the
proposed charter was the repeal of the Blaine Amendment, barring
state aid to parochial schools. At the rally, some speakers blamed
anti-Catholic bias for the strong opposition to the new charter, but
Bobby chose not to make that accusation. A Wendy's now stands on
the Southwest corner of the boulevard where the arena was located.

# JOHN F. KENNEDY INTERNATIONAL AIRPORT
## JAMAICA

IDLEWILD AIRPORT WAS RENAMED FOR JFK on December 24, 1963, one of the first of many places in the U.S. to be dedicated in his honor. Ted and Joan were here for the ceremony, where they were joined by New York Mayor Robert Wagner and New Jersey Gov. Richard Hughes. Bobby had been scheduled to appear but opted for an Aspen vacation with his family instead. Hughes stated that the renaming created:

> *"A perpetual message to those millions who will pass through this threshold to a great land, and those others who, leaving here, will represent the image and meaning of America in the far places of the earth."*

Bobby was photographed standing next to the new sign for the airport shortly after it was renamed. He complained of the facility's disrepair and poor maintenance while here in 1968.

## QUEENS TERRACE RESTAURANT
68-21 ROOSEVELT AVE. @ 69TH ST., WOODSIDE CLOSED

THIS WAS A POPULAR CATERING hall years ago. Bobby attended a rally here to drum up support for the new state constitution on November 4, 1967. The proposed overhaul lost at the polls three days later. According to an FBI airtel released in 2017, the Queens Terrace was the location of a planned meeting of organized crime figures in September 1967, but the meeting didn't take place on the appointed day. The original building was gutted by a fire that took the life of a 19-year-old female employee in June 1969. Today, the building houses the local congregation of the Universal Life Church.

## QUEENS COLLEGE
### 65-30 KISSENA BLVD., FLUSHING

BOBBY GAVE THE COMMENCEMENT ADDRESS to an audience of 2,105 gathered behind Jefferson Hall here on June 15, 1965. He told the students, "A revolution is now in progress ... a revolution for individual dignity, in societies where the individual has been submerged in a desperate mass." He praised "The sit-ins and Teach-ins, the summer projects (a reference to the Mississippi "Freedom Summer" voter registration campaign of 1964 that claimed the lives of three civil rights workers, one of whom was Queens College graduate Andrew Goodman), civil rights protests, organizing the poor, and marching on Washington as ways for "individual citizens ... to contribute to the public dialogue." With the Vietnam War escalating and Bobby, for now at least, in alignment with LBJ's policy, he cautioned, "It is not helpful ... to protest the war in Vietnam as if it were a simple and easy question, as if any moral man could reach only one conclusion." Vietnam, of course, was the issue that would compel Bobby to challenge LBJ less than three years later.

Today, the Robert F. Kennedy Community High School is located on Parsons Blvd. in Kew Gardens Hills, not far from where Bobby spoke that day.

www.qc.cuny.edu

# FLUSHING MEADOWS
## CORONA PARK

IT WAS A COLD AFTERNOON when JFK spoke at a ceremony marking the groundbreaking for the 1964-65 World's Fair here on December 14, 1962. He was greeted by master builder Robert Moses, the fair's president. This was to be the second World's Fair at this location; the first was held in 1939. Before the ceremony, JFK stopped to review the scale model of the fair in the administration building. In his remarks, he stated:

> "...The theme of this World's Fair — Peace Through
> Understanding — is most appropriate in these
> years of the 60s. ... I want the people of the world to
> visit this fair ... and come to the American exhibit —
> the exhibit of the United States — and see what we
> have accomplished through a system of freedom.
> ... So we begin today, with this ceremony. We'll
> begin again in April of 1964. And we'll show what
> we have done in the past and even more important,
> what America is going to be in the future."

On December 17, Moses wrote to thank JFK: "Your visit and

endorsement have done more than I can say to help the fair. I believe you will not be disappointed in the results."

On April 22, 1963, one year before the opening day, JFK remotely started the "Countdown Clock" that would be installed in the administrative offices and tick off the seconds until the fair opened. He told an assembled crowd of 800 in Flushing via telephone: "366 days from today, I plan to be there." Of course, JFK was gone by the time the fair opened. One of his aides said the only time he ever saw Moses cry was on November 22, 1963.[164]

The fair at first embodied the hope and optimism of the early 1960s. By the time it closed on October 17, 1965, the 60s had taken another dark turn with the escalation of the war in Vietnam and the Watts riots in Los Angeles during the summer of 1965.

Jackie and her children made an unannounced visit to the fair on April 30, 1964. They enjoyed the various pavilions while going largely unnoticed by the public, at least for a while. Bobby, Ethel, and seven of their eight kids came to the Fair on October 17, the day before it closed until the following spring. There, in the midst of his heated senate campaign, Bobby was photographed kissing each of his kids as they boarded the Glide-a-Ride car in front of the IBM Pavilion. Bobby and Ethel were at the Fair on Memorial Day 1965 before heading to Grand Army Plaza in Brooklyn for the dedication of a monument to JFK there.

The RFK Pro-Celebrity Tennis Tournament moved to Armstrong Stadium here in 1979. The tournament started in 1972 at the Forest Hills Tennis Stadium and was held there through 1978.

John Jr. attended the U.S. Open here on several occasions, including August 31, 1994, and on the evening of September 8, 1995,

164   www.nywf64.com/perspective03.shtml

the day he held his press conference introducing *George*. Two days later, he returned and was photographed watching the men's singles final between Andre Agassi and Pete Sampras, which Sampras won in four sets. Louis Armstrong Stadium was the primary venue here until 1997 when the new Arthur Ashe Stadium superseded it. John also watched the September 10, 1998, epic quarter-final match at Ashe Stadium between Thomas Johansson and Mark Philippoussis, which Philippoussis won in a 12-10 fifth-set tie-breaker. The original Armstrong Stadium was demolished in 2016; a new stadium of the same name with a retractable roof was opened in 2018.

## FOREST HILLS STADIUM

### 1 TENNIS PLACE, FOREST HILLS

THE RFK PRO-CELEBRITY TENNIS TOURNAMENT was played here for eight years, from 1972 to 1978. It relocated to the National Tennis Center in Flushing in 1979, which marked its last year in New York. Ethel organized the tournament to raise funds for the RFK Memorial Foundation. Muhammad Ali, Pelé, Dolly Parton, and Elton John were among the many celebs that participated, and the festivities were usually televised in condensed form on ABC-TV. All the Kennedys turned out in force for these events, including Jackie, Ted, Caroline, and John Jr. It was at the 1977 event that Maria Shriver first met Arnold Schwarzenegger. The Beatles, Bob Dylan, and the Doors played here back in the 1960s, and the venue has once again begun hosting concerts recently after not doing so for many years.

# CITI FIELD; FORMER SITE OF SHEA STADIUM
## 123-01 ROOSEVELT AVE. FLUSHING, QUEENS; DEMOLISHED

JACKIE,[165] ARI, JOHN JR., AND Caroline attended a game of the 1969 World Series here between the Mets and Orioles. John Jr. was photographed with new Met Willie Mays in the dugout here on June 3, 1972. Accompanied by singer Carly Simon and poet Allen Ginsberg, John attended a Rolling Stones concert here in late October 1989. According to Carly's then-husband Jim Hart,[166] she was seeking to cheer John up after he'd failed his bar exam for the second time. The Stones were on their *Steel Wheels* tour at the time, their first U.S. tour in eight years. Shea was demolished in 2009 to make room for a parking lot for the newly constructed Citi Field.

---

165   Jackie was quite a baseball fan, and quizzed filmmaker Ken Burns about his documentary on the game when she met him in the early 1990s. (Simon, *Touched by the Sun*.)

166   James Hart, *Lucky Jim*, Jersey City: Cleis Press, 2017.

# KAUFMAN ASTORIA STUDIOS

## 34-12 36ᵀᴴ ST. ASTORIA, QUEENS

SPORTS TALK RADIO STATION WFAN broadcast from studios in a windowless basement here before moving to Manhattan in 2009. John Jr. was a guest on the *Imus in the Morning* radio show here in May 1997. John's interview with Imus had been published in the June issue of *George*, an indication of the stature Imus enjoyed at the time. The show was a popular platform for Washington politicians, and Imus welcomed President Bill Clinton and regular guests such as Sens. John McCain, John Kerry, Joe Biden, and Al D'Amato. D'Amato would briefly write a column for *George*.

Known for his impertinent questions and irreverent humor, Imus brought up the current woes of his John's cousins, Rep. Joe Kennedy and his brother Michael. Joe's ex-wife Shelia claimed he'd tried to bully her into an annulment while Michael was said to have had an affair with his family's underage babysitter. Addressing his family's scandal, John said to Imus:

> *"So, when Michael's difficulties, or Joe's, or my uncle's, or my cousin's (William Kennedy Smith) — all those things tend to attract people's attention. Regrettably, maybe we keep providing them with material."*

Anyone aware of John's comments on the Imus show wouldn't have been surprised when, two months later, he would refer to Joe and Michael as "poster boys for bad behavior" in his editor's note in the September edition of *George*. John was actually making an obtuse argument in their defense, but that point was lost amidst the spectacle of one Kennedy criticizing other Kennedys. John was ruminating on temptation and the choices people make between living an upright — and possibly unexciting — life or risking one's reputation in pursuit of pleasure. (In his April 1999 talk at the Harvard Club, John opined that Joe and Michael had gotten a "raw deal" and that, "Anyone who read that letter would know I was not condemning my cousins.") In August, Joe announced that he would not make his expected race for governor of Massachusetts. On December 31, 1997, Michael was killed in a skiing accident in Aspen, Colorado.

Joe no doubt had Michael's death in mind when he cited "a new recognition of our own vulnerabilities and the vagaries of life" when announcing his retirement from the House of Representatives in the spring of 1998. His comment now seems eerily prophetic, considering the fate that awaited John a year later.

# AT&T BUILDING; FORMER SITE OF THE BOULEVARD RESTAURANT

## 94-05 QUEENS BLVD., REGO PARK

JFK HELD A RALLY AT the Boulevard while campaigning in New York just days before the 1960 election. An enormous crowd of supporters greeted him under cloudy skies. A silent movie of the rally can be seen on YouTube. The restaurant was torn down in 1973.

# LA GUARDIA AIRPORT
## EAST ELMHURST

JFK USUALLY FLEW IN AND out of the Marine Air Terminal here when visiting New York as President.

Perhaps the most heartbreaking event that the Kennedys endured in New York was the return of Bobby's body to La Guardia from Los Angeles on the night of June 6, 1968. He died earlier in the day after having been shot 24 hours earlier at the Ambassador Hotel in Los Angeles following his victory in the California primary. The scene at La Guardia was a macabre replay of what the nation witnessed at Andrews Air Force Base the night of November 22, 1963, when JFK's body returned to Washington. The scene at La Guardia was eerily similar in that they both took place at night; both times, the caskets were offloaded from a Presidential plane, and Jackie was present both times. The fact that another Kennedy brother had been assassinated just four-and-a-half years after JFK's death — and almost exactly two months after the assassination of Martin Luther King Jr. — was shocking and incomprehensible to many Americans. Bobby's casket was taken directly from La Guardia to lie in state at St. Patrick's Cathedral.

# LIBERTY ISLAND

## THE STATUE OF LIBERTY NATIONAL MONUMENT

ON OCTOBER 3, 1965, BOBBY and Ted were here for the signing ceremony at which President Johnson signed a bill overhauling the nation's immigration policies. The Immigration and Nationality

LBJ signs the Immigration Act of 1965 on Liberty Island. Bobby and Ted, Lady Bird Johnson, Vice President Hubert Humphrey and his wife Muriel, New York Mayor John Lindsay, W. Averell Harriman, and Hawaii Sen. Daniel Inouye are among those pictured. *LBJ Library photo by Yoichi Okamoto.*

Act of 1965 ended *de facto* prohibitions on immigrants from southern and eastern Europe, Asia, and Africa. The previous law favored immigrants from northern and western Europe. The new 1965 law resulted in a profound change to U.S. demographics in the ensuing decades and is one of the most important legacies of the JFK/LBJ era. JFK had supported the overhaul and Ted was instrumental in guiding the bill through the Senate. In his remarks given against the backdrop of the lower Manhattan skyline, LBJ cited "the vision of our late beloved President John Fitzgerald Kennedy" and the support Bobby and Ted had given the legislation.

# STATEN ISLAND

## SNUG HARBOR CULTURAL CENTER
## & BOTANICAL GARDEN
### 1000 RICHMOND TERRACE

JACKIE FAMOUSLY VISITED HERE ON July 30, 1976. The 80-acre site had served as a home for retired seamen via the bequest of the former landowner. Two old sailors who had refused to leave when the rest were transferred to North Carolina were on hand to greet Jackie. During the 1960s, the Greek Revival buildings here were the first structures in New York City to gain landmark status. The city purchased the property in the early 1970s. Jackie was quoted as saying, "The more attention that can be attracted to this lovely place, the better." Plans to turn this into the cultural center it is today were then in their infancy, but Jackie's visit certainly helped spur them into reality. On the way home to Manhattan, Jackie was photographed at the helm of the Staten Island Ferry. Today, the Center is thriving and includes the Botanical Gardens.

www.snug-harbor.org

# WILLOWBROOK STATE SCHOOL
## 2800 VICTORY BLVD.

SINCE GERALDO RIVERA'S 1972 REPORTS on WABC-TV in New York revealed the overcrowding and inhumane conditions for developmentally disabled patients here, the name Willowbrook has been infamous. Rivera's efforts brought the situation to national attention, eventually resulting in a consent decree to improve conditions. Willowbrook closed in 1987. Few recall that it was Bobby who first shined a light on the deplorable conditions here. In 1965, Bobby went here accompanied by a film crew on a surprise visit so officials wouldn't have the opportunity to deceive him. "At Willowbrook ... we have a situation that borders on a snake pit. ... I think all of us are at fault, and I think it's long overdue that something be done about it."

The "snake pit" term refers to the 1948 film *The Snake Pit* starring Olivia de Havilland. By depicting the harrowing conditions at a nursing home, the movie raised awareness about the deplorable conditions in these facilities and spurred successful reform efforts around the United States. Both JFK and Bobby decried the neglect of the mentally ill in the United States. JFK established the President's Panel on Mental Retardation, which called for increased federal funding to state mental hospitals. While Bobby's efforts surely raised public awareness of the problem, little had improved at Willowbrook by the time Rivera began his reporting.

## ST. GEORGE FERRY TERMINAL
### 1 BAY ST.

WITH FEWER THAN TWO WEEKS to go before the election, JFK took the ferry here for an early evening rally. This was part of a long day during which he was greeted by swarms of people as he toured all of New York's boroughs except the Bronx. Speaking from where taxis normally picked up commuters, he addressed an enthusiastic crowd of 15,000 for thirty minutes. The rally was one of the biggest gatherings of people ever on Staten Island.

# VERRAZZANO MONUMENT
## VERRAZZANO BRIDGE PLAZA,
## LILLY POND AVE. @ MAJOR AVE.

ON OCTOBER 12, 1966, BOBBY accompanied LBJ to a rally here in support of New York gubernatorial candidate Frank O'Connor and other Democratic candidates. 1966 marked the revival of the Republican Party's fortunes following the crushing defeats of 1964. This was fueled by the backlash against civil rights legislation, concerns about crime, and disenchantment with the war in Vietnam. The Democrats lost 47 House seats and 3 Senate seats, although they retained control of both chambers. O'Connor would lose to Gov. Nelson Rockefeller, and the Republicans would net seven governorships. In his remarks, LBJ called Bobby "one of the most able and outstanding men in the United States Senate."

In his book *Journals*, Arthur Schlesinger recounted a fall 1966 conversation in which Bobby recalled recently a spending a day (possibly the day of the Verrazzano stop) campaigning with LBJ in New York. At the end the day LBJ told Bobby: "Of all the things in life, this is what I most enjoy doing." An incredulous Bobby told Schlesinger: "Imagine saying that, of all the things in life, this is what you like most."[167] The anecdote speaks volumes about how different in style

---

167  Schlesiger *Journals.*

and temperament Bobby and LBJ were. Their personal enmity would have a profound effect on the history of the 1960s.

# LONG ISLAND

## GARDEN CITY HOTEL
### 45 SEVENTH ST., GARDEN CITY

THIS ELEGANT HOTEL HAS BEEN a Long Island landmark for over 150 years.

Bobby attended the Sky Island Club's "Fall Guy" Luncheon as the guest of honor here on Friday, March 15, 1968. It was a notable occasion because it was on this day that word had leaked out that, after months of indecision, Bobby was going to announce his candidacy for president. This would be his final public appearance as a non-candidate. The lunch was a sort of roast, with Bobby the target of light-hearted jibes. The next day, the New York Times carried a photo of Bobby sitting at the dais, which was adorned with a banner reading "Bobby Go Braugh" in reference to St. Patrick's Day, which was two days away. He appears to be trying to avert his eyes from a belly dancer doing her thing a few feet in front of him.[168]

During the speeches, Bobby spoke with former Republican National Committee chairman Len Hall, who asked him, "Are you going the primary route?" Bobby replied, "Yeah," which—like Hall's question—was picked up by a nearby microphone and thus con-

---

168    Richard Witkin, "Kennedy Decides to Run; Will discuss Plans Today," *The New York Times*, March 16, 1968.

firmed that he was running.

Asked to describe Bobby's mood at the prospect of an arduous campaign, an aide ominously described him as "fatalistic."

Following a stop at the Westbury Manor for a Democratic Party meeting (where he encountered a group of teenage McCarthy supporters gathered outside), it was off to LaGuardia Airport for a flight back to Washington, where he would prepare to formally announce his candidacy the following morning.

www.gardencityhotel.com

## UBS ARENA FORMER SITE OF THE MANICE MANSION/ TURF AND FIELD CLUB

### 2400 HEMPSTEAD TURNPIKE, ELMONT

HOUSED IN THE TURRETED 19TH-CENTURY Manice Mansion on the grounds of Belmont Park, the Turf and Field was one of New York's most exclusive country clubs. Every June, the club hosted the annual Belmont Ball, which raised money for charity. Jackie was photographed dancing with fashion designer Oleg Cassini at the 1954 ball. Belmont Park was familiar ground for Jackie. There is a photo of her there taken in 1939, the year she turned ten.

Cassini was not only Jackie's favored designer when she was First Lady, he was also a trusted friend. A month before moving into the White House, Jackie sent a letter to Cassini dated December 13, 1960, in which she poignantly pleaded: "Protect me - as I seem so mercilessly exposed and don't know how to cope with it."

The Manice Mansion was torn down in 1963, along with the old grandstand.

# VILLAGE OF BRONXVILLE, WESTCHESTER COUNTY

## KENNEDY FAMILY RESIDENCE
### 294 PONDFIELD RD., BRONXVILLE

JOE PURCHASED THIS FIVE-ACRE ESTATE known as "Crownlands" for nearly $250,000 in May 1929 when he moved the family from Riverdale in the Bronx. The main brick Georgian-style house had twenty rooms spread over three floors plus separate quarters for the gardener and chauffeur. JFK and Joe Jr. would sometimes invite their school friends here to play baseball and football on the sprawling lawns. On occasion, Joe would treat them to a showing of one of the latest Hollywood movies in the basement projection room.

Joe sold the property in January 1942. The house was torn down in 1953, and the property has since been subdivided into three parcels and redeveloped. One of those properties went on the market in 2023 with an asking price of $5.75 million.

In commemorating JFK's 100th birthday in May 2017, the Village of Bronxville and the Bronxville Historical Conservancy revealed a plaque in his honor. The memorial is located near the corner of Pondfield Rd. and Gramatan Ave.

## GRAMATAN COURT TOWNHOUSES;
## FORMER SITE OF THE HOTEL GRAMATAN
### LAWRENCE PARK, MOSTLY DEMOLISHED

THIS STATELY HOTEL ON TOP of a hill was a local landmark for decades. Built in a Spanish Mission style usually found in California rather than New York, the luxurious hotel had 300 rooms and amenities like riding stables. Theodore Roosevelt, Greta Garbo, and Gloria Swanson (visiting Joe Sr.) were among the notables who stayed there. JFK was said to have reluctantly attended a school dance here. Joe Sr. was said to have regularly used the hotel for furtive trysts while the family lived on Pondfield Rd.

The distinctive tower was spared from the wrecking ball when the rest of the hotel was torn down in 1972, and it still stands today.

# CHURCH OF SAINT JOSEPH
## 15 CEDAR ST.

THIS CHURCH WAS BUILT IN 1928, just a year before the Kennedys arrived in Bronxville. All the Kennedys attended weekly mass here while living in Bronxville from 1929 to 1941. Ted served as an altar boy here as a teenager. He married Joan here on November 29, 1958, with JFK serving as best man. All of the family except Peter Lawford, who was on a movie shoot, were in attendance. This day would mark the last time JFK would set foot in Bronxville. The reception was held at the Siwanoy Country Club on Pondfield Rd. A group photo was taken on this day with (almost) the entire family present. It's poignant to look at their smiling faces, knowing that JFK, Bobby, and Joe would all be gone in just a few short years.

# BIBLIOGRAPHY

Mimi Alford, *Once Upon a Secret: My Affair with President John F. Kennedy and Its Aftermath*, New York: Random House, 2012.

Christopher Anderson, *The Day John Died*, New York: Avon Books, 2001.

Christopher Anderson, *The Good Son: JFK Jr. and the Mother He Loved*, New York: Gallery Books, 2015.

Elizabeth Beller, *Once Upon a Time: The Captivating Life of Carolyn Bessette Kennedy*, New York: Gallery Books, 2014.

Michael Bergin, *The Other Man: A Love Story*, New York: William Morrow, 2004.

Matt Berman, *JFK Jr., George, & Me: A Memoir*, New York: Gallery Books, 2014.

Gerald Blaine and Lisa McCubbin, *The Kennedy Detail: JFK's Secret Service Agents Break Their Silence*, New York: Gallery Books, 2011.

Richard Blow, *American Son: A Portrait of John F. Kennedy, Jr.*, New York: St. Martin's Paperbacks, 2002.

The Richard Burton Diaries,

William D. Cohan, *Four Friends: Promising Lives Cut Short*, New York: Flatiron, 2019.

Peter Collier and David Horowitz, *The Kennedys: An American Drama*, New York: Summit Books, 1984.

James W. Douglass, *JFK and the Unspeakable: Why He Died and Why it Matters*, New York: Touchstone, 2008.

Judith Exner, *My Story*, New York: Grove Press, 1977.

Gerald Gardner, *Robert Kennedy in New York*, New York: Random House, 1965.

Steven M. Gillon, *America's Reluctant Prince: The Life of John F. Kennedy Jr.*, New York: Dutton, 2019.

Doris Kearns Goodwin, *The Fitzgeralds and the Kennedys*, New York: Simon and Schuster, 1987.

Richard N. Goodwin, *Remembering America: A Voice from the Sixties*, New York: Little Brown, 1988.

Liza M. Greene, *New York for New Yorkers: A Historical Treasury and Guide to the Buildings and Monuments of Manhattan*, New York: W.W. Norton & Company, 2001.

Edward O. Guthman and C. Richard Allen, *RFK: His Words for Our Times*, New York: William Morrow, 2018.

Christina Haag, *Come to the Edge: A Love Story*, New York: Random House, 2012.

Seymour M. Hersh, *The Dark Side of Camelot*, New York: Little Brown & Co., 1997.

David C. Heymann, *A Woman Named Jackie: An Intimate Biography of Jacqueline Bouvier Kennedy Onassis*, New York: Lyle Stuart, 1989.

Clint Hill with Lisa McCubbin, *Mrs. Kennedy and Me*, New York: Gallery Books, 2012.

Kitty Kelley, *Jackie Oh!*, New York: Ballantine Books, 1984.

Robert F. Kennedy Jr., *American Values: Lessons I Learned from My Family*, New York: Harper, 2018.

William Kuhn, *Reading Jackie: Her Autobiography in Books*, New York: Anchor Books, 2011.

Greg Lawrence, *Jackie as Editor: The Literary Life of Jacqueline Kennedy Onassis,* New York: Thomas Dunne Books, 2011.

Laurence Leamer, *The Kennedy Men 1901-1963*, New York: William Morrow, 2001.

Laurence Leamer, *The Kennedy Women: The Saga of an American Family,* New York: Ivy Books div Ballentine, 1995.

Richard Lertzman and William J. Birnes, *Dr. Feelgood: The Shocking Story of the Doctor Who May Have Changed History by Treating and Drugging JFK, Marilyn, Elvis, and Other Prominent Figures,* New York: Skyhorse, 2014.

Robert T. Littell, *The Men We Became: My Friendship with John F. Kennedy Jr.,* New York: St. Martin's Press, 2004.

Ward Morehouse III, *Inside the Plaza: An Intimate Portrait of the Ultimate Hotel,* New York & London: Applause Books, 2001.

Jay Mulvaney, *Kennedy Weddings: A Family Album,* New York: St. Martin's Press, 1999.

David Nasaw, *The Patriarch: The Remarkable Life and Turbulent Times of Joseph P. Kennedy,* New York: Penguin Press, 2012.

William Sylvester Noonan, *Forever Young: My Friendship with John F. Kennedy Jr.,* New York: Viking, 2006.

Jerry Oppenheimer, *The Other Mrs. Kennedy*, New York: St. Martin's Paperbacks, 1994.

James Patterson with Cynthia Fagen, *The House of Kennedy*, New York: Little, Brown & Co., 2020.

Barbara A. Perry, *Rose Kennedy: The Life and Times of a Political Matriarch*, New York: W.W. Norton & Co., 2013.

Jean Stein and George Plimpton, Ed., *American Journey: The Times of Robert Kennedy*, New York: Harcourt Brace Jovanovich, 1970.

Carole Radziwill, *What Remains: A Memoir of Fate, Friendship & Love*, New York: Scribner, 2007.

Richard Reeves, *President Kennedy: Portrait of Power*, New York: Simon and Schuster, 1993.

Arthur M. Schlesinger, *Journals: 1952-2000*, New York, Penguin Books, 2007.

Carly Simon, *Touched by the Sun: My Friendship with Jackie*, New York: Farrar Straus, and Giroux, 2019.

Amanda Smith, Editor, *Hostage to Fortune: The Letters of Joseph P. Kennedy*, New York: Viking, 2001.

Jean Kennedy Smith, *The Nine of Us: Growing Up Kennedy*, New York: Harper, 2016.

Stephen Spignesi, *J.F.K. Jr.*, New York: Citadel Press, 1999.

J. Randy Taraborrelli, *Janet, Jackie & Lee: The Secret Lives of Janet Auchincloss and Her Daughters Jacqueline Kennedy Onassis and Lee Radziwill*, New York: St. Martin's Griffin, 2019.

Rosemarie Terenzio, *Fairy Tale Interrupted: A Memoir of Life, Love, and Loss*, New York: Gallery Books, 2012.

Evan Thomas, *Robert Kennedy: His Life*, New York: Simon & Schuster, 2002.

Richard J. Whalen, *The Founding Father: A Study in Power, Wealth and Family Ambition*, New York: Dutton, 1964.

Chris Williams, Editor, *The Richard Burton Diaries*; New Haven and London: The Yale University Press, 2012.

Norval White and Elliot Willensky with Fran Leadon, *AIA Guide to New York City, Fifth Edition*, New York: Oxford University Press, 2010.